Henry Swinburne, Peter Elmsley, Francesco Giomignani, Carlo Nolli

Travels Through Spain

In the Years 1775 and 1776

Henry Swinburne, Peter Elmsley, Francesco Giomignani, Carlo Nolli

Travels Through Spain
In the Years 1775 and 1776

ISBN/EAN: 9783744759328

Printed in Europe, USA, Canada, Australia, Japan

Cover: Foto ©Andreas Hilbeck / pixelio.de

More available books at **www.hansebooks.com**

TRAVELS

THROUGH

SPAIN,

IN THE YEARS 1775 AND 1776.

IN WHICH SEVERAL

MONUMENTS OF ROMAN AND MOORISH

ARCHITECTURE

ARE ILLUSTRATED BY

ACCURATE DRAWINGS TAKEN ON THE SPOT.

By *HENRY SWINBURNE*, Esq;

RIEN N'EST BEAU QUE LE VRAI; LE VRAI SEUL EST AIMABLE.

BOILEAU.

LONDON:

PRINTED FOR P. ELMSLY, IN THE STRAND.

M.DCC.LXXIX.

PREFACE.

MOST travellers that favour the world with their obfervations on foreign countries, endeavour to foften the edge of criticifm by declaring, that they had orginally no intentions of appearing in print, but were betrayed into the prefs by the importunities of their friends. This excufe feldom anfwers the end; for when any effential defect raifes the indignation of the reader, as fevere a fentence is paffed upon the ftraggler decoyed into the literary walk, as upon the moft avowed voluntary trefpaffer. I fhall therefore be very ingenuous, and acknowledge, that when I fet out upon my Spanifh journey, I had thoughts of publifhing my remarks on that country. I had an earneft defire of purfuing a track almoft untrodden by travellers, that I might know how great a degree of credit was due to the accounts already given. In my plan of enquiry, an exact investigation of the soil, cultivation, government, commerce, and manners of that kingdom, was to be the grand primary object; but what I was more confident of my strength in, and what I own I found more suitable to my inclinations, was the study of its antiquities, especially the Moorish: in that line, my own eye and labour were sufficient helps to enable me to collect interesting materials for a publication.

The travels through Spain that have appeared in print, are either old and obsolete, consequently in many respects unfit to convey a proper idea of its present state; or only relations of a passage through particular provinces, where the authors had neither time nor opportunity to procure much information.

Not being under any restraint in point of time; being furnished with letters, and every thing necessary for rendering the tour easy, and my stay in the towns agreeable and instructive, with a sufficient knowledge of the language, I had some reason to hope I might
accomplish

PREFACE. v

accomplish my purpose, with satisfaction to myself, and utility to the public. How far I have succeeded, is submitted to the judgment of the candid reader; at least some little indulgence is due to me for having contributed my mite, however insignificant, to the common stock of topographical knowledge; which of late years has been so prodigiously increased by accumulated imports from all parts of the globe. There is but one merit I insist upon, that of a steady adherence to Veracity, as far as I was able to discern Truth from Falsehood. I may be detected in many mistakes; because a foreigner must often be exposed to receive partial accounts of things from the natives, who have an interest in hiding the nakedness of their country, and in exaggerating its advantages; but I shall never be detected in a wilful perversion of the truth, being as free from prejudices of all kinds as most men.

Many things in my private letters, of which the following sheets are almost exact copies, were not deemed proper for the public inspection; as there are many trifling occurrences that fill up a letter very agreeably,

agreeably, but when printed become ridiculous. The additions made to the correspondence consist chiefly of the historical, commercial, and literary parts; which I drew from the most esteemed Spanish authors, from some manuscripts, and from books in the public libraries. In these researches I was much assisted by the Reverend Mr. R. Waddilove, chaplain to the British embassy; who, I hope, will excuse my making him this slight acknowledgment.

I have been very particular in whatever regards the history and architecture of the Moors, as those are subjects not yet worn thread-bare: with the help of the prints, I hope to give the curious a satisfactory idea of their manner of building, distributing and adorning public edifices. The Alhambra of Granada is an *unique*, and its excellent preservation affords an opportunity of studying all the detail of their designs and ornaments.

I can answer for the exactness of the drawings; as I never took the liberty of adding or retrenching a single object, for the sake of improving the beauty or harmony of the landscape.

PREFACE.

Not to multiply notes and references in the body of the work, I thought proper to give at the beginning, a Chronological Table of the Kings of Spain; Tables of weights, coins, and meafures; and an Itinerary of our route, with the number of hours it requires to perform each ftage.

[ix]

A

Chronological Table of the Kings of SPAIN.

Invaded by the Carthaginians	—	239 before Chrift.
Conquered by the Romans	—	206 before Chrift.
Conquered by the Goths	—	409 after Chrift.
Invaded by the Saracens	—	712 after Chrift.

KINGS OF

Afturias and Leon.	Caftille.	Aragon.	Navarre.	Portugal.	Saracens.
Began to reign.					
718 Pelayo 737 Favita 739 Alfonfo 758 Froila 768 Aurelio 774 Silo 783 Mauregat 788 Bermudo 791 Alfonfo II.					755 Abdoulrahman 788 Hiffem 795 Hachem
845 Ramiro 851 Ordoño 862 Alfonfo III.			Garcias Ximenes 880 Fortun		822 Abdoulrahman 853 Mahomet 886 Almundar 888 Abdaliah
910 Garcias 913 Ordoño II. 923 Froila II. 923 Alfonfo IV. 927 Ramiro II. 952 Ordoño III. 956 Sancho 967 Ramiro III. 985 Bermudo II. 999 Alfonfo V.			905 Sancho 925 Garcias II. 970 Sancho Abarca 994 Garcias III.		912 Abdoulrahman 961 Alhacan 976 Hiffem

[xi]

A TABLE of WEIGHTS, MEASURES, and COINS.

WEIGHTS OF CATALONIA.

12 Ounces · · · · · · · 1 Pound
26 Pounds · · · · · · · 1 Arroba
4 Arrobas · · · make · · 1 Quintal
120 Pounds · · · · · · · 100 ℔ of Amsterdam
125 Pounds · · · · · · · 1 hundred weight English

WEIGHTS OF CASTILLE.

1 Quintal · · · · · · · · · · · · · · · 100 Libras, or 4 Arrobas
1 Arroba · · · · · · · · · · · · · · · · 25 lb.
1 Media Arroba · · · · contains · · 12 lb. 8 oz.
1 Quarto de Arroba · · · · · · · · · 6 lb. 4 oz.
1 Media quarto de Arroba · · · · · 3 lb. 2 oz.

1 Libra · · · · · · · · · · · · · · · · · · 16 Onzas
1 Mediatt · · · · · · · · · · · · · · · · 8 oz.
1 Quarteron · · · · · · · contains · 4 oz.
1 Medio quarteron · · · · · · · · · · 2 oz.
1 Onza · · · · · · · · · · · · · · · · · · 4 quartas

1 Quarta · · · · · · · · · · · · · · · · · 2 Medios quartas
1 Media quarta · · · · · contains · 2 Adarmes
1 Adarmes · · · · · · · · · · · · · · · 2 Medios Adarmes

N.B. The Valencian and Catalan lb. contains only 12 oz. but the oz. are larger.

LONG MEASURE.

12 Inches · · · · · · · · · 1 Castillian foot
3 Castillian feet · · make · 1 Vara
1648 Varas · · · · · · · · · 1 Mile
7680 Varas · · · · · · · · · 1 League

The Vara is about 33 Inches English. 1920 Varas make an English Mile of 1760 Yards.

COINS.

IMAGINARY.

Real de Vellon { equal to half a real de plata or eight quartos 2 maravidis
Escudo de Vellon — — — 10 reals de Vel.
Ducado de Vellon — — 11 r. V. 1 mar.
Ducato de Plata nuevo — — 16 r. V. 17 mar.
Ducato de Plata Antiguo — 20 — — 25 $\frac{15}{17}$
Dobla de oro Decabua, Peso — 14 — — 9

BRASS.

Maravadi, the least coin in Spain
Ochavo — — — — — — 2 }
Quarto — — — — = 4 } maravidis
Dosquartos — — — = 8 }

N. B. A Real de Vellon is worth 8 Quartos 2 Maravidis, or 17 Ochavos.

SILVER.

Medio real de Plata — — 1 r. de Vellon.
Real de Plata — — — 2
Real de 2, pesetta, pistreen — 4
Real de 4 Sevillano — — 8
Real de 8 Sevillano — — 16
Medio real columnario — 1 — 8
Real de Plata colum. — 2 — 17
Real de a 2 colum. — 5
Real de a 4 — — 10
Real de a 8 — — 20

GOLD.

Veintino, peso duro, hard dollar — 20 r. de Vellon.
Escudo de oro nuevo — — — 37 — 17
Escudo de oro Antiguo — — 37 — 22
Doblon de a 2 nuevo, pistola — 75
Doblon de a 2 Antiguo — — 75 — 10
Doblon de a 4 nuevo — — 150
Doblon de a 4 Antiguo — — 150 — 20
Doblon de a 8 nuevo, quadruple — 380
Doblon de a 8 Antiguo — — 301 — 6

ITINERARY.

Name.	Inns.	Hours in going.
Perpignan	Notre dame ; bad.	
Boulou	Dolphin ; tolerable	4
Junquiera	Town-house	3
Figuera	S. Joseph ; bad ; French house	3½
Coldoriol	Single house ; bad	3¼
Girona	Fontana d'Oro ; good	4
Mayorquien	Bad	4¼
Sanfalony	Bad	6½
Rincon	Single house	6
Barcelona	Fontana d'Oro	4½
Cipreret	Single house ; clean	4½
Villa Franca	Bad	5
Figuereta	Single	5⅓
Tarragona	Bad	3½
Reus	—	3
Hospitalet	Single ; no lodging	5
Venta del Platero	Single ; as bad as any in Spain	3¾
Venta Don Ramon	Tolerable ; new	4½
Torlofa	S. Joseph ; new inn	3
Ildecona	Poor	5
Benecarlo	—	3
Torreblanca	—	6½
Castillon	S. Francisco ; good	7
Nule	Good	3½
Morviedro	Clean	4
Valencia	S. Andrea ; not the best	4½
Alzira	French ; clean	6½
San Felipe	French ; new	3¾
Mojente	—	4½

ITINERARY.

Name.	Inns.	Hours in going.
Fuente de la Xiguera	Good	3
Villena	—	4
Monforte	—	6¼
Alicant	S. Francifco; pleafant	4
Elche	Bad	4½
Orihuela	Tolerable	5¾
Murcia	Tolerable	4¼
Venta San Pedro	Nothing	5¾
Carthagena	Aquila d'Oro; excellent	2½
Fuente del Alamo	Bad	4¼
Totana	Clean	6
Lorca	Tolerable	4
Puerto Horniera	Very bad	3¾
Velez el Rubio	—	6
Xirivel	—	3½
Cuellar	—	5
Baca	—	4½
Venta del Golpe	Wretched	6½
Guadix	—	3½
Ifnallos	Tolerable	11¾
Granada	Al Sol; there is a better	6¾
Loja	—	10
Antequera	Corona; clean	11
Venta de Almoyna	—	3
Malaga	Coffee-houfe	3
Venta de la Compania	—	3
Antequera	—	3
Podrera	—	11
Offuna	Good	3¾
Puebla	—	3½
Arajal	Good	4¾
Molares	Very bad	4¼
Cabecas	—	6
Venta del Bifcayno	Good	3
Xeres	Arroyo; good	6¾
Puerto S. Maria	Three Emperors; Italian	3¾
Cadiz	Cavallo Blanco; Italian	2
Chielana	Baudry; good	4
Cortijos	—	14
San Roque	—	12
Gibraltar	—	1½
San Roque	—	1½
Cara del Duque	—	12

ITINERARY.

Name.	Inns.	Hours in going.
Chiclana	—	14
Cadiz	—	4
Puerto	—	0¾
Xeres	—	3
V. Bifcayno	—	7
V. Alcantirella	—	6¼
V. Oran	Clean	2
Sevilla	La Reyna; Italian	5¾
Carmona	Good	7½
V. Monclova	—	5½
Eccija	S. Agoſtino	4
Carlotta	New; good	4
Cordova	Fonda; Italian	5
Carpio	—	6
Aldea	—	5
Anduxar	—	5
V. Rombla	—	4
Carolina	New; excellent	7¼
V. Miranda	—	3
Viſo	—	6
Santa Cruz	—	3¼
Valdepeñas	Good; new. Good wine	3¼
Mancanares	—	5
Villaharta	—	5¼
Puerto Lapiche	—	2½
Confuegra	—	3¼
Mora	Good	6
Toledo	Sangre de Chriſto; clean	6½
Illefcas	—	6¼
Getafe	—	4¼
Madrid	S. Sebaſtian; Italian	3
Aranjuez	Italian; good	4
Madrid	—	4
Efcurial	—	4½
V. S. Catalina	—	4
S. Ildefonſo	—	9
Segovia	Good	2
S. Maria	—	5¼
Villa S. Cruz	—	5½
Hornillo	—	4¼
Valladolid	Good	5¾
V. Trigeros	—	4
Torquemada	—	7

ITINERARY.

Name.	Inns.	Hours in going.
Villa Rodrigo	—	5
Burgos	Good	9¼
Torres	Poor place	3½
Birviesca	—	5½
Pancorvo	Tolerable	5½
V. S. Gaetan	Excellent	7
Victoria	Good	2
Montdragon	Dirty	6½
Vergara	Good	2¼
Tolofa	—	9½
Hernani	Good	3¾
Paſſage	—	6
S. Jean de Luz	Good	4
Bayonne	S. Etienne.	

Directions

Directions for placing the Prints.

Arch of Hannibal	To face Page 50
Arch of Barra	— 72
Tomb of the Scipios	— 74
Venta del platero } Saxe — }	— 109
Plan of the Alhambra	— 171
Gates of the Alhambra	— 172
Great bath of the Alhambra	— 177
Court of the Lions	— 178
Pieces of Architecture	— 179
Entrance of the tower of the two Hermanas	— 183
Plan of the mosque of Cordova	— 296
East front of the mosque	— 300
Chapel of the Koran	— 302

LETTERS

TABLE OF CONTENTS.

P<small>REFACE</small>.

Chronological tables — — — — Page ix

Tables of weights, coins, and measures — — xi

Itinerary — — — — xii

Letter
- I. Journey from Bagneres to Perpignan—wine of Rivesaltes—bay of Leucate—Perpignan — — — Page 1
- II. Pass into Spain by Bellegarde—cork woods of Junquiera—Figuera, and its fortress—Girona—wild country—accident in the river—mode of drinking in Catalonia. — — 3

A.   III. Landscape.

CONTENTS.

Letter

III. Landscape near la Rocca—governor of Barcelona—comedy—history of Catalonia — — — Page 8

IV. Barcelona described—port—Barceloneta —monument of La Mina— ramparts—Rambla—citadel—history of the Major—cathedral— palace—exchange—academy of drawing—antiquities — 15

V. Theatre illuminated—cabinet of natural history—lifts of the army— pay of the troops—story of the Valencian boys—journal of the expedition to Algiers — — — 23

VI. Environs of Barcelona—convent of Sariá—aloe lace—convent of Jesus—Campofanto—fandango — —. 43

VII. Castle of Montjuich — — — — 46

VIII. Journey to Montserrat—arch of Hannibal—abbey—church—treasure—story of brother John—camarines—miraculous image— walk up the mountain—hermitages—life of the hermits—plants and prospects — — — — 49

IX. Bargain with the muleteers—account of Catalonia—its inhabitants— taxes, and mode of collecting them—thieftakers—dress—character of the Catalans—harvest—produce—commerce—population—manufactures—devotion—inquisition—Jews — epitaph of the soldiers of Sertorius — — — 60

X. Journey to Reus—road—bridges—husbandry—arch of Barra—beautiful coast—tomb of the Scipios—Tarragona—antiquities—cathedral—Campo Tarragonés—Reus—its population and trade— story of the Monks — — — 70

XI. Journey through the desart—Venta del Platero—Ebro—bishop of Tortosa—liquorice-works—Tortosa—Valencian dress—journey along the coast—Benicarlo—wine-trade—vale of Margal—music

79

XII. Vale

CONTENTS.

Letter
XII. Vale of Almenara—Morviedro, the ancient Saguntum—ruins of the theatre—caftle—noble profpect—plain of Valencia   Page 88

XIII. Character of the intendant—climate of Valencia—character of the people—defcription of the city—Alameda—Grao or port—hackney-chairs—churches—ftyle of architecture—archbifhop—palaces—exchange—cuftom-houfe—hiftory of Valencia—exploits of the Cid—population—filk-trade—method of raifing mulberry-trees—productions—play-houfe — — 94

XIV. Journey over the plain—Albufera lake—agriculture—rice-grounds—tillage of rice—San Phelipe—caftle and order of Montefa—Villena—Saxe—ftyle of falutation—encampment of carriers—harbour of Alicant — — — — 105

XV. Englifh factory—climate—defcription of the town—caftle blown up with the Englifh garrifon—Las huertas—tent wine—watering of the grounds—trade—drefling of a ftatue—opera—colony of S. Polo — — — — 111

XVI. Method of lodging in Spanifh inns—foreft of palm-trees—Orihuela—fertility—vale of Murcia—defcription of the city of Murcia—cathedral—fteeple—trophies of the inquifition—plain of Carthagena — — — — 116

XVII. Arfenal—docks—ftores—engines and pumps worked by flaves—fevere ufage of the flaves—row round the harbour—defcription of it—play-houfe—hofpital—landing-place of Santiago — 122

XVIII. Account of the different forts of barilla—barilla—gazul—foza—falicor—manner of diftinguifhing them—culture—earth of Almazaron — — — — 129

XIX. Journey over the defart—drefs of a gipfy—ancient gold mine—guadix—clay cliffs—Cuefta yefma — — 134

A 2   XX. Defcription

CONTENTS.

Letter
XX. Description and history of the ancient kingdom of Granada—etymology of its name—description of the city of Granada—chronological account of the kings—siege of Granada—speech of the last king—situation of the conquered Moors—despair and rebellion—Ferdinand de Valor—his murder—submission of the Moriscos—their final banishment — Page 138

XXI. Story of the Sultana—plot of the Zegris—murder of the Abencerrages—trial of the Sultana—combat—victory of the Spanish champions — — — — 154

XXII. Ancient population—productions—character of the ancient Granadines—sugar-plantations—Moriscos — 162

XXIII. Description of the Alhambra—palace of Charles the Vth—Moorish palace — — — — 171

XXIV. Alameda—description of the city—cathedral—chancery—beggars—play — — — — 188

XXV. Vale of Dauro—reservoirs—generaliph—anniversary of the surrender of Granada—governor of the palace — 197

XXVI. Journey to Malaga—Soto—improvements made by General Wall—his character and way of life—Antequera—mountains—vineyards and plain of Malaga—description of the city—castle—harbour—pier—cathedral—foreign factory—commerce—sugar-mills — — — — 201

XXVII. Journey to Cadiz—banditti—brood mares—rich deep plain of Andalusia—Roman bridge—Xeres—Port S. Mary—passage to Cadiz — — — — 210

XXVIII. Description of Cadiz—streets full of rats—tower of signals—population—Fort S. Sebastian—cathedral—barracks—bay—custom-house—commerce—smuggling—robbers—amusements
2·5

XXIX. Dances

CONTENTS.

Letter
XXIX. Dances—hiftory of the gipfies—journey to Gibraltar—falt-pans—Chiclana—mills of Vegel—bad lodging at Los Cortijos — woods — Spanifh lines — defcription of Gibraltar—Jews — — — Page 228

XXX. Return to Cadiz—farms—dinner at Vegel—fail down the bay—dock-yards—General O Reilly—ride to S. Lucar—Guadalquivir—journey to Seville—Xeres—Carthufians — 242

XXXI. Alcazar defcribed—feat of juftice of Don Pedro—character of that prince—ramble to Italica—amphitheatre — 251

XXXII. Hiftory of Seville—defcription of the city—cathedral—Giralda —aqueduct—fnuff-manufactory — — 261

XXXIII. Journey to Cordova—caftle of Carmona—ancient road—new colonies — — — 272

XXXIV. Environs of Cordova—defcription of the town—bull-feaft—character of the Cordovans—hiftory of Cordova — 276

XXXV. Potro — mofque — cloyfters — children expofed — earthen jars — — — — 295

XXXVI. Journey to Madrid—king's ftud—beautiful birds — Moorifh mill—colony of la Carolina—paffage of the Sierra Morena 306

XXXVII. La Mancha—wine of Valdepenas—eyes of the Guadiana—dancing gypfy — defcription of Toledo— Mofarabic rite—approach to Madrid wretched — — 317

XXXVIII. Situation of Aranjuez—woods on the banks of the Tagus—gardens—palace—town—water party—way of life — 327

XXXIX. Character of the royal family—orders of knighthood - 333

XL. King's

CONTENTS.

Letter
XL. King's stallions—jack-asses—Campo Flamenco—bull-feast—dexterity of a negro—parejas, or games on horseback   Page 340

XLI. Description of Madrid—churches, and stile of architecture—pictures—royal palace—marbles—pictures—Armeria—Buenretiro—Prado—canal—bridges—diamonds—Casa del Campo — — — 350

XLII. Character of the Spaniards—story of a friar and a girl—education of the nobility—account of living authors—Voto de S. Jago—character of the women — — 366

XLIII. Escurial—description of it—church—burial-place of the kings—gallery of pictures—passage of Fuenfrio—St. Ildefonso—pictures—water-works—glass-manufactory — 388

XLIV. Aqueduct of Segovia—cathedral—Alcazar—Algerine prisoners—mint—wool—journey through Old Castille—Valladolid—Burgos—history of Castille—description of the cathedral—origin of Gothic architecture discussed—Biscay—chearful country and good roads—Victoria—passage of the Bidassoa, and entrance into France — — 404

INDEX

INDEX of PERSONS.

A.

ABDALLAH, king of Cordova, 284.
Abdallacis, a Saracen general, 11. 101.
Abdoulrahman I. king of Cordova, 280, 296.
———————— II. king of Cordova, 283.
———————— III. king of Cordova, 284, 286, 382.
Abenaboo, chief of the Morifcos, 153.
Abencerrage, a Moorifh family, 155, 181.
Abiabdallah, king of Granada, 145.
Abilhaffan, king of Morocco, 144.
Abilhaffan, king of Granada, 150, 151.
Abouabdallah, king of Granada, 151, 152, 155, 181, 185.
Abouhadjad, king of Granada, 145.
Abuabdalla, king of Granada, 143.
Abuhagiagi, king of Granada, 144, 173.
Abulhaxex, king of Granada, 146, 185.
Aboumelik, a vifier, 284.

Acton, Mr. a Tufcan officer, 40.
Aguilar, a Spanifh hero, 160.
Alabece, a Moorifh family, 155.
Albinhamet, a Moor, 156, 199.
Alexander VI. pope, 107.
Algardi, fculptor, 329.
Alihamed, a Moor, 160.
Alhamar, king of Granada, 142.
Alizeriab, a Moorifh mufician, 282.
Alkahem I. king of Cordova, 283.
———————— II. king of Cordova, 282, 292.
Almanzor, a vifier, 185, 293.
Almaoalnayar, king of Granada, 148.
Almoradi, a Moor, 159.
Almundar, king of Cordova, 284.
Alphonfus of Aragon, 12.
———————— VI. of Caftille, 324.
———————— IX. of Caftille, 315.
———————— XI. of Caftille, 144.
Arcos, duke of, a Spanifh champion, 160.
Afturias, prince of, 331, 337, 348.
———————— princefs of, 337.
Ataulph, a Goth, 11.
Ayxa, a fultana, 151, 152.
Azarque, a Moor, 159.

5   B. Balba,

INDEX of PERSONS.

B.

Balba, king of Granada, 146.
Barbara, queen of Spain, 352.
Barceló, D. Ant. 36, 38, 40, 87.
Baroccio, a painter, 394.
Bayer, D. Franc. 378.
Benalhamar, king of Granada, 144.
Benofmin, king of Granada, 148.
Berwick, duke of, 13, 45.
Bologna, John of, a ftatuary, 366.
Bowles, Mr. Mich. 382.

C.

Callot, engraver, 366.
Calderon, a poet, 378.
Cafiri, D. Mich. 379.
Campomanes, D. Rodr. 379.
Cervantes, Mich. 109, 309, 377.
Charlemagne, 12, 281.
Charles the Bald, emperor, 12.
——— V. emperor, 12, 102, 171, 201, 254, 391.
——— VI. emperor, 13.
——— I. king of England, 353.
——— III. king of Spain, 248, 334.
Charcon, D. Juan, a Spanifh champion, 153, 160.
Cid Ruy dias, 101.
Coello, painter, 397.
Conti, an author, 155, 382.
Cordova, D. Ferd. a champion, 161.
——— D. Martin, mafter of Calatrava, 272.
Corrado, a painter, 353.
Correggio, a painter, 353, 359, 396.

E.

Elazari, king of Granada, 147, 148.
Elzagal, a Moor, 151.
Elzugair, king of Granada, 147.
Effex, earl of, 216.

F.

Farinelli, a finger, 362.
Fatima, queen of Granada, 151.
Ferdinand Gonzales of Caftille, 414.
——— regent of Caftille, 12, 146.
——— de Valor, 153.
——— St. 142, 262, 323.
——— V. of Aragon, 12, 13, 151, 152, 193, 202, 406.
——— VI. of Spain, 5, 269, 352, 400.
Flores, an author, 72, 75.

G.

Garcias, Sanchez, of Caftille, 415.
Giles, Perez, an author, 154.
Gomeles, a Moorifh family, 155.
Gregory VII. pope, 323.
Grimaldi, marquis of, 332, 337, 348.
Guercino, a painter, 351.
Guido, a painter, 395, 396.
Guarin, John, a hermit, 54.

H.

Hadrian, emperor, 256.
Hamilcar, Carthaginian, 11, 50.
Hannibal, Carthaginian, 50, 92.
Henry Tranftamare, king of Spain, 255, 273.

Henry

INDEX of PERSONS.

Henry IV. king of Spain, 352.
Hermenegild, a martyr, 268.
Herrera, John, architect, 270.
Hiaya, king of Cordova, 101.
Hiſſem, king of Cordova, 283, 297.

I.

James I. king of Aragon, 102.
―― II. ―――――― 108.
Ibnbekir, a Moor, 292.
Ignatius, St. 58.
Ildephonſus, St. 323.
Infants of Spain, 338.
Joan, queen of Spain, 193.
John of Auſtria, 13, 199.
―― II. king of Caſtille, 265.
Iſabella, queen of Spain, 151, 152, 406.
Iſidore, St. 323.
Juan, George, author, 381.
Julian, count, a Goth, 140.
Iſmael, king of Granada, 149.
Juſef, king of Morocco, 261.
Juvara, Philip, architect, 354.

L.

Lago, king of Granada, 144.
La Mina, marquis de, 17.
Leo, emperor, 286.
Leovigild, a Goth, 268.
Lewis the Debonnair, emperor, 11.
―― XIV. king of France, 13.
Licinius ſura, 72.
Lopes la Vega, poet, 377.
Luca Giordano, painter, 353.
Lucan, poet, 279.
Luna, Peter de, antipope, 85.

M.

Mahomet, king of Morocco, 315.
Marti, dean of Alicant, 90.
Martin of Aragon, 12.
Mary, queen of England, 207.
Mayans, Gregory, author, 379.
Mengs, painter, 330, 355, 359.
Mudo, painter, 393.
Murillo, painter, 266, 353, 358.
Muza, a moor, 157, 159.
Muza, a Saracen general, 140, 261.
Muley, king of Granada, 142.

N.

Nata, daughter of Count Julian, 140.
Nazer, king of Granada, 143.

O.

Olavides, intendant of Seville, 271.
O Reilly, general, 27, 28, 29, 30, 41, 248.

P.

Padilla, Maria de, 273.
Pedraza, hiſtorian, 139.
Pedro, king of Caſtille, 144, 253, 254, 255, 272.
Pelayo, king of Aſturias, 140.
Peter, king of Aragon, 315.
Petronilla, of Aragon, 12.
Pharagi, king of Granada, 143.
Philip I. king of Caſtille, 193.
―― II. ―――――― 207, 330, 390, 391, 411.

B   Philip

INDEX of PERSONS.

Philip III. king of Castille, 154, 411.
—— IV. ———————— 13, 398.
—.— V. ——.———— 13, 107, 186, 253, 400.
Ponz, an author, 381.

Q.

Queen of Granada, 155, 160.

R.

Ramiro II. of Leon, 383.
——— III. ———— 414.
———— II. of Aragon, 12.
Raymund V. of Barcelona, 12.
Raphael, painter, 353, 395, 397.
Rodrigo, king of the Goths, 140.
Rubens, painter, 358, 394.

S.

Sabatini, architect, 363.
Sachetti, architect, 354.
Sancho, the brave, king of Castille, 265.
Sancho of Navarre, 315, 415.
Sarte, Andrea del, painter, 396.
Scipio, 74, 258.
Seneca, 279, 305.
Sertorius, 70.
Spagnolet, 358, 394.

T.

Tacca, statuary, 362.
Tarif, Saracen general, 140, 142.
Teresa, St. 398.
Tiepolo, painter, 355.
Theodosius, emperor, 256.
Tintoret, painter, 396.
Titian, painter, 330, 351, 357, 393.
Trajan, emperor, 256.

U.

Vandyke, painter, 358, 394.
Velasco, Lewis, 9.
Velasquez, painter, 353, 358, 394.
Veronese, painter, 394.
Veruguete, architect, 175.
Ulloa, author, 381.

W.

Walid, Caliph, 140.
Wall, general Richard, 180, 201, 328.
Wifred, the hairy, 12.

X.

Ximenes, Cardinal, 324, 325.

Z.

Zegris, a Moorish family, 155.

INDEX

INDEX of PLACES.

A.

ALCALA', 269.
Alcanterilla, 212.
Aldaya river, 410.
Alhama, 150.
Algiers, 31.
Alicant, 111.
Almazaron, 133.
Almenara, 89.
Almeria, 152.
Alpuxaras mountains, 139.
Alzira, 106.
Anduxar, 309.
Antequera, 204.
Aranjuez, 327.

B.

Baça, 152.
Balaguer, 80.
Barcelona, 11.
Bellegarde, 4.
Benicarlo, 84.
Besos river, 8.
Boulou, 3.
Bidassoa river, 427.
Burgos, 413.

C.

Cabeças, 213.
Cabeçon, 412.
Cadiz, 215.
Carlotta, 274.
Carmona, 272.
Carolina, 310.
Carpio, 309.
Carthagena, 122.
Casa Campo, 366.
Castillon, 86.
Cenia river, 84.
Ceuta, 238.
Chiclana, 232.
Conil, 233.
Cordova, 276.
Cortigos, 234.
Consuegra, 319.

D.

Dauro river, 141.
Duero river, 411.

E.

Ebro river, 81.
Eccija, 274.

Elche

INDEX of PLACES.

Elche, 118.
Elda, 109.
Escombrero island, 122.
Escurial, 389.

F.
Figuera, 5.
Francolis river, 75.

G.
Gaya river, 73.
Gibraltar, 237.
Girona, 6.
Granada, 141.
Guadalete river, 214.
Guadalquivir river, 248.
Guadaviar river, 98.
Guadiana river, 319.
Guadix, 136.

H.
Hornillo, 410.
Hostalric, 7.
Huertas of Alicant, 113.

I.
Ildefonso, St. 355.
Isla, 231.
Isnallos, 134.
Italica, 256.
Junquera, 5.

L.
Lebrixa, 213.
Llobregat river, 51.

Leucate bay, 2.
Loja, 204.
Lorca, 135.
Luisiana, 274.

M.
Madrid, 326.
Malaga, 205, 291.
Marbella, 169.
Martorel, 50, 60.
Mataro, 65.
Mejares river, 86.
Medina Sidonia, 221.
Miranda, 422.
Montesa, 108.
Montfort, 109.
Montserrat, 50.
Montjuich, 46.
Morviedro, 88.
Motril, 169.
Moxente, 108.
Murcia, 119.
Molares, 212.

N.
Narbonne, 1.
Navas de Tolosa, 315.
Nules, 79.

O.
Orihuela, 118.
Osmedo, 410.
Ossuna, 210.

P. Pancorvo,

INDEX of PLACES.

P.

Pancorvo, 422.
Pardo, 389.
Parillo, 81.
Pedrera, 210.
Peniscola, 85.
Perpignan, 2.
Puerto Lapice, 318.
Puerto Real, 221.
Puerto Santa Maria, 214.
Puiferga river, 412.

R.

Reus, 76.
Rota, 221.

S.

Salo, 77.
Salinas, 426.
San Lucar, 248.
San Felipe, 107.
San Polo, 115.
San Roque, 236.
Segovia, 404.
Seville, 133, 142, 250, 262.
Sierra Morena, 306, 309.
Sitges, 65.
Sijean, 2.
Sierra Elvira, 142.
Sierra Nevada, 141.
Simancas, 411.

Suaço bridge, 215.

T.

Tagus river, 320, 328*l*
Tangiers, 238.
Tarragona, 75.
Tech river, 4.
Tetuan, 238.
Toledo, 320.
Tortofa, 83.
Torquemada, 412.
Tolofa, 427.

U.

Valencia, 98.
Valdepenas, 319.
Valladolid, 411.
Vegel, 233, 245.
Ventaplatero, 80.
Villena, 109.
Villa Real, 86.
Ville Santa Cruz, 410.
Villa Franca, 72.
Victoria, 425.
Vinaros, 85.

X.

Xenil river, 141.
Xeres, 140, 214.
Xucar river, 106.

ERRATA.

ERRATA.

Page ix. for *Favita*, read *Favila*.
xi. for *Maravadi*, read *Maravedi*.
44. for *of such vermine*, read *of vermine*.
45. for *by an hollow*, read *by a hollow*.
65. for *Mataw*, read *Mataro*.
73. for *lowest trees*, read *locust trees*.
91. for *military architecture: a wall*, read *military architecture are; a wall*.
106. for *it is very shallow*, read *which is very shallow*.
113. for *las huertas; the gardens of Alicant lying*, read *las huertas, the gardens of Alicant, lying*.
119. for *Peric pepper*, read *Peru pepper*.
135. for *Lorea*, read *Lorca*.
135. for *metals*, read *medals*.
225. for *Alcade*, read *Alcalde*.
250. for *incorrupted*, read *uncorrupted*.
275. for *groves, clump and*, read *groves, clumps and*.
283. for *of the Narbonne*, read *of Narbonne*.
291. for *Murica*, read *Murcia*.
328. for *for the spring*, read *for spring*.
331. for *magnificient*, read *magnificent*.
341. for *in a grand scale*, read *on a grand scale*.
358. for *Saville*, read *Seville*.
364. for *there are three*, read *these are three*.
375. for *at San lucas*, read *at San lucar*.
380. for *lashes away*, read *dashes away*.
383. for *Compostilla*, read *Compostella*.
385. for *near Terragona*, read *near Taragona*.
394. for *tents, semitents*, read *tints, semitints*.
395. for *is presented, sitting with her right hand, holding*, read *is represented sitting, with her right hand holding*.
396. for *Corriggio*, read *Correggio*.
397. for *Viago*, read *Viage*.
399. for *Parnese*, read *Farnese*.
400. for *resembles modern*, read *resembles a modern*.
406. for *Nicestra*, read *nuestra*.
411. for *were the palace*, read *were the palaces*.
416. for *correspond exactly to the*, read *correspond exactly with the*.

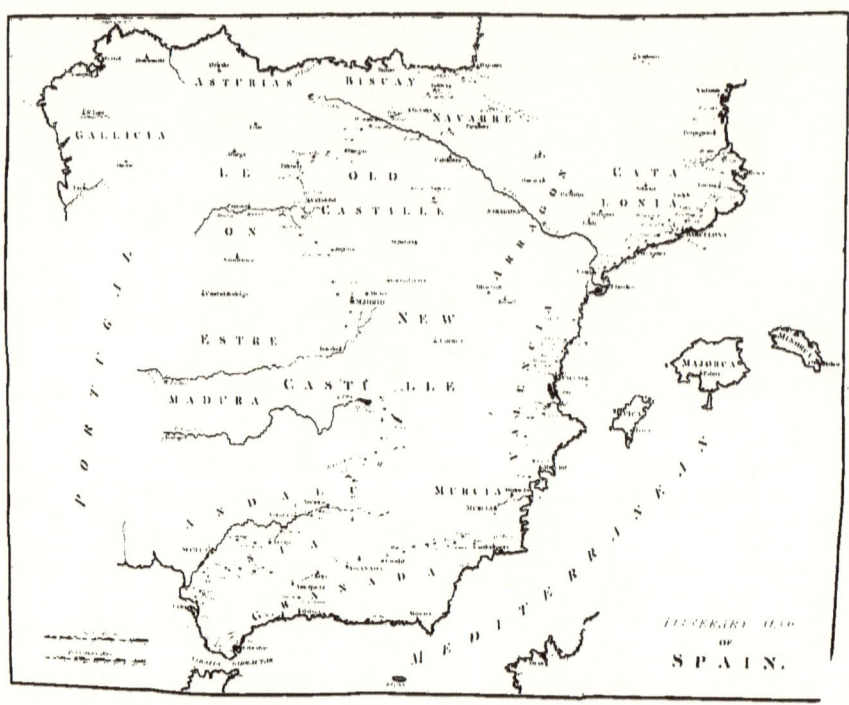

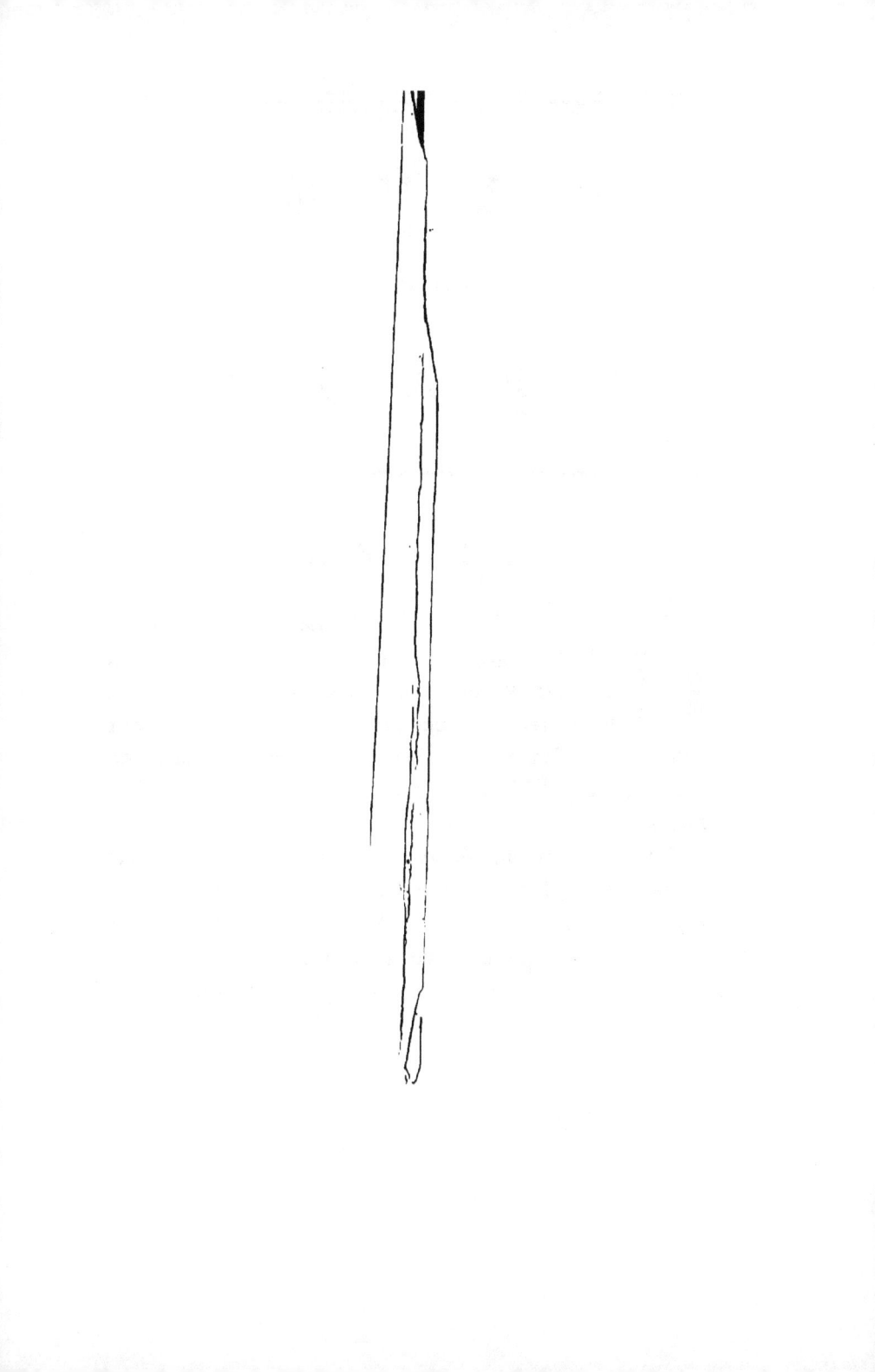

TRAVELS
THROUGH
SPAIN.

LETTER I.

Perpignan, October 23, 1775.

HERE we are, in hopes of setting out for Spain to-morrow, but many are the difficulties we shall have to encounter before we make our point good. Mules and horses are scarce and dear, and the roads are said to be much damaged by the late floods.

After a thousand delays, we left Toulouse at one o'clock on Sunday, and, travelling all night, reached Narbonne about noon next day. Having rambled over that small city, and perused the ancient inscriptions in the archiepiscopal archiepifcopal palace, we thought it advifeable to move on ; and accordingly came to fleep at Sigean, in order to have more leifure at Perpignan for arranging matters, and looking out for mules and other requifites for our Spanifh journey.

There is not a more barren country on the face of the earth, than that between Narbonne and Rivefaltes, famous for its mufcadine wine; yet I fufpect you would prefer thofe bleak grey hills to more fertile fpots ; for among the ftones, and through the crannies of the rocks, fhoot up innumerable tribes of aromatic plants, on which, as a botanift, your eye would feaft with rapture. The fuperior excellence of the Narbonne honey is, no doubt, owing to this profufion of ftrong-fcented flowers, on which the bees feed.

The bay of Leucate, and the plains that ftretch out from the fea to the foot of the Pyrenean mountains, form a noble fweep, that bears fome refemblance to the gulph of Naples.

Perpignan is a villainous ugly town, on the fkirts of an extenfive flat, that has juft olive woods enough to make a tolerable appearance from the ramparts. The grounds are inclofed with the tall yellow-flowering aloe.

LETTER

LETTER II.

San Salony, October 27, 1775.

AS I am informed the post passes by to-morrow from Barcelona, I write from this place, lest we should be delayed by any accident, and so miss the opportunity.

The weather hitherto has been very favourable; a clear sky and warm sun since the 24th, the day we left Perpignan. There was such a scarcity of mules, that we were forced to comply with the exorbitant demands of a French *voiturier* and two Italian rope-dancers, who insisted upon twenty Louis-d'ors for ten horses as far as Barcelona: one of the tumblers rides postillion to our carriage; and for want of a saddle-horse, my man S* G*** goes with the other in a crazy two-wheeled chaise; but any thing, to get away from Perpignan, a most disagreeable town, and, to a curious traveller, destitute of every kind of recommendation.

The heavy rains that fell about a month ago, swelled the torrents to such a degree, that in many places they spoiled the road; this rendered our evening journey very uncomfortable, and made it late before we could reach a poor inn at Boulou, near the mountains that separate Roussillon from Catalonia. By the help of our own beds, cook, and provisions, we rested very well in our hovel, and next morning fallied forth as burlefque a caravan as ever left inn fince the days of ¹ *Le Deſtin & La Rancune*. Several ingenious perfons travelling to the fair of Girona had joined company with us; we compofed the center; our vanguard was formed by a drummer and a tabor and pipe; the rear was brought up by a camel, loaded with five monkies, efcorted by two men who carried his portrait. Thefe, and three pedlars, whom we foon after overtook, were all come from the Milanefe. A few paces from the inn we croffed the Tech, a broad torrent, very dangerous after rain: in the late floods it caufed immoderate damage to the country. A few miles farther, we came to the chain of mountains that divides France and Spain, which are of no very confiderable elevation.

The road over the pafs is a noble work, and reflects great honour on the engineer who planned it. It is now very wide; the rocks are blafted, and fpread out, and bridges are laid over the hollows, which formerly were moſt dangerous precipices. It then required the ftrength of thirty men to fupport, and almoſt as many oxen to drag up a carriage, which four horfes now draw with eafe.

Exactly on the limits of France, in the higheſt part of the pafs, ſtands the fort of Bellegarde, on a round hill, commanding a boundlefs view over both kingdoms: an officer

¹ Scarron's Comic Romance.

officer of invalids has a lodge below, where he examines and signs the paſſports.

At La Junquiera, the firſt Spaniſh town, an officer of the cuſtoms made a ſhew of examining our baggage; but a piece of money ſoon put an end to his ſearch. Near this place a bloody battle was fought in 920, between the Chriſtians and Moors, in which the former were defeated with great ſlaughter. This was once a conſiderable city, a colony of the Maſſilians, or people of Marſeilles, and afterwards an epiſcopal ſee: but now it is a paltry village, ſubſiſting on what little is ſpent in it by paſſengers, and on the produce of the cork-woods, which ſeem to turn to good account. The ſurrounding mountains are covered with thoſe trees; moſt of them are of great ſize and age: their trunks, lately ſtripped of the bark, are of a duſky red colour: the operation of peeling them cannot be repeated above once in ſeven or eight years; but in the ſouthern parts of Spain, they do it every fifth year.

From hence to Figuera, an ugly ſtraggling town, the country improves every ſtep; the hills are cloathed with evergreen woods; the plains, in the fineſt cultivation, are divided by hedges of aloe, chriſtthorn, or wild pomegranate. The inhabitants are well-clad, good-looking fellows; the women much comelier than their neighbours on the French ſide of the Pyrenees. Ferdinand the Sixth began a moſt ſpacious fortreſs above Figuera, capable of containing 12,000 men: it is far from being finiſhed,

finished, and indeed it is difficult to guefs what fervice it can be of when completed.

Our journey to Girona was very pleafant, through a well-laid-out country, diverfified with fertile plains, and gentle eminences crowned with ever-green oaks and pines. The view ftretches down over the olive plantations, in the low grounds, as far as the fea; flender towers on the points of the rocks, and white fteeples rifing out of the woods, add great life to this charming fcene.

In every village, we found the people bufily employed in making ropes, bafkets, and fhoes, of a fmall rufh or reed called *efparto*.

Girona, where we lay laft night, is a large clean city, with fome good ftreets; but poorly inhabited, and for the moft part gloomy. The churches are darker than caverns; the gothic cathedral is grand, but fo very dark at the upper end, that but for the glimmering of two fmoky lamps, we fhould not have difcovered that the canopy and altar are of maffy filver.

The road was all this morning very hilly, but the dryneſs of the weather prevented it from being at its ufual pitch of badnefs. Every thing, as Panglofs fays, is for the beft: had we left Bagneres when we intended, we fhould have had thefe deep roads to pafs immediately after exceffive rains; and, ten to one, fhould have been delayed many days by the fwelling of the torrents. Great part of this day's journey has been through the moſt ſavage wilds in nature: nothing but mountains upon mountains, covered with pines; a rambling ſandy river fills up the hollows, winding through all the turns of the hanging woods and narrow dells; a ſlight track on the ſand is the only thing that conveys any idea of the footſteps of man. The caſtle of Hoſtalric, a modern fortreſs, commands the outlet of this deſart, and overlooks the turrets and walls of an old ruinous village, wildly ſituated on the brink of a precipice.

This morning, on leaving Girona, we met with a laughable accident. S* G*, who travels in the vehicle of the mountebank, was rouſed from his nap by the bottom of the chaiſe ſuddenly giving way, and dropping them both into the river Ter. They were obliged to walk in the chaiſe (literally *ſe promener en voiture*) quite through the water, before their horſes could be prevailed upon to ſtop.

The peaſants have brought us partridges for ſupper, though it be Friday, and ſeem very well accuſtomed to ſee meat eaten on faſting days; however, the maid of the inn thinks to atone for this irregularity, by placing before us on the table a well-dreſt image of the Virgin, to whom ſhe expects we ſhould behave with proper liberality.

The mode of drinking in this country is ſingular: they hold a broad-bottom'd glaſs bottle at arm's length, and let the liquor ſpout out of a long neck upon their

tongue;

tongue; from what I see, their expertness at this exercise arises from frequent practice; for the Catalans drink often, and in large quantities, but as yet I have not seen any of them intoxicated.

LETTER III.

Barcelona, October 31, 1775.

OUR journey of the 28th was by much the most severe as to roads; the cross ones in Sussex are not worse. The pass called *El Purgatorio* had very near proved a *Hell* to us; for we thought at one time that the carriages must have remained jammed in between the rocks. The prospects on each side of the way are for the greatest part delightful; nothing can be more agreeable to the eye than the gothic steeples towering above the dark pine-groves, the bold ruins of La Rocca, and the rich fields on the banks of the Besos; but the passes are so bad, the roads so cut up, deep, and dangerous, that it was not possible to enjoy the beauties that surrounded us.

We got into this city just before the shutting of the gates. Upon the whole, this four days journey, though attended

attended with some disagreeable circumstances, was far from unpleasant; the weather was charming, and our health and spirits excellent, with which it is easy to bear up against the little rubs and vexations of an expedition like ours. The obstinacy of our coachmen, by taking the inland road, deprived us of the satisfaction of seeing the towns and orange-gardens along the coast.

We have paid the necessary visits to those in command. The governor of the place is a Velasco, brother to that Don Lewis who was killed at the surprize of the Moro castle. It is strange enough that the king should bestow the title of *Conde del Asalto* on the brother; it might with more propriety be conferred on the English general, who commanded the attack.

Our first entertainment here was the Spanish comedy. Alas! most of its glorious absurdities are vanished, and Dulness has established her throne on this stage. I was quite tired, and longed to have seen Harlequin carrying relics in procession, saints and devils engaged in doubtful conflict, and Lucifer acting the part of a prior of a convent, as they did formerly in the Loas and Autos sacramentales*.

---

* Autos and mysterios are prohibited on the theatres of Madrid, but are frequently represented upon all others in the kingdom, and even in the puppet-shews at the royal country residences. A friend of mine saw one acted last year at San Lucar, called the Conversion of Saint Barbara; a friar, by way of proving to her the mystery of the Trinity, gathered up three folds in the skirt of his habit, and then let them fall. The three plaits in one cloth were the image of three persons in one God.

I am afraid we are come here a century too foon, or a century too late, and that the old original caft is worn off the character of the Spaniards, without their having thoroughly acquired the polifh of France or England: this will render them a much lefs interefting race of people: in this province they are faid to advance apace; Barcelona feems to be a bufy, thriving town, and the Catalans an induftrious fet of men.

The playhoufe is handfome, and well-lighted up. The firft piece we faw acted was a tragedy, in which there were no parts for women in the dramatis perfonæ; fo, in order to make it ridiculous, the actreffes put on breeches and performed the play, without allowing any males to appear among them. The declamation was bombaftical and whining. The prompters (for they have them in many parts of the ftage) read aloud, verfe by verfe, what the player repeated after them, with the addition of a final twang, or an occafional fwing of the arm. Between the firft and the fecond acts we had a feguidilla fung, as wild and uncouth as any thing can be, but now and then fome very moving paffages ftruck the ear. After the fecond, we had, for interlude, an attack made upon the actreffes by the actors from a corner of the front boxes. The wit was bandied about very brifkly, and made the audience roar again, but, as far as I could underftand, it was very poor quibbling.

Before I proceed to give you any information concerning

ing the present state of the country, you perhaps will not be sorry to know something of its particular history.

The account of the original inhabitants of Catalonia, and of the foundation of Barcelona, are, with the rest of the early history of Spain, involved in such a cloud of fables, that nothing satisfactory relative to those dark ages can be discovered. The Massilians appear to have carried on a great trade, and to have been much connected with these provinces. Hamilcar Barcas is said to have founded Barcino, now Barcelona; but the Carthaginians did not long keep possession of it, for we find their boundary fixed at the Ebro, so early as the end of the first Punic war. After the fall of the Carthaginian commonwealth, the Romans turned their whole attention towards Tarraco, and neglected Barcino, though they made it a colony by the name of Faventia.

In the fifth century, the barbarians of the north of Europe, having pushed their conquests as far as this peninsula, divided it among the different nations that composed their victorious armies. Catalonia fell to the lot of the Goths under Ataulph, in 414. It remained under their dominion to the year 714, when it was forced to submit to the yoke of the Saracens; who, under the command of Abdallah Cis, made themselves masters of all the coast, as far as the Pyrenees. Tarragona being now no better than an heap of ruins, Barcelona became imperceptibly the capital of the province. Lewis the Debonnair,

nair, fon of Charlemagne, took it from the Moors in 800. From that period, the emperors, kings of France, governed Catalonia by appointing counts or vicegerents, removeable at pleafure, till the government was rendered hereditary in the family of Wifred the Hairy : whether this happened by a conceffion of Charles the Bald, or by ufurpation, remains a doubt among the learned. It con-tinued in his pofterity for many generations. This prince having been grievoufly wounded in a battle againft the Normans, received a vifit from the emperor, who dipping his finger in the blood that trickled from the wound, drew four lines down the gilt fhield of Wifred, faying, " Earl, be thefe thy armorial enfign." Four pallets Gules, on a field Or, remained from that time the coat of arms of Catalonia, and afterwards of Aragon, when Raymund the Fifth married Petronilla, only daughter and heirefs of Ramiro the Second, king of Aragon. Their fon Alfonfo fucceeded to that crown in 1162. The heirs male of Aragon failing in Martin, the Cortes or ftates elected Ferdinand of Caftille, whofe grandfon Ferdinand the Catholic, by his marriage with Ifabella heirefs of Caftille, and by the conqueft of Granada, united all the Spanifh kingdoms into one compact formidable monarchy, which devolved upon the houfe of Auftria, in the perfon of his grandfon Charles.

The violent fpirit of the Catalans, and their enthufi-aftic paffion for liberty, have often rendered their country
the

the seat of civil war and bloodshed : insurrections have been more frequent here than in any other part of Europe. The most remarkable were ; first, that in the time of Ferdinand the Fifth, when the peasants rose in arms to deliver themselves from the oppression of the nobles. Secondly, that under Philip the Fourth, about the time that the Portuguese shook off the Spanish yoke ; the issue of the war was not equally favourable to the Catalans, who failed in their attempt of becoming independent, and after having been twelve years under the protection of France, were reduced to obedience by Don John of Austria. Thirdly, that during the war of the succession, the most famous rebellion, as the French and Spanish writers stigmatize it ; or, in the language of a republican, the most obstinate struggle they ever made to break their chains and become a free nation. They attached themselves to the party of the archduke Charles, whose coin is still current in the province. In 1706, Barcelona sustained a siege, which Philip the Fifth was obliged to raise on the appearance of an English fleet. Though shamefully deserted by England at the peace of Utrecht, and afterwards by the emperor, the Catalans persisted in their revolt, and, having no longer the protection of any foreign prince to expect, resolved to form themselves into a commonwealth.

Lewis the Fourteenth sent the Duke of Berwick, in 1714, with a formidable army, to reduce Barcelona. The
trenches

trenches were opened in July, and the works carried on with the greatest vigour for sixty-one days; a French fleet blocked up the port, and prevented any succours or provisions from getting in. Yet, notwithstanding the famine that raged within, the terrible fire kept up by the enemy's batteries, and the despondency of the regular troops, who were inclined to a capitulation, the burgesses, animated by despair, rejected all offers of accommodation, and seemed determined to bury themselves under the ruins of their city. The very friars, inspired by the same enthusiasm, ran up and down the streets exhorting their fellow-citizens to die like brave men, rather than live the despicable slaves of a despot. The women, the children breathed the same spirit, and shared the labours of the defence with their husbands and fathers.

After sustaining four bloody assaults, and disputing the breach inch by inch, being at last driven from the ramparts, and from a breastwork they had thrown up behind the walls, they were obliged to fly for refuge to the new part of the town, where they made a kind of capitulation. Their persons were to remain untouched, but every privilege abolished, and heavy taxes laid upon them to recompense the soldiery. Since this epocha, Catalonia has borne the yoke with sullen patience, except when, a few years ago, the mode of raising recruits by *quintas* or ballot was ordered to be adopted in this as well as the other provinces of Spain. The Catalans, to whom such a
regulation

regulation was new, and confequently odious, were upon the point of taking up arms; but, a few rioters being killed by the cannon of the citadel, the commotion was quelled in the capital, and, the king having given up the project for the prefent, the reft of the principality was pacified. However, no arms are allowed to be carried by the common people, and very ftrict difcipline is kept up in Barcelona.

LETTER IV.

Barcelona, November 3, 1775.

THIS city is a fweet fpot; the air equals in purity, and much excels in mildnefs, the boafted climate of Montpellier. Except in the dog-days, they have green peafe all the year round. The fituation is beautiful, the appearance both from land and fea remarkably picturefque. A great extent of fruitful plains, bounded by an amphitheatre of hills, backs it on the weft fide; the mountain of Montjuich defends it on the fouth from the unwholefome winds that blow over the marfhes at the mouth of the Llobregat; to the northward, the coaft projecting into the fea, forms a noble bay; it has the

Mediterranean

Mediterranean to clofe the profpect to the eaft. The environs are in a ftate of high cultivation, ftudded with villages, country houfes, and gardens.

The form of Barcelona is almoft circular, the Roman town being on the higheft ground in the center of the new one; the ancient walls are ftill vifible in feveral places, but the fea has retired many hundreds of yards from the port gates; one of the principal gothic churches, and a whole quarter of the city, ftand upon the fands that were once the bottom of the harbour. The immenfe loads of fand hurried down into the fea by the rivers, and thrown back by wind and current into this haven, will, in all probability, choak it quite up, unlefs more diligence be ufed in preventing the gathering of the fhoals. A foutherly wind brings in the fand, and already a deep-loaden veffel finds it dangerous to pafs over the bar. Some years ago a company of Dutch and Englifh adventurers offered to bring the river into the port by means of a canal, if government would allow them a free importation for ten years. This project might have cleared away the fand-banks, but might alfo have given a fatal check to the infant manufactures of the country, for which reafon the propofal was rejected. The port is handfome; the mole is all of hewn ftone, a mafter-piece of folidity and convenience. Above is a platform for carriages; below, vaft magazines, with a broad key reaching from the city gates to the lighthoufe. This was done

done by the orders of the late Marquis de La Mina, captain-general of the principality, where his memory is held in greater veneration than at the court of Madrid. He governed Catalonia many years, more like an independent sovereign, than like a subject invested with a delegated authority. Great are the obligations Barcelona has to him; he cleansed and beautified its streets, built useful edifices, and forwarded its trade and manufactures, without much extraordinary expence to the province; for he had more resources, and made money go farther than most other governors can do, or indeed wish to do. On the neck of land that runs into the sea, and forms the port, he pulled down some fishermen's huts, and in 1752 began to build Barceloneta, a regular town, consisting of about two thousand brick houses, quarters for a regiment, and a church, in which his ashes are deposited under a tastelefs monument, with the following barbarous epitaph.

D.   O.   M.
Hic Gufmannorum jacet Epitome
Exc. Dom. Marchio de la Mina,
Dux, Princeps, fummus Imperator, Præfes,
In Acie Fulmen, in Aulâ Flamen,
Obiit heu! Homo, at non abiit Heros
Cui Infcriptio, Virtus omnis
Die 30 Jan. Anno 1768.
R.   I.   P.

As the land was given gratis, the houfes were foon run up on a regular plan; a ground-floor and one ftory above, with three windows in front and a pediment over them; the whole confifting of about twenty ftreets, and containing nigh ten thoufand inhabitants.

The lighthoufe at the end of the pier is a flender tower, near which fhips lie when they perform quarantine. The old one ftood much nearer the land, but was fwept away in a dreadful hurricane.

Another of La Mina's improvements, is the rampart or great walk upon the walls, extending the whole length of the harbour. It is all built upon arches, with magazines below, and a broad coach-road and foot-path above, raifed to the level of the firft floor of the houfes in the adjoining ftreet. In thefe clear, warm evenings, it is very pleafant to walk along this pavement, to the arfenal at the fouth-eaft angle of the city; where they are bufy raifing new fortifications, to prevent a furprize, in cafe of an infurrection. The late expedition againft Algiers, has drained thefe magazines fo completely, that fcarce a cannon, or even a nail, is to be feen. The work-fhops are built upon a grand fcale, but little bufinefs is going forward at prefent.

At this corner the rampart joins the Rambla, a long irregular ftreet, which they have begun to level and widen, with the intention of planting an avenue down the middle. Here the ladies parade in their coaches,

and

and sometimes go quite round the city upon the walls, which are of brick, lately repaired and enlarged. The drive is charming, having a sweet country on one side, and on the other, clusters of small gardens and orange-yards. You descend at the north gate into a very spacious square before the citadel, just where the grand breach was made, when the duke of Berwick besieged the town.

The citadel has six strong bastions, calculated to over-awe the inhabitants, at least as much as to defend them from a foreign enemy. The lowness of its situation renders it damp, unwholesome, and swarming with mosquitos. The major of this fortress owes his promotion to a singular circumstance. When the present king arrived at Madrid in 1759, a magnificent bull-feast was given in honour of that event: as it is necessary upon such occasions, that those who fight on horseback should be gentlemen born, the managers of the exhibition were greatly at a loss; till this man, who was a poor, starving officer, presented himself, though utterly ignorant both of bull-fighting and horsemanship. By dint of resolution, and the particular favour of fortune, he kept his seat, and performed his part so much to the public satisfaction, that he was rewarded with a pension and a majority.

The streets of Barcelona are narrow, but well paved; a covered drain in the middle of each street carries off the filth and rain-water. At night they are tolerably well lighted-up, but long before day-break every lamp is out. The houses are lofty and plain. To each kind of trade a particular diſtrict is allotted.

The principal edifices are, the cathedral, Santa Maria, the general's palace, and the exchange. The architecture of the cathedral is a light gothic, which, in the ornaments of the cloyſters, is inimitably airy. The ſtalls of the choir are neatly carved, and hung with eſcutcheons of princes and noblemen, among which I remarked the arms of our Henry the Eighth. The double arches under the belfry are deſervedly admired, for bearing on their center the whole weight of two enormous towers. In the cloyſters various kinds of foreign birds are kept, upon funds bequeathed for that purpoſe, by a wealthy canon. I could not learn what motives induced him to make ſo whimſical a deviſe.

Santa Maria is alſo a gothic pile.

The palace is ſquare and low, without out-courts or gardens, and contains nothing worthy of remark but a noble ball-room.

Oppoſite to its ſouth front, they are now erecting, out of the ruins of an old habitation of the earls of Barcelona, a new exchange upon an extenſive plan, but in a heavy taſte. The architect aſſured us the ſhell would not coſt above 300,000 Catalan livres; but he muſt either have impoſed upon us, or do very extraordinary

juſtice

juſtice to the truſt repoſed in him, if he builds ſuch a maſs of ſtone for that ſum. The work is carried on by means of a tax upon imports. In the old part of the building yet left ſtanding, the board of commerce has inſtituted an academy for drawing, in which five hundred boys are taught that art, and furniſhed with all proper implements, gratis. A maſter from Paris is the director of their ſtudies; and every month prizes of fifteen and twenty dollars are diſtributed to the moſt deſerving.

The Roman antiquities in this city are: 1. A moſaic pavement, in which are repreſented two large green figures of tritons, holding a ſhell in each hand; between them a ſea-horſe, and on the ſides a ſerpent and a dolphin. The common opinion is, that this church was a temple of Eſculapius; but the ornaments ſeem to prove very clearly that it belonged to ſome fane dedicated to Neptune. 2. Many vaults and cellars of Roman conſtruction. 3. The archdeaconry, once the palace of the prætor or Roman governor. From the ſolidity of the walls, and the regularity of the work, I am inclined to believe the tradition; but there is neither grandeur nor elegance to recommend it to notice. Some medallions and inſcriptions fixed in the wall, apparently at the time of its erection, rather invalidate the idea of ſuch remote antiquity. 4. In the yard, a beautiful ciſtern, or rather ſarcophagus, which now ſerves as a watering-trough for mules. They call it the coffin of Pompey's
father,

father, and it may as well be his as that of any one elſe, for we have no proof to the contrary. A large baſs-relief runs round it, of hunters, dogs, and wild beaſts. The chief perſon is on horſeback, bareheaded, in a military dreſs. The figures and animals are executed in a maſterly ſtyle, and the whole is a fine monument of antiquity. 5. In the houſe belonging to the family of Pinos, which was almoſt levelled to the ground by the bombs during the ſiege, are many excellent buſts and medallions. An *Auguſtus Pater*, with a *corona radialis*, a ſmall elegant Bacchus, and a woman holding a rabbit, ſuppoſed to repreſent Spain, the Provincia cunicularis, are the moſt remarkable. The owners of this houſe have always remained ſo true to their principles in politics, that they have conſtantly reſided in a poor dwelling hard by, and left their palace in ruins, as a *memento* to their fellow-citizens, and a monument of their own ſpirit and misfortunes.

LETTER

LETTER V.

Barcelona, November 10, 1775.

YESTERDAY, being the feftival of Saint Charles Borromeo, the king's patron, it was kept as a day of *Gala*. All the officers waited upon the governor in grand uniform; the theatre was illuminated, and crowded with well-dreft company, which made a very handfome fhew; the price of admittance was raifed from half a piftreen to a whole one. The pit is divided into feats, let by the year, each perfon keeping his own key; the boxes are taken for the feafon, and the upper gallery is filled with women in white veils, and no men allowed to fit among them; fo that a ftranger is at a lofs for a place.

The play was the *Cid Campeador*, an hiftorical tragedy, written with a great deal of fire, and force of character. The actors, in the old Spanifh habit and Moorifh garment, feemed to enter more than ufual into the fenfe of the author. In all tragedies they drop a curtefy, inftead of bowing, to kings and heroes. A pretty ballad was fung by a woman, in the fmart drefs of a *Maja* or coquette: fhe wore her hair in a fcarlet net, with taffels; a ftriped gauze handkerchief crofled over her breaft; a
rich

rich jacket, flowered apron, and brocade petticoat. I observed the pit was crowded with clergymen.

I passed the morning in the cabinet of natural history, belonging to Mr. Salvador. The botanical specimens are the most perfect part of the collection, though he possesses many rare things in every other branch of that study.

This afternoon has been employed in copying out lists of the Spanish forces, with their regulations; a succinct account of which may perhaps be interesting to you at this period, when our politicians in England seem so much afraid of them, and whilst their late unsuccessful attempt against Algiers still renders them the general topic of conversation.

If we are to credit the printed lists, the Spanish army consists of above an hundred and thirty thousand men; but the real number falls far short of this amount, and it is a matter of doubt, whether the regular troops exceed the number of fifty thousand.

The king's houshold is composed of three troops of gentlemen horse-guards, Spanish, Italian, and Flemish; one company of halberdiers; six battalions of Spanish, and six of Walloon foot-guards; and one brigade of carabiniers.

There are six regiments of Spanish infantry of two battalions; and twenty-seven of one battalion; two Italian, three Irish, four Walloon, and four Swifs regiments

ments of one battalion; one regiment of artillery of four battalions; six thousand seven hundred and twelve marines; and one company of engineers.

Each battalion of foot is composed of one company of grenadiers of sixty-six men, and of eight companies of fusileers of eighty men each, including three commissioned officers.

White or blue is the colour of their regimentals, except one Spanish and three Irish, who are dressed in red.

The cavalry consists of fourteen regiments, of which six are in blue, four in red, three in white, and one in green.

The dragoons form eight regiments, of which one is in blue, one in red, and six in yellow.

A regiment of cavalry and dragoons contains four squadrons, each composed of three companies; in each company are three commissioned officers, and forty-five soldiers.

Besides the regulars, they once a year assemble forty-three regiments of militia, and twenty companies of city-guards. The corps of invalids contains forty-six companies on duty, and twenty-six disabled. The African and American garrisons have also their respective militia.

Their uniforms are ugly and ill made; the soldiers abominably nasty in their cloaths, and their black greasy hair

hair feldom dreft. Till very lately, they were commonly in rags, and often mounted guard with half a coat, and almoft bare breeched; but now they are rather better clad, and kept in a fomewhat more decent trim.

The pay of a foldier is five quartos and an half, and twenty-one ounces of bread a day. After fifteen years fervice, he has an increafe of five reals of Vellon a month; after twenty, nine reals; and after twenty-five, he may retire, and receive a pezzetta per diem, and be cloathed as if he was ftill on actual fervice. If he remains thirty years in the army, he is allowed the rank and pay of a fubaltern officer. Every forty months, he receives new regimentals, two fhirts, two ftocks, one pair of fhoes, two pair of ftockings, a cap, and a hat.

The rank of any officer may be known at firft fight, by a particular badge of diftinction. A captain-general wears blue, embroidered with gold down the feams, and three rows of embroidery on the fleeves: a lieutenant-general has nothing on the feams, and but two rows on the cuffs; a marifcal de campo, but one: a brigadier has red cuffs, with one row of filver embroidery on his coat: a colonel has three narrow bindings on his fleeve, of the colour of his regimental button; a lieutenant-colonel, two; and a major, one: the mark of a captain is two epauletts; of a lieutenant, one on his right fhoulder; and of an enfign, one on the left.

The pay of a lieutenant is two pezzettas and a half per

per diem; that of an enfign, two. As every thing has trebled in price fince their pay was eftablifhed, it is become infufficient for the maintenance of the officers. In the guards, all fubalterns muft live upon their own fortune, till they get a company, which they may perhaps wait thirty years for.

About feven thoufand men form the garrifon of Barcelona, of which four thoufand two hundred are guards; the reft Swifs and dragoons. Each corps has its quarter appointed, which it provides with centries, and therefore they never interfere with each other.

Moft of thefe troops are lately returned from the Algerine expedition, where they fuffered great hardfhips; this has made them outrageous againft Count O Reilly, their commander. Converfation, at prefent, turns entirely upon that fubject, and it would hardly be fafe to undertake his juftification. In all this there may be a great deal of jealoufy, againft a foreigner that has made fo rapid a fortune, and enjoys fo large a fhare of the confidence of their common mafter. A fingular inftance of the national hatred, was exhibited a few months ago at Valencia. Some hundreds of boys got together, and, having divided their numbers into an army of Chriftians, and one of Moors, pitched upon the lame, deformed fon of a French barber, to perfonate O Reilly, the chief of the Spanifh party. The infidels obtained a compleat victory; and a court-martial was held upon the Chriftian commander.

commander. He was found guilty of cowardice and mifmanagement, and condemned to be whipped. The fentence was executed with fuch rigour, that the unhappy actor expired under the lafh.

The accounts given by the gazettes, are very unfatisfactory, I therefore flatter myfelf I fhall make you an agreeable prefent, by tranfmitting the following journal; the notes were taken down on the fpot by an officer, who was all day in the action, or very near it. This may fuffice to evince the authenticity of the narration. I have omitted all his farcafms upon the general, for I cannot help attributing many of them to paffion and refentment; and an impartial byftander muft not adopt fentiments palpably dictated by envy or difappointment.

JOURNAL OF THE SPANISH EXPEDITION
Againft ALGIERS, in 1775.

THE Conde Alexander O Reilly is an Irifhman, who began by a fub-lieutenancy in the regiment of Hibernia: he was major of that corps; when he obtained leave to ferve a campaign in the French army in Germany. At his return, he was promoted to the rank of lieutenant-colonel; and afterwards the poft of adjutant or aide-major-general of exercife was created for him, in confideration of his having introduced the German exercife into our army. In the Portuguefe war, the command of a
body

body of light troops was given to O Reilly, who was made a brigadier before the end of the campaign, and foon after fent out as marifcal de campo, to fuperintend the rebuilding of the fortifications of the Havannah; which had been lately reftored to Spain, by the treaty of Fontainebleau.

His commiffion being ended, he returned from Cuba; and, being named infpector-general of the Spanifh infantry, formed a camp, where the king affifted at the manœuvres in perfon. The monarch was fo well pleafed with the performance, that he raifed the infpector to the rank of lieutenant-general, and difpatched him to fettle the difputes in New Orleans, where the French planters refufed to fubmit to the Spanifh government. He is the projector of the prefent fcheme, and come to Carthagena to put it in execution; being appointed commander in chief of all the troops affembled in this port. If he is fuccefsful, no doubt he will be immediately named captain-general. An order is iffued out, prohibiting all difcourfe on the fubject of this expedition, the deftination of which remains a profound fecret. Count O Reilly has under his command nineteen thoufand eight hundred and twenty foot, and thirteen hundred and fixty-eight horfe. Caftejon brings him forty-feven king's fhips, of different rates, and three hundred and forty-fix tranfports.

June

June 15.

The proceſſion of *Corpus Chriſti* paſſed along the mole of Carthagena, and the fleet received the benediction. The ſhips, dreſt out with flags and ſtreamers of various colours, ſaluted the Hoſt with a triple diſcharge of all their artillery. Our generals, O Reilly and Ricardos, came on board at five in the afternoon. We remained till the

23d,

expecting every day to ſail, except that very one we actually did ſail. We had ſeen the wind ſo often favourable, without our making the leaſt motion, that I began to have my doubts about our departure; which however took place in the night betwen the 22d and 23d. We kept beating about before Carthagena in the utmoſt diſorder, till the

27th,

when we bare away from that harbour; and, after two days of the ſtrangeſt manœuvres ever known, by which the fleet was ſeparated into an hundred diviſions, all ſteering different ways, we began to ſuſpect we were bound for Algiers.

30th.

At ten this morning, found ourſelves off Cape Cercely, fifteen leagues weſt of Algiers. All our ſcattered fleet got together in the night, and made for the land, between Cape Tenez and Cape Cercely, where we lay-to the

remainder

remainder of the night. We faw fires on all the hills, and along the fhore; fignals, no doubt, to alarm the country.

July 1ft,
at three in the morning, the admiral fired a gun, for us to keep on our courfe, and at nine we were about fix leagues from Bocmeo. At eleven, we doubled Cape Pefcado, and a little before twelve, the bay of Algiers opened upon us, where we faw our men of war and miffing fhips lying at anchor. At one we could diftinguifh the town with a fpying-glafs. Soon after, the Algerines fired fome fhot from the town and caftles, and hoifted feveral red flags. Came to an anchor in twenty-five fathom water. The reft of the fleet came up foon, and formed a moft beautiful and formidable fhew; but I muft confefs, that the fortifications of Algiers, and the dangerous appearance of the coaft, were to the full as tremendous. We were in the belief, that we had feen a confiderable camp on the eaft of the river Inrac, and about nine at night we were confirmed in our opinion, by the lighting-up of many fires; which in lefs than a quarter of an hour ran along, and fet the whole ridge of hills in a blaze. The dead calm which then reigned, and the fweet harmony of two clarinets, that were playing aboard a neighbouring fhip, made me pafs a moft delicious hour, and forget that all thofe charms were foon to be changed into horrors. Till midnight we heard a
continual

continual firing of muſkets, which we were told was the Mooriſh method of paſſing the parole. I now learned that the men of war had come up the preceding evening; that our generals, diſguiſed in ſailors jackets, had reconnoitred the coaſt, and on their return had held a council of war.

2d.

At ſeven, the general ſent for the captains of the tranſports, to withdraw a ſealed paper they had received at Carthagena, which they were not to open, unleſs driven off by ſtreſs of weather. At five in the evening, he gave out the order for landing next morning; but the ſea running rather high about eight, the expedition was put off. Our commanding officers had orders, not to ſend for cartridges till next day. They are to be delivered out at the rate of ſixty for each ſoldier; which, with twenty-two he received at Barcelona, a pick-ax, a knapſack for proviſions, and a tin box for vinegar and water, beſides his arms, will prove an intolerable burthen at this hot ſeaſon of the year.

3d.

All this day it blew a freſh gale from the E. N. E. which ruffled the ſea ſo much, as to prevent our landing the following night, as the general had propoſed. We diſcovered ſome new camps of Moors, one in particular to the eaſtward of Algiers, which could neither annoy us, nor ſuccour thoſe we intended to attack; but we inferred from

from it, they were in no want of troops, since they had posts on every side.

4th.

At noon we had notice given us, that our four companies were to pass on board another vessel, but which it was to be, we were not informed till three; when we were told that five galliots were to take in fifty men each, and the surplus to be passed on board other ships; the captains of which were ordered to send their boats for them immediately. The cartridges not being delivered, occasioned a delay of two hours, spent in great confusion. This affair being at length settled, we went on board the galliots, where we soon had a lively sense of the misery that awaited us. The orders of the day were, that the officers and soldiers should carry four days provisions; and that at eight at night they should put off, in order to be able to land next morning on the beach of the gulph of the *Badwoman*, which is five leagues west of Algiers. Our generals had so often boasted of the plenty that was to follow us ashore, that we longed with the utmost impatience for the order for landing, as we looked upon it as the only thing that could put an end to our sufferings, which hourly encreased on board the galliots, whither we had carried nothing but a little bad biscuit, some cheese, and wine. Most wretched food! besides the horrid inconvenience, of not having room to lie down, or even to get up from the bench we first sate down upon. A dead calm all night. The breeze failed, and our landing was once more deferred, by which means both officers and men passed a cruel night.

5th.

Received orders to comply with those given out on the 2d, for the mode of disembarking, now no longer to be attempted at the gulph of the *Badwoman*; where we should, indeed, have been in the greatest danger of perishing. The very name denotes the dangers we should have had to encounter. All day a smart gale from the east, and another demur; and a second most fatiguing night for the soldiers.

6th.

The plan being now changed, we were ordered, at eight, to pass into the galliot that was to be placed on the left wing, with an hundred men of the Walloon guards on board. By some strange arrangement or other, our hundred was made up of two half companies, instead of one whole one. At ten, saw some men of war working out of the line of battle, to get near the shore. The slowness of their motion was, no doubt, regulated by the desire they had of attacking three forts on the coast, which it was deemed necessary to silence, before we could approach the land; but for what reason had this been deferred for so many days?

We had received orders to land so long ago as the 2d, which

which would have been put in execution but for the weather, that proved unfavourable, although no such precautions had been taken, nor even any floats prepared for the artillery. Indeed since that time they had been at work patching up some rafts.

At noon, the lesser of the two Tuscan frigates bore down within half a cannon-shot of a fort that fired upon her. After having examined it, she tacked about, and came along-side of her commodore. At half past three, the *Saint Joseph* steered towards the land, and drove within reach of three batteries that began to cannonade her; she returned the fire, but theirs growing very brisk, the *Oriente* was sent to take off the shot of a fort that annoyed her very much on her starboard quarter. This engagement lasted till eight, without much harm done on either side. The *Saint Joseph* had four men killed, and some wounded, among whom was the captain slightly bruised by a splinter: some of the cannon of the fort were dismounted. The galliots towed away the two ships which were becalmed. During this action, the Tuscan frigate sailed in again close under the shore to cannonade some straggling parties of Moors, and a fort at some distance on the left. A Spanish man of war and a frigate had already attacked this fort, but had prudently placed themselves out of the reach of all mischief; their caution was exemplary, and his Catholic Majesty may safely entrust such doughty captains with the command of his ships, being well assured they will bring them back to his ports whole and untouched. At seven, we descried three Algerine barks and about twelve shallops, with heavy cannon, bearing down upon the Saint Joseph. The half-galley of D. Ant° Barceló got under sail in an instant to give them chace, and was followed by five of our galliots. The chace lasted till half after eight, when the enemy retired under the cannon of Algiers. The galliot I was in was one of those sent out to tow a bombketch up to the admiral's ship; but the breeze was so strong, that we could not row against it, and were obliged to give up the point, and come alongside of the admiral to wait for our orders.

7th.

At four, saw several shallops full of troops going and coming under the stern of the admiral. The major of the Walloon guards, whom I saw upon deck, called out to me, that the affair was put off to the next day, and that he would take care to have boats for our hundred men. The poor soldiers were now quite cast down with the wretchedness of their situation; and it must be acknowledged, that to leave them four days and as many nights on a bench, exposed to the violent heats and unwholesome damps of the coast of Africa, and to give them nothing to eat but bad bread and cheese, was but a sorry preparation for an enterprize that required strength of body and vigour of mind. Their officers were not much

better

better off: the master of our bark did every thing in his power to alleviate our distresses; but this kind of vessel is so exceedingly inconvenient, that we were obliged to lie on the floor; and his cookery so nauseous, that, even in our miserable condition, we never could get any thing down but a little soup.

At nine, I went on board the ship where general O Reilly was, and learned that the attack had been deferred, because many detachments had not been punctual to their hour. On this account, he ordered all the barks with the grenadiers and battalions destined for the first embarkation, to be along-side of the admiral precisely at eight in the evening, in order to set off at day-break, when the signal was to be given. The bombketches were put in readiness, and the galliots had orders to range themselves behind them exactly at ten. Our commanders seemed to intend bombarding Algiers, but the design was not put in execution, nor have I learnt the reason. 'Till ten, the boats kept rowing up to the rendezvous, whilst the rest of the fleet drew near the batteries they were to cannonade to cover our landing. Our inaction this whole day, had given the Moors time to repair the damage done the foregoing one, and to put their forts in proper order. The boats our major promised us did not yet appear, so our master told us we should have his, which, however, could only land part of us at a time.

8th. At

8th.

At half paſt three, the men of war began the attack, with ſufficient prudence not to be under any apprehenſions of the enemy's balls reaching them. The two Tuſcan frigates, and the chebec commanded by Barceló, by drawing too near the land, deſtroyed the beautiful uniformity of the line formed afar by our men of war and frigates; whoſe fire was perfectly well kept up, but unfortunately of no manner of ſervice, on account of their vaſt diſtance from the enemy. At half after four, the admiral hung out the ſignal for going aſhore. Seven galliots advanced to clear the beach; they were followed by ſeven diviſions of boats, each diviſion carrying a brigade of ſoldiers, which was to form itſelf into a line of battle ſix deep, as ſoon as landed; but the boats were thrown into confuſion, as they had not been properly ſeparated and diſpoſed before they left the place of rendezvous. This diſorder, which might have occaſioned our total overthrow, would have been prevented, had we been provided with boats proper for ſuch an operation. Luckily for us, we met with no obſtacles, the leaſt of which would have been fatal to us; and we landed about eight thouſand men on the ſhore eaſt of Algiers: the boats left us immediately, and went back to fetch the ſecond diviſion, which did not arrive till an hour after, and then only part of the troops could get on ſhore.

The

The grenadiers of the army drew up in front, and advanced; but they had not marched an hundred yards before many of their men, and almost all their officers, were killed or wounded. Those next them moved forward to support them, without having time to form their ranks, a necessary consequence of the manner in which they had been put into the boats and disembarked. Some companies never could get together, having landed in different places, and by parcels. The light infantry was by this time cut to pieces. The unevenness of the ground we occupied, rendered every sand-heap a small breastwork, from behind which the Africans fired upon us by platoons, as they kept retiring towards the foot of the hills, about six hundred paces from the sea, where they hid themselves among the woods and gardens.

The general now ordered the left wing to advance. It was just six o'clock, and his scheme was to march the left wing to the brow of the hill, (the right resting on the sea shore) and then to form a column and advance about a league farther, to the attack of the castle of Charles the fifth, which commands the whole town. The storming of this fort would have ensured the conquest of Algiers. Whilst our left wing marched on with an intrepidity scarce to be expected in so dangerous a position, some battalions of the center being rather before the rest, drew up in battle array, and with the Spanish

guards

guards faced to the right, that they might defend us from the cavalry of the bey of Mafcarà. This body of horfe was foon difperfed by their fire, and that of the chebec of Antº Barcelò. But the bey of Conftantina, who commanded a large detachment of cavalry on our left, feized this opportunity to drive a herd of camels againft the head of the Walloon guards. By this unexpected affault, he was in hopes of drawing off their attention, whilft he difpatched a body of fifteen thoufand horfe to cut off their communication with the fea, from which we were now pretty far diftant. Our corps de referve wheeling off to the left, drew up to fill the fpace between the fea and the column of Walloons, who were forming their lines to repel the enemies that attacked them from behind the camels; but the greateft fteadinefs would have availed us little, nor could we have avoided being broken and flaughtered to a man, as our formation was too weak to refift the impetuofity of fuch a body of horfe, had not Mr. Acton, the Tufcan commander, cut his cables, and let his fhips drive in to fhore, juft as the enemy was coming on us full gallop. The inceffant fire of his great guns, loaded with grape-fhot, not only ftopt them in their career, but obliged them to retire with great lofs.

Being delivered from this danger, we made our retreat towards the fea-fide, in fuch diforder as muft enfue from a want of proper commanders, abandoning to the fury

of

of the barbarians our unhappy fellow-foldiers, that were unable to keep up with us.

Our general had been bufy for the laſt two hours, throwing up an entrenchment with faſcines, earth-bags, and chevaux de frize. We continued the work, and, to cover our front and flanks, placed a few eight and twelve pounders, that had been of great ſervice to us all the morning, in our different operations. We remained thus the beſt part of the day, pretty ſecure from all attacks of the Mooriſh cavalry, but by no means ſheltered from the balls of their carabines, which, carrying at leaſt one third farther than our firelocks, killed upwards of four hundred of our men, in this kind of camp. Here I ſaw our general on horſeback going about to encourage the ſoldiers; who, ſtretched out on the burning ſands, ſeemed heedleſs of the dangers around, and only anxious to procure a little reſt to their weary limbs.

By one o'clock, the Moors had finiſhed a battery on the right of our camp; and we were ſo pinched for room, and huddled together, that every ſhot took place. General O Reilly, having called for a return of the killed and wounded, aſſembled a council of war, in which it was decided, that at four we ſhould reimbark, as the enemy was raiſing another battery in front, which we muſt paſs under if we perſiſted in the undertaking. The Algerines, for want of experience in theſe matters, ſuffered us to accompliſh our ends undiſturbed; and about

G three

three in the morning the laſt diviſion of the army reimbarked, leaving behind them fourteen field pieces, two howitzers, ſome cheſts of ammunition, and the materials of our encampment, which the enemy broke into the moment the grenadiers of the rear guard puſhed off from the ſhore. We left on the field of battle one thouſand three hundred men, and brought off three thouſand deſperately wounded.

There being unfortunately hoſpitals only for four hundred men, the boats that had landed the Walloons, were taken up for the reception of the wounded; this occaſioned the greateſt diſorder imaginable in our battalions, who came off as well as they could, in the firſt boats or tartans they could meet with. They remained in this confuſion above four-and-twenty hours, employed, as well as many other regiments, in getting together their disjointed companies.

The Moors, as ſoon as they had burſt into our camp, cut off the heads of all our ſlain, and carried them off in bags, to demand the premium offered by the dey, for every chriſtian head; they afterwards heaped up the corſes upon the faſcines of the entrenchment, and ſet fire to the pile, which we ſaw burning for two days and two nights.

10th, and 11th.

All hurry; no water to be had, though there were ſhip-loads of it in the fleet.

12th. At

12th.

At six, a. m. signal for weighing anchor. Soon after most of the fleet sailed out of the bay.

15th.

At seven, a. m. came to an anchor in Alicant road.

31st.

The Walloon guards were ordered ashore, and quartered at Sanjuan.

August 10th.

We reimbarked, and

20th.

Landed at Barcelona.

LETTER VI.

Barcelona, November 11, 1775.

WE shall postpone our departure from this city a few days longer, to give the roads time to dry. There has been of late a very uncommon run of bad weather; it has thundered and lightened, with many showers, for several days together.

Our time has not hung heavy upon our hands, for all our acquaintance vie with each other in loading us with civilities.

civilities. The intendant has shewn us every possible mark of politeness, and rendered easy to us the access to the arsenal, magazines, &c. which in this military town, they are very chary of shewing to strangers.

Yesterday we took advantage of a gleam of sunshine, to accompany the consul to his villa in the *playa*. The moist warmth of the day brought out such swarms of insects as almost devoured us; I am afraid the great quantity of such vermin must make the summers in this delightful country very uncomfortable. However, it must be allowed to be a very fine climate, for, in spite of all the foulness of the sky, the air has always been mild and balmy. This plain abounds with gardens and orchards of oranges and other rich fruits. Few spots of the globe can surpass it in fertility, but they tell us wonders of the environs of Valencia and Granada.

In the afternoon the weather was heavenly, a prelude, I hope, to a total change for the better; we employed it in riding up to Saria, a convent of capuchin friars on the hills. The city and port of Barcelona appear finely from hence, collected into a most perfect landscape. The garden, on the slope of the hill, is truly romantic; the walks are shaded and sheltered by sweet-scented evergreens; streams of clear water run down on every side in all the wildness of nature, or spout through the eyes of a little Magdalen, or the *stigmata* of a Saint Francis. As the Romans had many villas on these eminences,

nences, we may presume that these limpid rills were then wont to gush out of the breasts of the Graces, or trickle from the quiver of the God of Love. Don't be surprised, that in November I speak feelingly of these walks being shady; I can assure you we found the rays of the sun very powerful, and relished much the shade of the bowers, and the coolness arising from the running water.

Our return to town was by an hollow way, under banks of Indian figs and aloes, when the butterflies were as brisk as in the middle of spring. The women in the little hamlets were busy with their bobbins making black lace, some of which, of the coarser kind, is spun out of the leaf of the aloe; it is curious, but of little use, for it grows mucilaginous with washing.

We passed by the convent of Jesus, belonging to the cordeliers or grey friars. The duke of Berwick razed it to the ground in 1714, to punish those fathers for their zeal in the revolt of Catalonia. Their present habitation is small. They have a fine spring of water, and an extensive garden surrounded with a wall of lemon-trees; adjoining is the Camposanto, where those that died in the last plague were buried. It now serves as a flower-garden, and contains some curious plants; among the rest the *aroma*, a species of *mimosa* or spunge-tree, bearing a round yellow flower with a faint musky smell, to which they attribute many odd qualities. If you

chew

chew the feed, and breathe it out into a room, it will immediately fill it with an overcoming ftench, and turn all white paint black.

Our evening ended with a ball, where we had for the firft time the pleafure of feeing the Fandango danced. It is odd and entertaining enough, when they execute with precifion and agility all the various footings, wheelings of the arms, and crackings of the fingers; but it exceeds in wantonnefs all the dances I ever beheld. Such motions, fuch writhings of the body and pofitions of the limbs, as no modeft eye can look upon without a blufh! A good Fandango lady will ftand five minutes in one fpot, wriggling like a worm that has juft been cut in two.

If the day proves clear, we fhall go to-morrow up the mountain to the caftle.

LETTER VII.

Barcelona, November 12, 1775.

I Am this moment returned from the fortrefs of Montjuich, where the finenefs of the day and the beauty of the profpect afforded me much real fatisfaction; but it fell greatly fhort of what I felt on finding a letter from you

you on my table. I have not met with the book you mention, nor indeed ever heard of Mr. T * * * 'till now. By your account, he has not been in this part of Spain, therefore my letters as yet convey something new to you; perhaps, even in those provinces where he has travelled, the difference of our difpofitions, ftudies, and purfuits, may ftrike out a fufficient fund of variety for my future correfpondence, to make it entertaining to you, though you have read his tour. I am fure I fhall be no plagiarift; for it is highly improbable the book fhould fall in my way for fome time to come.

Montjuich, a name corrupted either from *Mons Jovis* or *Mons Judaicus*, is a mountain that ftands fingle, on the fouth-weft point of Barcelona. This eminence is happily placed for the city, as it intercepts and diffipates the putrid exhalations pumped up by the fun from the ponds near the Llobregat, which are fometimes fo ftrong as to affect with great violence the centinels on duty. The extent of its bafis is very great. Large crops of wheat are reaped on the north and eaft fides, and all bought up at an high price for feed-corn, the quality being particularly found. A good deal of ftrong wine is made on the fouth-eaft angle; but it is faid to be medicated with lime, and mahogany chips, to give it fpirit and colour. The face of the mountain towards the fea is already by nature, or foon will be made by art, an in-

furmountable

furmountable precipice. The road up to the top is very steep; about half way, is the ancient burial-place of the Jews, where many large stones, with Hebrew infcriptions, are still lying scattered about the field.

Every part of the old castle is deftroyed, and large works in the modern manner built upon its foundations, on the crown of the hill. From hence you command a view over the coast, plain, and harbour; not a house in Barcelona but lies expofed to your fight. They are floping off the glacis at an incredible expence, fo that no approaches can be made under shelter, as every part is open, and liable to be raked by the cannon of the batteries. All the walls are of stone, and multiplied to an extravagant number. Spain cannot afford men to garrifon fuch overgrown fortreffes.

The main body of the place is bomb proof, very neatly finifhed; two ftone ftaircafes, with iron railing fit for a palace, lead down to the vaulted quarters for the foldiers, which are near four hundred yards long. One of the principal baftions is fcooped out into a ciftern capable of containing feventy thoufand cubic feet of water, of which only a fmall quantity is let off at a time into a draw-well, to prevent any traitor from poifoning the ftock of water. Above the quarters is a grand terrace round a court, with turrets at each angle. On the center of the fouth line ftands the tower of fignals; if one

fhip

ship appears, a basket is hung out; if two or more, it is raised higher, and if a Spanish man of war, they hoist a flag.

This castle has already cost immense sums in the space of fifteen years, and in all probability will not be finished in as many more, tho' above three hundred workmen are employed at the works. Each new engineer alters the plan and counteracts the scheme of his predecessor, which occasions such a delay and waste of treasure as is scarce to be credited.

Besides the inconvenience of requiring so large a garrison, the situation appears to me too elevated to annoy an enemy encamped in the plain.

LETTER VIII.

Barcelona, November 17, 1775.

I Expected to have been by this time in the kingdom of Valencia; but the badness of the mountain-road having determined us to take the new one, along the coast, we last Wednesday hired mules for Montserrat, which is not in the line of that lower route. This has retarded our departure for some days.

For about five or six miles the road is finished with a magnificence equal to the best in France, but after that, it relapses into its original state; however, though rough for carriages, it is very soft and pleasant for riding. The country up the Llobregat is well cultivated, but subject to frequent inundations, that make cruel havock. As you approach the mountain, the number of vineyards diminishes, that of olive-grounds increases.

At Martorel, a large town, where much black lace is manufactured, is a very high bridge with Gothic arches, built in 1768, as we are informed by the inscription, out of the ruins of a decayed one, that had existed 1985 years from its erection, by Hannibal, in the 535th year of Rome. At the north end is a triumphal arch or gateway, said to have been raised by that general in honour of his father Hamilcar. It is almost entire, well proportioned, and simple, without any kind of ornament, except a rim or two of hewn stone. The large stone-casing is almost all fallen off.

After dinner we continued our journey through Espalungera, a long village full of cloth and lace manufacturers; and about three arrived at the foot of the mountain of Montserrat [3], one of the most singular in the world, for situation, shape, and composition. It

---

[3] Monte ferrado means a mountain sawed; and the arms of the abbey are, the Virgin Mary sitting at the foot of a rock half cut through by a saw.

stands

HANNIBAL'S ARCH.

stands single, towering over an hilly country, like a pile of grotto work or Gothic spires. Its height is about three thousand three hundred feet.

We ascended by the steepest road, as that for carriages winds quite round, and requires half a day's travelling. After two hours tedious ride from east to west, up a narrow path cut out of the side of gullies and precipices, we reached the highest part of the road, and turned round the eastermost point of the mountain, near the deserted hermitage of Saint Michael. Here we came in sight of the convent, placed in a nook of the mountain; it seems as if vast torrents of water, or some violent convulsion of nature, had split the eastern face of Montserrat, and formed in the cleft a sufficient platform to build the monastery upon. The Llobregat roars at the bottom, and perpendicular walls of rock, of prodigious height, rise from the water edge near half-way up the mountain. Upon these masses of white stone rests the small piece of level ground which the monks inhabit. Close behind the abbey, and in some parts impending over it, huge cliffs shoot up in a semicircle to a stupendous elevation; their summits are split into sharp cones, pillars, pipes, and other odd shapes, blanched and bare; but the interstices are filled up with forests of evergreen and deciduous trees and plants. Fifteen hermitages are placed among the woods; nay, some of them on the very pinnacles of the rocks, and in cavities hewn out of the

loftiest

loftiest of these pyramids. The prospect is not only astonishing, but absolutely unnatural. These rocks are composed of limestones of different colours, glued together by a sand, and a yellow calcarious earth. In some parts they consist of freestone and white quartz, mixed with some touchstone. There may perhaps be reason to suspect fire to have been a principal agent in the formation of this insulated mountain.

Having brought a letter for the abbot, whom we found a polite, sensible ecclesiastic, a native of Estremadura, we were lodged and entertained in the convent. I cannot say much in favour of the cookery; it cost us some wry faces to get down the saffron soup and spiced ragouts. After dinner a plate of caraways, and a salver of wine, was handed about; which brought to my mind the treat Justice Shallow offers Sir John Falstaff in his orchard.

This is one of the forty-five religious houses of the Spanish congregation of the order of Saint Benedict; their general chapter is held every fourth year at Valladolid, where the deputies choose abbots and other dignitaries for the ensuing Quadrennium. In this monastery, they elect for abbot a Catalan and a Castillian alternately. Their possessions are great, consisting of nine villages lying to the south of the mountain; but the king has lately curtailed their income about six thousand livres a year, by appropriating to his own use the best

house

house in each village, some of which, with their tythes, are worth 200 dollars per annum. Their original foundation, in 866, gave them nothing but the mountain; and to donations and œconomy they owe the great increase of their landed property. They are bound to feed and harbour, for three days, all pilgrims that come up to pay their homage to the Virgin; the allowance is a luncheon of bread in the morning, as much more, with broth, at noon, and bread again at night. About three years ago, the king proposed to them to abolish this obligation of hospitality, on condition that the convent should subscribe a fixed sum towards the establishment of a poorhouse in Barcelona. The principals of the abbey were inclined to accept of the proposal, but the mob of monks opposed it vehemently; and, such a scheme being very contrary to the interests of the miraculous image, she resented it highly, and, according to her old custom, vanished in anger from the altar. Soon after, she was discovered in the cave where she was originally found, nor would she stir, till the intended innovation was overruled. It was thought expedient to wink at this juggling, not to alarm the common people, who are not sufficiently enlightened to see through such gross impositions.

The number of professed monks is 76, of lay-brothers 28, and of singing-boys 25, besides physician, surgeon, and servants.

Having

Having breakfasted very early, a German monk waited upon us to shew us the church. It is gloomy, and the gilding much sullied with the smoke of eighty-five lamps of silver, of various forms and sizes, that hang round the cornice of the sanctuary. Funds have been bequeathed by different devotees for furnishing them with oil.

The choir above stairs is decorated with the life of Christ in good wooden carving. A gallery runs on each side of the chancel, for the convenience of the monks. A large iron grate divides the church from the chapel of the Virgin, where the image stands, in a nich over the altar, before which burn four tapers in large silver candlesticks, the present of the duke of Medina Celi. In the sacristy, and passages leading to it, are presses and cupboards full of relicks and ornaments, of gold, silver, and precious stones; they pointed out to us, as the most remarkable, two crowns for the Virgin and her Son, of inestimable value, some large diamond rings, an excellent cameo of Medusa's head, the Roman emperors in alabaster, the sword of Saint Ignatius, and the chest that contains the ashes of a famous brother, John Guarin, of whom they relate the same story as that given in the Spectator of a Turkish santon and the sultan's daughter. They differ however in the following circumstance—The Catalan anchoret repents of his crime, and lives seven years on all fours like a wild beast. The earl of Barcelona, whose daughter John had ravished and murdered,

catches

catches the savage in his hunting-toils, and brings him as a shew to the city; when behold! the earl's son, only a month old, speaks aloud, and bids John arise, for his sins are forgiven. The easy prince pardons him also, and all of them go in quest of the body of the Princess. To their great astonishment, they meet her restored to life by the Virgin Mary, and as beautiful and young as ever. It is not said that she recovered her virginity; that is a miracle never once attempted by any saint in the calendar; however, she liked the mountain so well, that she there founded a monastery, in which she ended her days as a nun.

Immense is the quantity of votive offerings to this miraculous statue; and, as nothing can be rejected or otherwise disposed of, the shelves are crowded with most whimsical *Ex votos*, viz. silver legs, fingers, breasts, earrings, watches, two-wheeled chaises, boats, carts, and such-like trumpery.

From the sacristy we went up to the *Camarines*, small rooms behind the high altar, hung with paintings, several of which are very good. A strong silver-plated door being thrown open, we were bid to lean forward, and kiss the hand of *Nuestra Senora*. It is half worn away by the eager kisses of its votaries, but we could not ascertain whether it be marble or silver, as it is painted black. The face of the mother is regularly handsome, but the colour of a negro-woman.

Having

Having seen every place about the convent, where they are now building a new wing, and blasting a great deal of the rock to enlarge the gardens, we set out for the hermitages, and took the short way, up a crevice between two huge masses of rock, where in rainy weather the waters dash down in furious torrents. We counted six hundred holes or steps, so steep and perpendicular that from below we did not discern the least track. A hand-rail, and a few seats to take breath upon, enabled us to perform this scalade. Soon after, we arrived, through a wilderness of evergreens, at the narrow platform where the first hermit dwells. His cells, kitchen, chapel, and gardens, are admirably neat and romantic, built upon various patches of level on the tops of precipices. The view from it is wild, and in such a fine clear morning most delightful. The hermit seemed a chearful, simple old man, in whose mind forty years retirement had obliterated all worldly ideas. The hermits are all clad in brown habits, and wear long beards; their way of life is uncomfortable, and their respective limits very much confined. They rise at two every morning, ring out their bell, and pray till it is time to go to mass at the hermitage, called the *Parish*; it is always said at break of day: some of them have above two hours walk down to it. The convent allows them bread, wine, salt, oil, one pair of shoes, and one pair of stockings a year, with twenty-five reals a month for other necessaries. A couple

of

of men are kept to affift them in their labour, each in their turn. A mule carries up their provifions twice a week, and is occafionally driven to Barcelona for falt-fifh, and other things, which they buy by clubbing together. They get fome helps from the convent, in return for flowers, greens, &c. which they fend down as prefents. They never eat meat, or converfe with each other: their novicefhip is very fevere, for they muft undergo fix months fervice in the infirmary of the abbey, one year among the novices, and fix years further trial, before they are fuffered to go up to an hermitage; which they cannot obtain but by the unanimous confent of the whole chapter. They make every vow of the monks, and, over and above, one of never quitting the mountain; but none of them are allowed to enter into orders. Their firft habitation is always the moft remote from the convent, and they defcend according as vacancies happen in the lower cells.

Having left a fmall prefent in the chapel-window, we continued our walk: wherever the winding paths are level, nothing can be more agreeable than to faunter through the clofe woods and fweet wilderneffes that fill up the fpaces between the rocks. It is impoffible to give you an adequate idea of the fublime views and uncouth appearance of the different parts of the mountain; a painter or a botanift might wander here many days with pleafure and profit. There are few evergreens in Europe

rope that may not be found here, befides a great variety of deciduous plants. The apothecary of the houfe has a lift of four hundred and thirty-feven fpecies of plants, and forty of trees. The greateft hardfhip here is a fcarcity of good water. Except one fpring at the parifh, and another at the convent, they have no other than ciftern-water, and that bad enough; this in fummer is a terrible inconvenience, and gives the lye to the florid defcriptions I have read of the purling ftreams and beautiful cafcades tumbling down on every fide from the broken rocks. The want of water is fo great, that neither wolf, bear, nor other wild beaft, is ever feen on the mountain.

The fecond hermitage we came to, ftands on a point of the rock, over a precipice that defcends almoft to the very bed of the river; my head was near turning with looking down. The profpect is inimitably grand, extending over the northern and eaftern parts of the province, which are very hilly and bare, bounded by the mountains of Rouffillon. The true Pyreneans appear only through fome breaks in that chain. Manrefa, where Inigo de Loyola made his firft fpiritual retreat, is the principal town in the view. In a clear day, they affured us they could fee Majorca, which is one hundred and eighty-one miles diftant. Upon the round rock that hangs over the hermit's cell was formerly a caftle, with its cifterns and drawbridge, where fome banditti harboured.

ed. From this strong hold they made excursions to pillage the neighbouring vallies. By rolling down stones, they kept the monks in perpetual alarm, and obliged them to send up whatever provisions were wanted in the garrison. At last, a few miquelets climbed up the rock from tree to tree, like so many squirrels, surprized the fort, and destroyed this nest of robbers. In commemoration of this event, the hermitage is dedicated to Saint Dimas, a saint, I presume, you never heard of in your life. You must know he is the good thief in the gospel.

At la Trinidad, the next cell we walked to, the monks by turns go up to pass a few days in summer by way of recreation. The hermit has many rooms, and is allowed a boy to wait upon him. He gave us a glass of good Sitges wine, and a pinch of admirable snuff, made from tobacco raised in his own garden. The officers of the customs have extended their tyranny even to these solitudes, and sent orders that no more tobacco be suffered to grow.

Having scrambled up to one or two more hermitages, we found our curiosity satisfied, as, except in point of extensiveness of prospect, they varied very little from those we had already seen; and therefore we turned down another path, which led us to the dwelling of the vicar, a monk who during four years takes upon him the direction of the hermits.

Lower down we arrived at Santa Cecilia, the parish church, where every morning the silent inhabitants of this *Thebais* meet to hear mass, and perform divine service, and twice a week to confess and communicate.

About eleven, we got down to the abbey for dinner; and, having received the customary donation of blessed crosses and holy medals, mounted our mules and came to lie at Martorel. We reached Barcelona early this morning, and have been ever since making ready for our departure.

LETTER IX.

Barcelona, November 18, 1775.

ALL our affairs are settled for beginning our journey to Valencia to-morrow afternoon. We have agreed with a master muleteer, to furnish us with mules at the rate of fifteen reales de vellon a day for each mule, clear of all other expences whatever. If we part with him at Valencia, he is to be paid for his return, eight days; if at Alicant, ten; at Cadiz, thirty; at Madrid, fifteen; and at Lisbon, thirty. We have also hired a miquelet, compleatly accoutred, to attend us. You see we are fitted

ted out in good earnest for a long journey, which I hope will afford us some pleasant hours, to compensate for the trouble and fatigue that we foresee must frequently fall to our share. I believe you are not sorry to find I am on the point of leaving Catalonia, which must by this time be a subject my frequent letters have rendered rather tiresome to you; however, I entreat your indulgence one letter more, while I endeavour to bring together the remarks I have made on the character of this people, and all the material information my friends have furnished me with.

Catalonia is almost throughout extremely mountainous. The nature of the country appears to have great influence on that of the inhabitants, who are a hardy, active, industrious race, of a middle size, brown complexion, and strong features; their limbs well knit together, and by education and practice inured to the greatest fatigues; there are few lame or distorted persons, or beggars, to be met with among them. Their *Mocos* or mule-boys are stout walkers; some of them have been known to go from Barcelona to Madrid, and back again, in nine days, which by the high road is six hundred miles.

The loss of all their immunities, the ignominious prohibition of every weapon, even a knife, and an enormous load of taxes, have not been able to stifle their independent spirit, which breaks out upon the least stretch of arbitrary power; but within these few years, many of

their

their ancient privileges have been gradually reftored; and this is at prefent one of the moft flourifhing provinces of Spain. Their taxation is ftill very high. All trade is affeffed according to the bufinefs you are fuppofed to tranfact in the courfe of the year, without regard to your lofs or gain. One mode of collecting the revenue is fomewhat fingular;—the intendant (who manages all the finances, and, befides numberlefs emoluments and fecret profits, receives one third of all feizures of contraband goods) has a certain number of clerks or apprentices, with a ftipend for each allowed by the king. Thefe young men are fent out into the villages to gather the taxes; an operation which they fpin out to the utmoft, as their profits, and thofe of their mafter, are encreafed by every delay, the communities being obliged to find them food, lodging, and two pefos a day. When the peafantry of a place proves refractory or dilatory in its payment, an order is given by the treafurer to an officer, who goes with his foldiers to the fpot, to receive his own and his regiment's pay, and live at difcretion upon the poor wretches until full fatisfaction be made.

Amongft other reftrictions, the ufe of flouched hats, white fhoes, and large brown cloaks, is forbidden. 'Till of late, they durft not carry any kind of knife; but in each public houfe there was one chained to the table, for the ufe of all comers. The good order maintained by the police, and the vigilance of the thieftakers, fupply the

the place of defensive weapons, robberies and murders being seldom heard of; you may walk the streets of Barcelona at all hours unarmed, without the least apprehension, provided you have a light; without it you are liable to be carried to prison by the patrol.

The minones, or thieftakers, are men of trust and consideration, and of approved courage; their dress is that of the miquelets or mountaineers, who so cruelly harrassed the French armies in the wars at the beginning of our century. They wear their hair in a net; a broad silver-laced hat, squeezed flat like those of the English sailors, hung on one side of their head; an handkerchief loosely tied round the neck; a short striped waistcoat, and over it a red jacket, with large silver buttons like bells dangling from it; a blue skirt, bound with yellow tape, rolled several times round their waist, in which they carry their knife, handkerchief, &c. Over this jacket they wear two cross belts, one for an ammunition-pouch, the other for their broad sword and pistols; on the left shoulder hangs a blue great coat embroidered with white thread; their breeches are blue and white striped; their stockings, rolled below the knee, and gartered with an enormous buckle, and bunch of black ribbons, reach only down to the ankle, where they tie several rounds of blue fillet very tight, to keep on their packthread sandals, that seem scarce to cover their toes.

The

The common dress of a Catalan sailor or muleteer is brown, and the distinctive mark by which they are known in Spain, is a red woollen cap, falling forwards, like that of the ancient Phrygians. The middling sort of people and artificers wear hats and dark cloaths, with an half-wide coat carelessly tossed over the shoulders.

The dress of the women is a black silk petticoat over a little hoop, shoes without heels, bare shoulders, and a black veil stiffened out with wire, so as to arch out on each side of the head, something resembling the hooded serpent.

The Catalans are excellent for light infantry, on the forlorn hope, or for a *coup de main*; but tho' brave and indefatigable, they are averse to the strictness of regular discipline, unless it be in their own national regiments. They cannot brook the thoughts of being menial servants in their own country, but will rather trudge it all over with a pedlar's pack on their shoulders, or run about upon errands, than be the head domestic in a Catalan family. Far from home they make excellent servants, and most of the principal houses of Madrid have Catalans at the head of their affairs. They are the general muleteers and calessieros of Spain; you meet with them in every part of the kingdom: their honesty, steadiness, and sobriety, entitle them to the confidence of travellers, and their thirst after lucre makes them bear

with

with any hardships. With good words, you will always find them docile, but they cannot bear hard usage or opprobrious language.

Those that remain at home for the labours of the field, are exceedingly industrious. Their corn-harvest is in May or early in June; but, as those crops are liable to frequent burstings and mildews, they have turned their attention more to the vine, which they plant even upon the summits of their most rugged mountains. In many places, they carry up earth to fix the young set in; and in others, have been known to let one another down from the brow of the rock by ropes, rather than suffer a good patch of soil to remain useless. Their vintages are commonly very plentiful. This autumn, there was such a superabundance of grapes in the valley of Talarn, in the neighbourhood of Pallas, that whole vineyards were left untouched for want of vessels to make or hold the wine in; notice was pasted upon the church-doors, that any one was at liberty to take away what quantity he pleased, on paying a small acknowledgment to the proprietors. The best red wine of Catalonia is made at Mataw, north of Barcelona, and the best white at Sitges, between that city and Tarragona.

The scarcity of corn is sometimes very great, the principality not producing above five months provision. Without the importation from America, Sicily, and the north of Europe, it would run the risk of being famished.

From four hundred thousand to six hundred thousand quarters of wheat are annually imported. Canada alone sent this year about eighty thousand quarters. There are public ovens, where the bakers are bound by contract to bake every day into bread one thousand bushels of flour, or more, at a stated price, and, in case the other bakers should refuse to work, they are under the obligation of furnishing the city with bread.

The number of the inhabitants of Barcelona is made to amount to one hundred and fifty thousand souls, and those of Barceloneta to ten thousand; but, although trade and population have increased surprizingly in the course of a few years, I doubt there is some exaggeration in this reckoning.

The great export-commerce consists in wine, brandies, salt, and oil, which are mostly taken in by foreign ships at the little ports and roads along the coast, and not brought to be shipped off at the capital.

There are mines of lead, iron, and coal, in the mountains, but they are ill wrought, and turn to poor account. The manufactures are of more importance. Barcelona supplies Spain with most of the cloathing and arms for the troops. This branch of business is carried on with much intelligence; they can equip a battalion of six hundred men compleatly in a week.

A great trade is driven in silk handkerchiefs, stockings, &c.; in woollens of various qualities; in silk and
thread

thread lace; in fire-arms. The gun-barrels of Barcelona are much esteemed, and cost from four to twenty guineas, but about five is the real value; all above is paid for fancy and ornament: they are made out of the old shoes of mules. Several manufactures of printed linens are established here, but have not yet arrived at any great elegance of design or liveliness of colour.

The imports are, besides corn, about eighty thousand hundred-weight of Newfoundland cod, which pays three pesettas per hundred-weight duty, and sells upon an average at a guinea; beans from Holland, for the poor people, and an inferior sort from Africa, for the mules; salted conger eel from Cornwall and Britany, sold at forty or fifty shillings per quintal; this is an unwholesome, luscious food, which they cook up with garlick and spices: English bale goods, and many foreign articles of necessity or luxury. House-rent and living are dear; provisions but indifferent: the fish is flabby and insipid; the meat poor; but the vegetables are excellent, especially brocoli and cauliflower. I believe their meat and fish are much better in summer than at this season of the year.

The devotion of the Catalans seems to be pretty much upon a par with that of their neighbours in the southern provinces of France, and, I am told, much less ardent than we shall find it as we advance into Spain; but they still abound with strange practices of religion and local worship. One very odd idea of theirs is, that on the 1st of November, the eve of All Souls, they run about from houſe to houſe to eat cheſnuts, believing that for every cheſnut they ſwallow, with proper faith and unction, they ſhall deliver a ſoul out of purgatory.

The influx of foreigners, increaſe of commerce, and protection granted to the liberal arts, begin to open the underſtanding of this people, who have made great ſtrides of late towards ſenſe and philoſophy.

There are now but one or two churches at moſt, in each city, that are allowed the privilege of protecting offenders, and murderers are excluded from the benefit of the ſanctuary. The proceedings of the Inquiſition are grown very mild. If any perſon leads a ſcandalous life, or allows his tongue unwarrantable liberties, he is ſummoned by the Holy Office, and privately admoniſhed; in caſe of non-amendment he is committed to priſon. Once a year you muſt anſwer to that tribunal for the orthodoxy of your family, and of every ſervant you have, or they muſt quit the country; but the foreign proteſtant houſes are paſſed over unnoticed. Avoid talking on the ſubject of religion, and with a little diſcretion you may live here in what manner you pleaſe.

Every Jew that lands in Spain muſt declare himſelf to be ſuch at the Inquiſition; which immediately appoints a familiar to attend him all the time he ſtays aſhore, to whom he pays a piſtole a day. Were he to neglect giving this information, he would be liable to be ſeized. Yet I have

have been assured by persons of undoubted credit, that a Jew may travel incognito from Perpignan to Lisbon, and sleep every night at the house of a Jew, being recommended from one to another; and that you may take it for granted, that wherever you see a house remarkably decked out with images, relics, and lamps, and the owner noted for being the most enthusiastic devotee of the parish, there it is ten to one but the family are Israelites at heart.

If a stranger is desirous of becoming acquainted with Spain, the manners and disposition of its inhabitants, he must proceed further; for I am told this province bears so little resemblance to the rest of the kingdom, that he will derive no real knowledge on that score from travelling in Catalonia. Here it is not uncommon to hear them talk of a journey into Spain, as they would of one into France; and their language is not understood by the Spaniards, being a dialect of the ancient Limosine tongue, a kind of Gascon.

I cannot close this sketch of the character of the modern Catalans more properly, than with the epitaph of their countrymen who served under Sertorius, and after the murder of that great man, disdaining to obey another leader, sacrificed themselves to his manes. It is taken from the annals of Catalonia.

> ⁴ *Hic multæ quæ se manibus*
> *Q. Sertorii Turmæ et Terræ*
> *Mortalium omnium Parenti*
> *devovere dum eo sublato*
> *superesse tæderet et fortiter*
> *pugnando invicem cecidere*
> *Morte ad præsens optata jacent.*
> *Valete Posteri.*

LETTER X.

Reus, November 24, 1775.

WE left Barcelona on Sunday the 19th instant. Our first day's journey was very short; the road good, but made upon too expensive a plan to be continued far. The bridge over the Llobregat is grand, but unluckily so placed as never to be seen by travellers in an oblique direction.

⁴ Here lie the bones of many companies of soldiers, who devoted themselves to the manes of Q. Sertorius, and to the common mother Earth, as loathing all thoughts of surviving him. Fighting bravely with each other, they fell, and met the death which they then wished for. Farewell Posterity.

We stopped at Cipreret, a neat house in a wild mountainous country, with a few pines scattered about, seldom enough to form a grove, much less a wood. We here for the first time saw a true Spanish kitchen, viz. an hearth raised above the level of the floor under a wide funnel, where a circle of muleteers were huddled together over a few cinders.

Next morning we passed a broad glen or hollow, over which they intended to convey the high road in a strait line, by means of a bridge of three rows of arches one above the other. Had they turned a little to the left by a gradual slope, the descent had been trifling, and a single arch sufficient for the passage of the water. This great work has failed, and seems abandoned. I should suspect they built here for the diversion of future antiquaries, not for the use of the present generation, which feels all the weight of the expence, without reaping any benefit from such ill-calculated undertakings. In the present state of things the pass is very dangerous, and further on the road grows worse, in a large forest of pines, where the rocks and gullies render it next to impossible for a carriage to get through without damage. On account of the great number of bridges necessary among these broken hills, and of the obstinacy with which the engineers (whose profits increase by delays and difficulties) persist in carrying the road strait through rocks and torrents, the work
advances

advances so slowly, that before a second mile be finished, the first is ruined for want of repairs.

The country at the foot of the mountains is fertile and populous. About Villa Franca de Panades the soil is remarkably light. The husbandmen shovel up the stubble, weeds, and tops of furrows, into small heaps, which they burn, then spread them out upon the ground, and work them in with a plough, which is little more than a great knife fastened to a single stick, that just scratches the surface. In this country all the corn is trod out of the sheaf by means of horses and mules driven backwards and forwards over it on a stone or stucco area.

In the evening we passed by torch-light under a Roman arch, which I returned next morning to examine, our inn not being more than a mile beyond it. This arch is almost entire, elegant in its proportions, and simple in its ornaments; the gateway lofty; the entablature is supported on each side by four fluted Corinthian pilasters. All I could read of the inscription was EX TEST; which Flores, in his Espana sagrada, makes out to be part of

EX TESTAMENTO L. LICINII. L. F. SERGII. SURAE CONSECRATUM.

This Licinius was thrice consul under Trajan, and was famous for his extraordinary wealth. No reasonable conjecture

jecture has been made why he ordered by his will this monument to be erected, or what was the use of it when built. Some think it was the entrance of the Campus Tarraconensis, and that a wall ran from the sea, which is about half a mile distant to the south-east, through the olive-grounds quite up to the hills. There appear some remnants of a wall in that direction, but I won't pretend to say they are of so ancient a date.

The next day was the most delightful of our whole journey. The sun shone out in all his splendor; the sea was smooth and calm; the prospect was incessantly varying as we moved on, sometimes along the rich level on the shore, where the bushy heads and glossy leaves of the lowest trees, contrasted with the pale green of the olive-woods, made it appear quite a summer scene; sometimes over gentle eminences, from which we commanded views of numberless bays and promontories, crowned with towers and antique fortifications. The little river Gaya distributes its waters in stone channels to all parts of the valley, and gives vigour to its productions, which otherwise would be parched up by the drought. Here the tender olive-sets are nursed up in long baskets, till they get out of the reach of goats and other enemies. As we descended the hill of Bara to the beach, Tarragona presented itself to our view, like a ruined fortress, on a round point projecting into the sea; and a little further on we turned off the road to the right, into a wood of pines and shrubs, to visit a monument that tradition has named the tomb of the Scipios. They were the father and uncle of Scipio Africanus, both killed in Spain.

This building is small, being about nineteen feet square and twenty-eight high. In the front, facing the sea, are two statues of warriors in a mournful posture, roughly cut out of the stones of the sepulchre, and much worn away by the sea air. The inscription is so much defaced, that it is hard to make any thing of it: what remains is as follows:

ORN...TE...EAQVE....L..O...VNVS...VER..BVSTVS...I..S..NEGL.
VI...VA..FL...BVS..SIBI..PERPETVO REMANERE.

I think it has been erected by some priest, for himself and family, as the fragments of the last line may be interpreted in that manner. Some take the first word of the first line to have been Cornelius, a name belonging to the Scipios. The top of the monument, which probably ended in a pyramidal form, is fallen off [5].

From the heavy sands of the sea-shore, where a great many fishermen were hauling in their nets, we ascended the naked rock of Tarragona. It produces nothing but the dwarf palm or palmeto. This plant grows among the stones to the height of one or two feet: the leaves are stiff and sharp, spread out like fingers, or the sticks of a

[5] The tomb of Theron, at Girgenti in Sicily, resembles this in form.

fan,

fan, and very much refembling the leaves of the date palm. This alfo produces fruit, and the infipid pith of its root is a favourite eating of the peafants. The leaves make good brooms and ropes, and are a great fattener of cattle.

The ancient Tarraco is now contracted to a very trifling city, that covers only a fmall portion of the Roman inclofure, and is an ill-built, dirty, depopulated place. Many antiquities have been found, and are ftill to be feen in the town, and almoft all round the walls. A few veftiges remain of the palace of Auguftus, and of the great circus: an arch or two of the amphitheatre, and fome fteps cut in the folid rock, ftill exift, impending over the fea. About three miles from the city, is the Puente de Ferriera, an ancient aqueduct, which we did not go to fee, not having heard of it till we had paffed too far on to turn back. Father Flores has given a plate of it. The cathedral, dedicated to Saint Thecla, is ugly, but the new chapel of that tutelar faint is beautiful. The infide is cafed with yellow and brown marbles, dug up in the very center of the town, and ornamented with white foliages and bafs-reliefs. The architecture is accounted heavy, but I confefs I did not think that fault very glaring. The whole together has a very pleafing effect.

In Queen Anne's war, the Englifh were in poffeffion of this poft, and intended to keep and fortify it, by bringing the river Francolis quite round it. For this purpofe they threw up vaft outworks and redoubts, of which the ruins are yet very vifible. Having fecured Minorca and Gibraltar, they renounced the project of fixing a garrifon in Tarragona.

From this city we defcended into the Campo Tarragonés, a plain of about nine miles diameter, one of the moft fruitful fpots in Europe: there is not an uncultivated part in the whole extent. The abundance and excellence of its productions have induced all the foreign houfes fettled in Barcelona to eftablifh agents and factors at Reus, the principal town, pretty near the center of the plain.

Here we have again been loaded with civilities by our friends, and detained fome days in feafts and amufements. Indeed the crazy vehicle our fervants travel in, contributed much toward the facility with which we yielded to their entreaties; for, about an hundred yards before we reached this place, both its fhafts fnapped in two, fo that very little, except the hind wheels and fome braces, now remains of the original carriage that left Pafcal's coach-houfe, in the Rue Guenegaud, at Paris.

It has blown for three days a moft bitter north wind; the froft is pinching and the ice thick, but no kind of vegetation feems affected by it, and the fun fhines out burning hot every day.

Reus increafes daily in fize and population; the number

ber of its inhabitants has within thefe fifteen years rifen above two thirds, and now amounts to twenty thoufand fouls. The fuburbs are already twice as large as the old town. They have begun to build a very pretty theatre, and have engaged a company of comedians.

Wines and brandies are the ftaple commodities of Reus: of the former, the beft for drinking are produced on the hills belonging to the Carthufians; thofe of the plain are fitteft for burning. The annual exports are about twenty thoufand pipes of brandy, all very pale, but afterwards, by mixtures in Guernfey and Holland, brought to the proper colour for our market. There are four degrees of proof or ftrength—common, oil, Holland, and fpirit. Brandy of common proof froths in the glafs in pouring out, and remains fo. Oil proof is when oil finks in the brandy. Five pipes of wine make one of ftrong brandy, and four make one of weak. The king's duty is ten pefettas a pipe on the high proofs, and twelve on the low: the town dues come to three fols, and both duties are paid by the exporter. This branch of trade employs about one thoufand ftills in the Campo, of which number the town contains an hundred and fifty. It is all carried in carts, at half a crown a pipe, down to *Salo*, an open but fafe road five miles off. Here it is left on the beach till it pleafes the Catalan failors to float it off to the fhips: as they are paid by the year, they only work when they choofe, and in fair pleafant weather.

weather. Nuts are likewife an article of exportation, upwards of fixty thoufand bufhels from the woods at the foot of the weft mountains having been fhipped off laft year. Every thing here wears the face of bufinefs, but it is greatly at the expence of the inland villages, many of which are left almoft deftitute of inhabitants.

Not far behind the mountains that furround this plain ftands a rich convent of Bernardine monks. Had the weather been milder we fhould have paid them a vifit, there being many fine views and natural curiofities in its neighbourhood. As they are far removed from the eye of the world, we have been affured that they lead a moft diffolute life: the immenfe lordfhips they poffefs are faid to ferve as fo many nurferies and feraglios for them, where the wives and daughters of their vaffals are humbly devoted to their pleafures. A modeft woman would run great rifk of being infulted by the lufty friars, fhould fhe venture within their territories without proper attendance. Some years ago, a fet of wild young officers, who owed the holy fathers a grudge, carried thither a bevy of common ftrumpets dreft out like ladies, and contrived matters fo, that while the men of the party went up the hills to fee profpects, the females were left to be comforted by the Bernardines. The hot-livered monks employed the time of abfence to the beft advantage, but fmarted fo feverely for the favours they obtained from the good-humoured nymphs, that for many months afterwards

wards the chief dignitaries of the house were dispersed about in the neighbouring towns, under the care of the barber-surgeons.

LETTER XI.

Nules, November 29, 1775.

YOU will not find upon the common maps the name of the place I date this from, though it is a considerable town, inclosed with walls and towers *alla morisca*, with two handsome suburbs. This is all I can tell you of it, as we are just arrived by moon-light. I am now melting with heat, and sitting close to the window for air, but I fear the twanging of a wretched guitar will soon drive me away. How wonderfully fortunate we have been in the weather! not a drop of rain on the road from Perpignan hither, and we are to reach Valencia to-morrow.

Last Saturday we took an affectionate leave of our friends, and left Reus loaded with provisions of all sorts. The road through the plain hollow and bad, the view confined on every side by groves of locust and olive trees, till we entered the desart near the sea-shore, at

a ruined

a ruined tower called the *Casa yerma*. In the afternoon we came through a rocky paſs under the fort of Balaguer, lately built to command the defile and the coaſt. The evening journey lay among bleak uncomfortable hills, covered with low ſhrubs, where nothing but the proſpect of the ſea, and watch-towers placed as beacons along the ſhore, afforded the leaſt variety; the road moſt abominably rough and trying for carriages. The approach of night, and the danger of venturing in ſuch broken ways in the dark, obliged us to ſtop at the Venta del Platero, a hovel that *beggars all deſcription*; ſo ſuperlatively wretched, that I thought an exact drawing of its outward appearance would be a real curioſity. We were lodged in part of a ground-floor, the remainder of which was occupied by the mules and pigs; the ſervants ſlept in the carriages. A pool of water behind the houſe, and above the level of our floor, made our apartment ſo damp, that the next morning our cloaths might have been wrung. Thanks to the wholeſomeneſs of the climate, we felt no bad effects from it. Several companies of fiſhermen, that hawk their fiſh about theſe ſcattered cottages, kept all night a perpetual knocking at the gate of our court, and brought to my mind very lively ideas of the enchanted caſtles of Don Quixote.

As ſoon as it was light we left our inn, and found the waſte grow more and more barren. The ſteepneſs and roughneſs of the deſcents made the road exceſſively jolting

ing and dangerous; the chaifes cracked and groaned, and we either rode on horfeback, or walked, all the way. Torrents that rufh from the adjoining ridge of mountains, after every heavy fhower, have fwept away all bridges and caufeways, and wafhed the road to the very rock. We paffed through Parillo, a fmall village, which is the ufual baiting-place, and feems, by the ruins near it, to have been formerly a place of greater confequence than it is at prefent.

In a few hours we emerged from this defart, which is at leaft ten leagues long. In fome places it produces locuft and olive trees, which, when the underwood is cleared away, and the earth moved about the roots, become productive of good fruit. A little turn of the road to the weft brought us in fight of the mouth of the Ebro, which appears to wafte itfelf before it reaches the fea, by running through various channels, in a tract of flat lands containing near one hundred thoufand acres. This land is very capable of improvement, and the miniftry have actually before them a plan for draining thefe grounds, and properly diftributing the wafte water for the purpofes of cultivation. There are two good harbours at the mouth of the river, which is navigable for veffels of fifty tons, up as far as Tortofa, and for fmall craft much higher, into the kingdom of Arragon. The waters of the Ebro, though muddy, are conftantly drunk by the inhabitants; the flime they leave after great floods is efteemed as beneficial to the lands they overflow as those of the Nile are to Egypt. The rich narrow vale along the banks is laid out in corn-fields and mulberry-plantations. An amphitheatre of bleak gloomy mountains shuts up the valley to the west, where the river makes its way through a narrow breach in the vast chain of rocks. Just before we entered Tortosa, we met the bishop of that see, clad in the plain simple manner of the inferior clergy of the province. His lank black hair was cut close to his ears, and covered by a great hat, squeezed up on each side into the form of a boat. The order of bishops in this kingdom leads a very exemplary life, much retired from the world, expending their great revenues in feeding the poor, building and endowing churches, convents, and hospitals, and allowing very scantily for their own expences. Their charity, however laudable as to the intention, is certainly most prejudicial to the public welfare, as it encourages beggary and idleness; for who will work in a country where he is sure of a good dinner every day at the gates of a monastery or palace, besides the chance of occasional alms; and where the softness of the climate renders cloaths and lodging objects of luxury rather than of prime necessity. Perhaps it would be better for Spain, were its prelates as extravagant as those of France, as their wealth would then be divided among the industrious and honest, and not lavished to support the existence of the idle, and often of the profligate. In spite of

so

so good an example, the inferior clergy, and above all the monks, (one or two orders excepted) are notorious for the loosenefs of their morals. The bishopric of Tortosa is worth about thirty thousand dollars a year.

A little further on we came to a liquorice-work, carried on by an Englishman. The liquorice plant grows in great plenty on all the low grounds near the river. He employs above an hundred hands in gathering it, and about fifteen at constant work in the mills. He pays a certain sum to the proprietors of those lands; yet such is their envy, that this season they would not suffer him to pluck a single stick, though the loss falls upon themselves, and the very extraction of the root brings the ground almost to a state of cultivation. This conspiracy obliged him to send up into Arragon for liquorice, at a great additional expence. Much of it also is found about Villanova, and other places along the coast. Four hundred tons of root make fifty of cake, which in England sells at about three pounds fifteen shillings per hundred weight: this year he expects to export about that quantity.

Tortosa is an ugly town on the declivity of a hill, north of the Ebro, over which there is a bridge of boats. Its commerce in silk and corn is but at a low ebb. We purchased of some nuns the most delicate silk gloves I ever beheld, made of what they call the flower of silk.

We next traversed the rich vale of Garena, where the

olive-trees grow to a great fize, their luxuriant branches not being fo clofely pollarded as in France. Here the peafants wear the Valencian drefs, which differs totally from that of Catalonia; a monftrous flouched hat, cropt hair without a net, a fhort brown jacket, white waiftcoat and trowfers, ftockings gartered below the knee, and packthread fandals.

At the paffage of the Cenia, a pretty brook in winter, but dry in fummer, we entered the kingdom of Valencia. After croffing a large tract of heath, we came to the fea-fhore, which is beautifully planted to the water-edge with olive, mulberry, fig, and *algarrobo* trees. We found a rich red foil, and vineyards neatly trimmed in rows, without ftakes, in the diftrict of Benicarlo, a fmall place entirely fupported by the wine trade. Eight thoufand pipes of a very ftrong, fweet, red wine, bought in the country at the rate of five guineas per pipe, are annually fhipped in this road for Holland, Germany, and Bourdeaux, where they are mixed with the fecond-rate claret, to give it colour and body. The wine for Bourdeaux is conveyed along the coaft to Cette, on board Spanifh barks, which are exempt from all duties on exportation. By reafon of their apprehenfions of Moorifh corfairs, and the chance of bad weather, they come to an anchor every night, and commonly make it a voyage of a month at leaft. At Cette thefe wines are put upon the great canal of Languedoc, and fmuggled into Bourdeaux

deaux as high-country wines; for foreign ones are not allowed to be entered at that port. A fociety of mariners float all the cafks from Benicarlo to the fhips, and, from the time of their taking charge of them, become anfwerable for all loffes by weather or mifmanagement. A good deal of wine goes likewife from Vinaros, a neighbouring town to the north; but the quality of that wine is much inferior to thofe of Benicarlo and Penifcola, a town and fort fituated fouth of Benicarlo, on a rock in the fea, where the famous antipope, Peter de Luna, took refuge.

In this plain they fuffer much for want of water; the vintage is frequently diminifhed by the exceffive heats, which dry up all the fprings. It was once in agitation to bring a canal from the Ebro to water this country, but the project ended in fmoke, like feveral others propofed for the amelioration of many parts of Spain. Wherever they can procure water from wells, by means of a wheel turned by a mule, they have fine vegetables all the year. They cut lucerne every week in fpring, and every fortnight in winter, and mix it with the fweet bean of the locuft, for the provender of their mules. Provifions are very fcarce here, no kind of meat being killed except kid. In fpring, goats milk is plentiful; but the peafants in the adjacent mountains live moft part of the year upon the roafted acorns of the ever-green oak, a food which we found furprifingly favoury and palatable,

latable, but not very nourishing. The gentlemen, proprietors of vineyards, reside up in the mountain villages, in a poor style, always distressed for money, notwithstanding the sure and ready sale of their wines. The sea hereabouts is full of sharks.

From Benicarlo we had much stony road, alternately skirting the shore, or climbing up wild rocky hills. Few vales surpass in beauty that of Margal, a noble plain, full of trees, villages, and towns. The sea forms a picturesque bay before it, and the mountains run behind in a vast semicircle. The locust and olive trees are old and branchy, the soil deep, and the grounds fertile, as being well drenched with water. We dined at Castillon de la Llana, the largest and best built town in our route. The women are very ugly, and render themselves still more uncomely, by frizzling their hair all round the forehead, and twisting it on the crown of the head round a nasty brass bodkin. Villa Real is another large town, near the Mijares, a river of a green colour, in a large plain.

The moment we entered this petty kingdom of Valencia, we began to feel a sensible change in the climate: the days are troublesomely hot, the nights soft and mild, like our fine summer evenings. Early and late in the day I walk an hour or two, to enjoy the sweetness of the morning and evening breeze, and contemplate at leisure the enchanting prospects along the calm Mediterranean. The numberless creeks and bays, the bold promontories,

with

with each its slender tower, of various shapes and dimensions, the green woody vales, with rocks impending over them, are scenes that can seldom be met with, and never outdone in any country, and such as no description of mine can do justice to. But, as all human pleasure is allayed with some mixture of pain and distress, these charming coasts are not without their calamities; till lately, they were cruelly infested by the Barbary rovers, who frequently cut barks out of their roads, and carried off whole families from the small villages. At present Barceló keeps so sharp a look-out, that their appearance is less frequent in these seas. The scarcity of water is another misfortune, and severely felt almost every summer. Of the innumerable beds of rivers and torrents that we have crossed between Barcelona and Nules, six only have any water in them, viz. the Llobregat, Gaya, Francolis, Ebro, Cenia, and Mijares: two of these are dry during the hot weather. Hereabouts the little canals from the hills supply the lands with a greater plenty of water.

All these nights past we have heard the people singing doleful ditties under our windows, to the sound of a guitar, which they strike with their nails, without any notion of air, but merely as a kind of an accompaniment, sometimes high, sometimes low, but very coarse and monotonous. I can compare their music to nothing so well as to the beating of a frying-pan, to call down a swarm of bees.

LETTER

LETTER XII.

Valencia, November 30, 1775.

THIS morning, like many of the foregoing ones, was delicious; the sun rose gloriously out of the sea, and the air all around was perfumed with the effluvia of the aloe, as its rays sucked up the dew from the leaves.

From an eminence we had a noble view of the valley of Almenara, a kind of land bay, surrounded by lofty mountains, and adorned with six pretty towns, rising out of the bosom of a forest of dark and light greens, varied in a multitude of tints. The long range of turrets upon the hill of Murviedro (once the too faithful Saguntum) juts out towards the sea, from the chain of mountains that runs parallel with the coast, and divides the vale of Almenara from that of Valencia.

We halted at Murviedro, to view the ruins of so celebrated a city, and to take drawings of its most remarkable remains. The present town is very considerable, and seems to stand upon the same ground as the ancient Roman city, but in all probability the Saguntum which was destroyed by Hannibal was built upon the summit of the hill. That the Romans also had a fortress on the top,

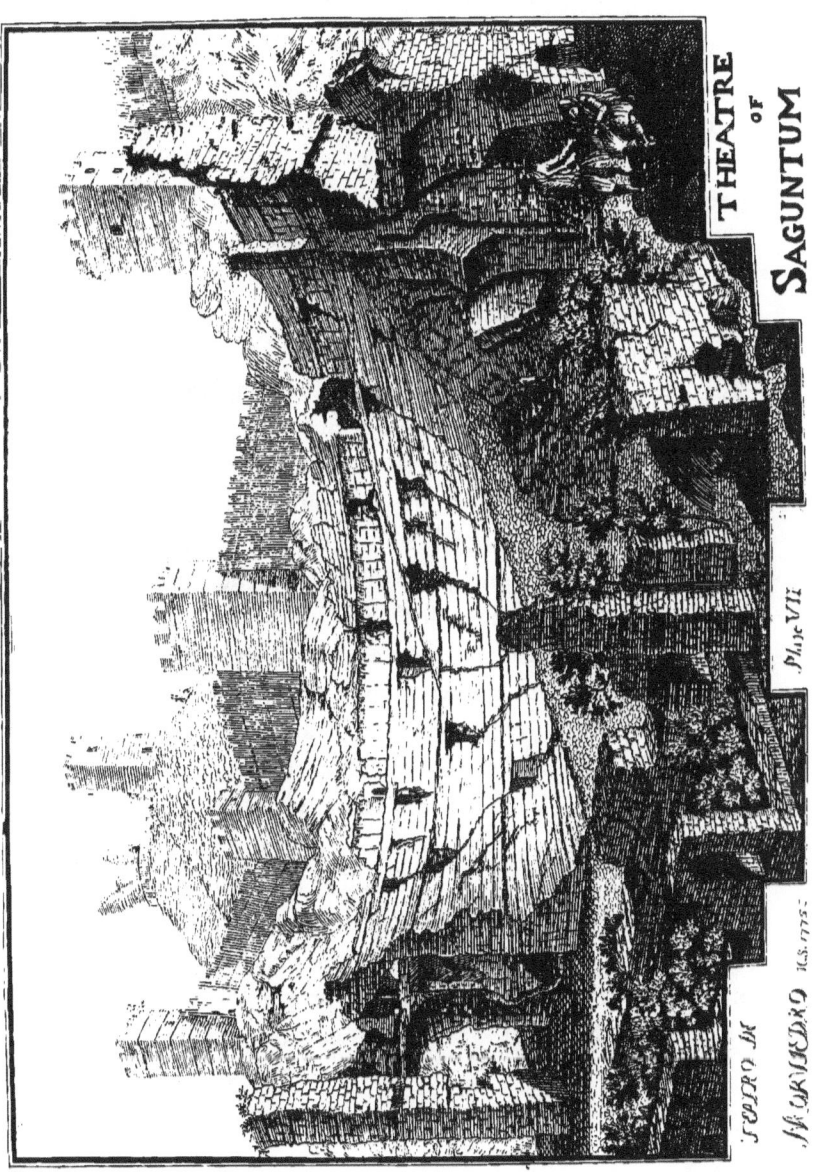

TEATRO DE
MORVIEDRO M.S. 1775

THEATRE OF SAGUNTUM

Plate VII

top, is clear, from the large stones and regular masonry, upon which the Saracens afterwards erected their castle.

Half way up the rock are the ruins of the theatre, in sufficient preservation to give a tolerable idea of its size and distribution. It is an exact semicircle, about eighty-two yards diameter from outside to outside; the length of the orchestra, or inner diameter, twenty-four: the seats for the audience, the staircases, and passages of communication, the vomitoria, and arched porticoes, are still easy to trace. The back part rests against the hill, and some of the galleries are cut out of the rock. Two walls going off at an angle serve to turn off the rain-water that washes down from the cliff behind. As the spectators faced the north and east, and were sheltered from the west and south, nothing could be more agreeable in this climate than such a place of entertainment; open to every pleasant and salubrious breeze, and defended from all winds that might bring with them heat or noxious vapours. It is computed that nine thousand persons might assist without inconvenience at the exhibitions in this theatre. I passed some time in taking an oblique drawing of the present appearance of the ruins; but, in spite of all my attention, I found it a very difficult task, the heaps of rubbish, broken porticoes, and vaults, and remnants of walls, creating such a perplexity, that my eye could scarcely distinguish the proper form and situation of each object. The silence that reigns in this auguſt ruin, which anciently reſounded with the applauſes of proconſuls, and Roman citizens, is now broken only by the *ſeguidillas* of a few rope-makers, who have patched up a ſtraw ſhed againſt the ſtage, and ſpin out their work acroſs the *proſcenium*, regardleſs of the ſurrounding ſcenery [6].

From the theatre we climbed up to the ſummit of the mountain, which is about half a mile in length, and not a tenth part as wide; quite a narrow ridge, covered with ruins and Mooriſh bulwarks. A few unintereſting inſcriptions, two mutilated ſtatues, the veſtiges of the floor of a temple, and ſome Roman arches thrown over a large ciſtern, are all the antiquities we found. One of the in-

---

[6] In the Latin Letters of Em. Marti, dean of Alicant, written about the year 1720, is a long and learned diſſertation on this theatre. He gives the following meaſures:—Perimeter of the ſemi-circle, 564 palmos; diameter, 330; diameter of the orcheſtra, 94; height from the orcheſtra to the top of the higheſt wall remaining, $144\frac{1}{2}$; breadth of the upper portico, $15\frac{1}{4}$; height, $12\frac{1}{4}$; diſtance of the pulpitum from the orcheſtra, 12; height of the pulpitum, $6\frac{1}{4}$; diſtance from the orcheſtra to the ſcena, 28; breadth of the proſcenium, 12; breadth of the pulpitum, $16\frac{1}{4}$. The palmo he uſes contains about nine Engliſh inches. He adds, that great part of this theatre is ſtill entire; and that we ſhould ſee it in a much more perfect ſtate, if the barbarous hands of the Morviedreſe had ſpared it as much as time has done; for they have purpoſely deſtroyed this ancient monument, by wrenching off all the caſing-ſtones for the purpoſes of building convents. There is no doubt but they intended to demoliſh the whole, if the obſtinate hardneſs of the cement had not wearied them out. Marti extorted from the magiſtrates a public decree, inflictive of ſevere penalties on all ſuch as ſhould injure it in any manner whatſoever.

ſcriptions

scriptions is placed topsy-turvy over a gate. The fortifications divide the hill into several courts, with double and triple walls, erected upon huge masses of rock, laid in regular courses, by the Romans. The characteristics of the Moorish military architecture:—A wall built by means of square forms of wood, into which a mortar, composed of pebbles mixed with a strong cement, is run, and left a certain time to harden; then the boards are taken away, but the marks remain, and give the wall an appearance of regular masonry. Battlements perpendicularly placed on the wall, not projecting over, nor with borders round, as in the Norman and Gothic castles, where the hollows behind the battlements served to throw stones and combustibles through, as the enemy approached to scale them. A gateway turned in an arch, neither pointed like what we call Gothic, nor semicircular like the Grecian; but one, the parts of which resting upon the imposts, come much farther in towards each other, and form the figure of a horseshoe. Sometimes, but very seldom, the Moors employed stones of a large size, and more regular cut; and some few of their arches may be found that are sharp like the Gothic; but I suspect them to be of the latter times of the Moorish empire in Spain.

What was wanting in interesting antiquities in the castle, was amply made up to us in prospect, which was so surprisingly fine, that I dare hardly attempt to specify its beauties, lest you should think me too easily enraptured,

tured, or too unequal to the tafk of imparting to others the fenfations it raifed in me. This laft accufation I plead guilty to, for no pen can convey an adequate idea of this view, and few painters ever poffeffed that richnefs of touch, and clearnefs of manner, fuch a fubject would require. The vale of Almenara, on the north, is fo delightful, that from any other ftation it would have engroffed all our attention; but we foon neglected its beauties, and, gliding rapidly over the immenfe volume of fea ftretched out before us to the eaftward, where the funbeams played in full force, we fixed our eyes on the almoft boundlefs plain of Valencia, that lay to the fouth. It is four leagues in breadth from the fea to the hills, in the wideft part, and in length five times that extent, lofing itfelf in a ridge of diftant mountains. The yellow green of the mulberry plantations, and the paler hue of the olive-trees, regularly planted in fields of bright green corn; that regularity now and then broken by large plots of dark-coloured algarrobos; villages and convents, thick fcattered over this great expanfe, with numberlefs gay flender fteeples; the city of Valencia, about twelve miles off, with all its fpires: thefe objects, united, form the moft inimitable landfcape it is poffible to conceive. The day was fo clear, the air fo pure, as to add infinitely to the charms of the profpect. Hannibal is a great favourite of mine, but I cannot forgive him for having dealt fo hardly by fo fweet a place: had he

come

come upon this hill in such a day as this, the softness of the air, and beauty of the view, would have melted the obduracy of his heart, and opened it to pity and forgiveness.

From hence to Valencia is one perfect garden, so thick of trees, that there is no seeing at any distance on either side. Villages and monasteries every hundred yards, and such crouds of people on the road, as I scarce ever saw but in the neighbourhood of London. All the grounds are divided into small compartments by water-channels, the work of the Moors, who understood the art of watering land in the utmost perfection. The ruinous state these drains are now in, proves the indolence and inferiority of the present proprietors; what little skill they still shew in agriculture is nothing but the traditional remains of the instructions left by their masters in husbandry, the Arabians. Our pleasurable ideas were a little ruffled by the sight of some hundreds of women in the villages, sitting in the sun lousing each other, or their husbands and children. When a young woman condescends to seek for lice in a man's head, it is supposed that the last favours have been granted by the fair one, or at least that he may have them for asking.

Valencia is situated in so dead and woody a flat, that we were in the suburbs before we thought ourselves near it, and, having made half the round of the walls,

came

came to an inn on the Alicant road, as it was late, and we did not choose to be detained at the gates by the cuftomhouse officers.

LETTER XIII.

Valencia, December 3, 1775.

OUR firft morning here paffed very ftrangely, in a vifit to the old intendant of the province, to whom we brought a letter of recommendation from his *confrere* of Catalonia. The old ufurer, whofe figure refembles that of the bandy-legged apothecary in Hogarth's *Marriage à la mode*, received us very ungracioufly, took our letter and flung it on the table, without faying a word to us, or even offering us a feat. Having waited fome time, we began to look at each other and laugh. Upon this the intendant looked up, and afked me if we were not Catalans? No, replied I, we are Englifh gentlemen upon our travels. This anfwer produced a wonderful effect. Oh, oh, you come from a better country; Can I be of any fervice to you? Bring thefe gentlemen chairs. Do you choofe to take any refreshment?

freshment? said he, pulling off his hat with great reverence, and making us a most profound bow. We asked him for the only thing we stood in need of, a protection against the people of the customhouses, who, though they do not meddle with your baggage, pester you at every gate for something to drink, or buy tobacco with. The intendant's character is very little respected, nor indeed does it deserve the love or esteem of the Valencians, if the traits they relate be true. Many are the stories they tell of his avarice and hardness of heart; but one will suffice to set him in his proper light. Not long ago he was confined to his bed by a severe fit of illness, and positive orders were given, that he should not be disturbed by applications, petitions, or any thing appertaining to his employment. It so happened, that a tradesman who had been taken up for smuggling, and kept in prison for some weeks, was discovered to be perfectly innocent of the crime laid to his charge. One of the magistrates thought, that for so just a cause as that of restoring an honest man to his liberty, and to his distressed and indigent family, whose very existence depended upon his industry, he might venture to break through the injunction of the intendant, and accordingly procured admittance, and presented the proper paper requisite to be signed, before the jailor could deliver up his prisoner. As soon as the old rogue understood the purport of the visit, he flew into a most violent rage, and obstinately
refused

refufed to fign. Another officer, feeing the door open, took that opportunity of handing up an order for the commitment of a fellow that had been detected in illicit practices. The intendant no fooner read it, than he called for a pen, and fet his hand to it with great pleafure, at the fame time perfifting in his refufal to comply with the firft requeft.

We fhall leave Valencia to-morrow, being heartily tired of our quarters. The climate is mild and pleafant, but there is fomething faintifh and enervating in the air. Every thing we eat is infipid, and void of fubftance; the greens, wine, and meat, feem the artificial forced productions of continual waterings and hot-beds. It puts me in mind of the *Ifle frivole* of the Abbé Coyer, where things were fo feeble and unfubftantial, that they were little better than the fhadows of what they are in other countries. Here a man may labour for an hour at a piece of mutton, and, when he has tired his jaws, find he has been only chewing the *idea* of a dinner. The meat, as foon as cut into, yields abundance of gravy, and may be faid to bleed a fecond time to death, for nothing remains but a mere withered *caput mortuum*, as our fervants know by woful experience. Vegetables, with the fineft outward fhew imaginable, tafte of nothing but water. This wafhy quality feems alfo to infect the bodies and minds of the Valencians: they are largely built, and perfonable men, but flabby and inanimate. We have feen no women

men out at work in the fields; but this may proceed from their conſtant employment within doors, as much as from any remnants of the Mooriſh jealouſy, though the Valencians ſtill retain much of the features and manners of their old Saracen maſters. To this day the farmers won't allow their wives to ſit at table, but make them ſtand at their elbow and wait upon them. The Caſtillians and Catalans hold the Valencians in ſovereign contempt, and ſtigmatize them with many opprobrious appellations, dictated, as we muſt in charity ſuppoſe, by the rancour of national antipathy. The inhabitants of this province are ſaid to have more of the filth, and ſullen unpoliſhed manners of the old Spaniards, and to have adopted leſs of foreign improvements in civilization, than moſt other parts of Spain. They ſtrut about all day in *redicillas,* or nets, monſtrous hats, and dark-brown cloaks, which give the crowd in the ſtreets the appearance of a funeral proceſſion. Scarce any ſociety is kept up amongſt them, tho' the ſalubrity of the climate, and reaſons of œconomy, induce ſeveral very conſiderable families to make this city the place of their abode. In ſome ſtrange way or other they ſpend very large incomes, without doing themſelves the leaſt credit. Their chief expence lies in ſervants, mules, and equipages; low, obſcure amours often conſume the beſt part of their fortunes; and they live in ſo pitiful a manner, that moſt part of them send out to the wine-vault for a pint of wine to their meals.

This city is large, and almost circular; its lofty walls have towers remaining in one quarter, the rest have been demolished: a fine broad road goes quite round: the two suburbs are considerable. Several large, clumsy bridges cross the bed where the river should run; but either from drought, or from the many bleedings it undergoes above, for the purpose of watering the fields, there is scarce water enough in the *Guadaviar* to wash a handkerchief; but in rainy seasons the floods are very tremendous. The captain-general resides in the suburbs, in an uncouth Gothic palace, at the entrance of the *Alameda*, a long double avenue of poplars, cypresses, and palms, where, on great festivals, the nobility take the air in their coaches. About a mile below is the *Grao*, or port of Valencia, which, properly speaking, is only an open road, the mole having been long ago swept away by some violent storm. The dusty highway from the city hither is the fashionable drive; and, for the accommodation of such as have no carriages of their own, several single-horse chairs wait at all hours at the gates. This vehicle is very uneasy, and open to all weathers; but the horses are excellent, and run along like lightning. The driver sits sideways at your feet, and all the way keeps chattering to the horse,
and

and patting him on the buttock. Having occasion one day for a coach to carry us about, the stable-boy of our inn offered his services, and in a quarter of an hour brought to the door a coach and four fine mules, with two postillions and a lacquey, all in flaming liveries; we found out they belonged to a countess, who, like the rest of the nobility, allows her coachman to let out her equipage when she has no occasion for it: it cost us about nine shillings, which no doubt was the perquisite of the servants.

The streets of Valencia are crooked and narrow; not being paved, they are full of dust in dry weather, and in wet knee-deep in mud. The reason alledged for this scandalous neglect, is, that by these means a greater quantity of manure is produced, which, in a plain so full of gardens, is of inestimable value. Various and overpowering are the stinks that rise up in every corner; in which respect, as well as in many others, this country resembles Lombardy.

The houses are filthy, ill built, and ruinous; most of the churches tawdry, and loaded with barbarous ornaments both without and within; the most agreeable architecture I met with, is in the church of the *Escuelas pias*, and of *nuestra Señora de los Desamparados*, both rotundas. In the multitude of sacred edifices, some may be found that excel in particular parts; as, one may please the eye by the just proportions of its dimensions, another ſtrike by the richneſs of its marbles and paintings; but in all, the judicious obſerver will be diſguſted with loads of garlands, pyramids, broken pediments, and monſtrous cornices; a taſte too gothic and trifling for any thing but the front of a mountebank's booth, or a puppet-ſhew in a fair. Some churches have domes, but the greater part tall ſlender turrets, painted and bedecked with all ſorts of pilaſters and whimſical devices: every thing is gilt and bedaubed with incredible profuſion; the Spaniards underſtand the gilder's buſineſs perfectly, and the purity of their gold, with the dryneſs of the climate, preſerves their work for years in its primitive luſtre. The convent of the Franciſcan friars has ſomething very grand and pleaſing in its double court, which is divided by a light wing, upon an open portico, with fountains playing in each diviſion.

The cathedral is a large gothic pile; its archbiſhopric one of the beſt in Spain, ſaid to bring in about forty thouſand pounds ſterling a year, paid in caſh into the hands of two receivers. The revenues of Toledo are much greater, but alſo more troubleſome to collect, and more precarious, as being paid in kind, and requiring a great number of bailiffs and ſervants. The preſent archbiſhop of Valencia, as well as the laſt one, is the ſon of a peaſant; the ruling paſſion of both has been convent building: the late prelate built and endowed a magnificent habitation for the Franciſcans, the champions of

the

the immaculate conception of the Virgin Mary; the prefent archbifhop, whofe fcholaftic tenets are diametrically oppofed to thofe of his predeceffor, has done as much for the fathers of the *Efcuelas pias.*

Priefts, nuns, and friars, of every drefs and denomination, fwarm in this city, where fome convents have more than an hundred monks, all richly provided for.

Among the profane buildings, many of which are prettily fet off with painted architecture, after the Italian manner, the palaces of *Dofaguas* and *Jura real* deferve the moft notice; the former for its ftatues and frefco paintings, the latter for the elegant fimplicity of its front.

The *Lonja*, or exchange, is a very noble gothic hall, built about the latter end of the fifteenth century, with all the beauty and richnefs that ftyle is fufceptible of.

The cuftom-houfe, where the intendant and other officers of the revenue are lodged, is a new large edifice in a great fquare, a very clumfy mafs of brick and ftone.

This kingdom and city were conquered by the Moors under Abdallah Ciz, and loft by them in 1094, when the famous Cid Ruy dias de Vivar, taking advantage of the confufion and civil war that raged in Valencia, after the murder of Sultan Hiaya, made himfelf mafter of the city by ftorm, at the head of a chofen band of valiant knights. This was the laft exploit of that hero, so long the terror of the muſſulmen. A few years after his death, the king of Caſtille, finding it too far diſtant from his other dominions to be conveniently ſuccoured in caſe of a ſudden attack, thought proper to withdraw his troops, and ſuffer the Moors to repoſſeſs themſelves of it. It was again taken from them by James the Firſt, king of Arragon, in the year 1238, and for ever united to that crown, the fate of which it has ever ſince followed through all its various revolutions. In the beginning of the reign of Charles the Fifth, this province was diſtracted by civil commotions and ſtruggles between the nobility and commons.

Since the laſt conqueſt, Valencia has been much enlarged; for the gate through which the Cid made his triumphal entry, is now very near the center of the town.

The number of inhabitants is computed at one hundred thouſand; but, to ſpeak more exactly, according to the laſt authentic enumeration, made in 1768, which allows four perſons to each *vecino*, at twenty thouſand vecinos, or fathers of families; which makes the number to be eighty thouſand inhabitants. The population of the whole kingdom of Valencia amounts to one hundred and ſeventy-nine thouſand two hundred and twenty-one vecinos, or ſeven hundred and ſixteen thouſand eight hundred and eighty-four ſouls, reſident in five hundred and ſeventy towns and villages. The manufactures of
ſilk

silk are the cause of a population that may be reckoned considerable, if compared to that of other provinces of Spain. The produce of this article came this year to one million pounds, but one year with another the average quantity is about nine hundred thousand pounds, worth a doubloon a pound in the country. The crop of silk this last season was very abundant. Government has prohibited the exportation of Valencian raw silk, in order to lay in a stock to keep the artificers constantly employed in bad years; for it has happened in some, that half the workmen have been laid idle for want of materials. As they are not so strict about Murcian silk, which is of an inferior quality, I am told that some from Valencia is sent out of Spain under that denomination. The great nurseries of mulberry-plants, in this plain, are produced from seed, obtained by rubbing a rope of *esparto* over heaps of ripe mulberries, and then burying the rope two inches under ground. As the young plants come up, they are drawn and transplanted. The trees, which are all of the white kind, are afterwards set out in rows in the fields, and pruned every second year. In Murcia, only every third year, and in Granada never. The Granadine silk is esteemed the best of all; and the trees are all of the black sort of mulberry.

The fruit exported from Valencia to the north of Europe may be estimated, *communibus annis*, at two millions.

lions of pefos, about three hundred and thirty-four thoufand pounds.

The annual crop of hemp may be worth three hundred thoufand pefos, at three pefos per *arroba*.

One hundred and forty thoufand loads of rice, at ten pefos a load, make one million four hundred thoufand pefos.

The vintage of 1767 produced four million three hundred and nine thoufand meafures of wine, which, at three reals a meafure, come to about eight hundred and fixty-one thoufand one hundred and thirty-three pefos.

There is alfo much cotton made in this province, from the cotton-plant, which rifes to the height of three feet at moft, and very much refembles the rafp-berry-bufh. They make in good years four hundred and fifty thoufand arrobas, worth one million three hundred and fifty thoufand pefos, and in middling years two hundred and eighty-five thoufand fix hundred arrobas.

Notwithftanding all this abundance, nothing can be more wretched than the Valencian peafantry, who can with difficulty procure food to keep their families from ftarving.

We were laft night at the play, which gave us no very refpectable opinion of the tafte and politenefs of a Valencian audience. The houfe was low, dark, and dirty; the actors execrable; and the pit full of men in cloaks and

and night-caps, driving such puffs of tobacco out of their *cigarros*, as filled the whole room with smoke, and at last forced us to make a precipitate retreat. We there met with our old acquaintance the duke of C. P. who a few months ago came post from France, to embark for the expedition against Algiers. When he arrived at Valencia, he found the fleet was sailed, and an order for him to remain in exile here. The derangement of his finances, and some amorous connections, have procured him this order from court. His fate is truly ludicrous, but he did not drop the least hint to us of this unkind return for his patriotic spirit, and eagerness to serve the king.

LETTER XIV.

Alicant, December 8, 1775.

WE set out early on Monday morning, without regretting in the least the rich gardens or brilliant sky of Valencia, which would be an admirable last retreat for our consumptive countrymen, were the approach by sea or land less difficult.

We travelled that day in a plain, as fertile as nature and frequent waterings can render it. At some miles distance

distance from the city the soil is a red, sandy loam; near the Albufera, a lake about four leagues long, it is very shallow, and communicates with the sea only as often as they open the sluices, to let in a supply of water in dry seasons, or to give vent to the overcharge of water brought down in winter by the land floods. On the edge of it are salt-pans. It supplies the city with fish and water-fowl. Once or twice in a season all the shooters in the country assemble upon it in boats, and make prodigious havock among the flocks of birds, that almost cover the surface of the pond. Sometimes they meet with flamingos here.

Before we arrived at Alzira, a large town in an island of the Xucar, a deep, muddy river, we crossed a large tract of land astonishingly fruitful. The peas and beans in the fields were very high, and in full blow. The husbandmen use in their tillage a shovel-plough, with which they turn the soil from the roots of the olive-trees, that they may benefit by the moisture of the season. We were stopped several times by long droves of mules, carrying corn to Valencia; their conductors, most savage-looking fellows, all clad in leather; their broad belts were fastened round their waist with seven buckles.

In the afternoon, at the entrance of a more mountainous country, we came to the rice-grounds, now in stubble. The process of that tillage is as follows:—In winter they plow out a piece of land, and sow it with beans

that

that come into blossom about March, when they plow them in for manure; water is then let in upon the ground about four inches deep. It next undergoes a third ploughing, after which the rice is sown. In fifteen days it comes up about five inches out of the earth, and is pulled up, tyed in bundles about a foot diameter, and carried to another well-prepared field, covered with water to the depth of four inches. Here each planter sets the plants of his bundle in the mud, in rows at about a foot distance one from another. Every stem ought to produce from ten to twenty-four fold, and grow so close, that the ears may touch. When ripe, it is gathered in sheaves, and put into a water-mill, where the lower grinding-stone is covered with cork; by which means the chaff is separated from the grain without bruising. The rice of Valencia is yellower than that of the Levant, but much wholesomer, and will keep longer without growing musty.

We entered the highlands, and came to lie at Xativa, which was a strong fortress, till destroyed by Philip the Fifth, who ordered it to be rebuilt by the name of San Felipe. That monster Rodrigo Borgia, pope by the name of Alexander the Sixth, was a native of this town. The farmers hereabouts have a very sturdy, good-looking breed of horses.

Our route from San Felipe lay up long winding vales, between ridges of high bleak mountains. On the right hand.

hand ſtands the caſtle of Monteſa, head of the military order of Monteſa, inſtituted in 1317, by James the Second king of Arragon, after he had driven the Moors as far back as the territories of Granada. All the poſſeſſions of the knight-templars in the province were beſtowed upon the new order, into which none but natives of Valencia were to be admitted. They wear a plain red croſs. The commanderies belonging to the foundation are thirteen in number; and their yearly income, according to the king's books, where they are very low rated, amounts to four hundred and four thouſand one hundred and twelve reales de vellon. In 1748, an earthquake overthrew the caſtle, and all the adjacent buildings; burying under the ruins the greateſt part of the chaplains, ſervitors, &c. belonging to the congregation. The remainder were removed to Valencia, where a new church is building for their uſe.

We did nothing the whole day but aſcend through olive plantations, pine foreſts, and bare chalky hills, up the courſe of a little brook, till we came to its ſource, which breaks out in the middle of a town on the confines of Caſtille. Hitherto, the olives I have ſeen are all of the ſmaller ſort.

Next morning the froſt was very ſmart on the high, bare hills, where there is much corn-land, but no trees; the farm-houſes are ſcattered about pretty much as they are in the uncloſed parts of England.

Juſt

Venta del Platero, in Catalonia.

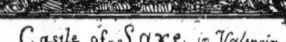

Castle of Saxe in Valencia.

Just as we were going into Villena, a little, round, squat figure, in a brown montero cap, jacket, and breeches, with a yellow waistcoat, caught my eye. It is not possible to paint a better Sancho Pança; and we were actually in a corner of the country of that 'squire, which makes me conclude Cervantes drew the picture from real life, in some of his journies through La Mancha. All the inhabitants of the town wear the same dress, which is neat enough. The castle of Villena is large, well situated, and has been strong. I never saw a country so full of ruined towers, as these skirts of Valencia and Castille; not a village without its rocca perched upon some almost inaccessible cliff; none more singular than that of *Sax*. The hills here are broken, the landscape bleak; but about Elda the plain is improved to the best advantage. We passed by a string of ponds and caves, where the inhabitants of that town keep their provision of ice, for the summer's consumption. As there was a thin coat of ice on the surface of the water, they were very busy carrying it off with the greatest expedition, lest a sudden thaw should deprive them of it.

Before we came into the plain of Montfort, we had a vile piece of road, through a broken range of marly hills. We now found the style of salutation quite altered. Hitherto the peasants were wont to accost us as they passed, with a *Dios guarde usted:* " God keep your worship;" but here they begin, twenty yards before they come up to you, and

and bawl out as loud as they can, *Ave Maria puriſſima*; to which you are expected to anſwer, either *Sin pecado concebida*, or *Deo gratias*.

Late in the evening, we paſſed a large encampment of carriers of ſalt-fiſh. Their carts formed an outer circle, and their oxen a ſmaller one, round a roaring fire, where ſome of the men were cooking, others working at their tackle, but the greater part ſtretched out faſt aſleep. The moon ſhone very bright, and all was ſoft and ſtill; I quite envied the pleaſant ſenſations of thoſe fellows.

Our road this morning was bad, the country abominable, a white clay in powder, and not a ſtick of wood. In rainy years the crops of corn are extremely plentiful. Though it was a bitter cold day, the clouds of duſt almoſt ſtifled us.

We got in here very early, and took up our lodgings at an inn, which hangs over the ſea; the waves beat gently againſt the walls under our windows, and the whole road and harbour lie beautifully ſtretched out before us. Unfortunately, the warmth and ſtillneſs of the ſituation tempt the boat-men to make uſe of this part of the beach as a neceſſary, and we cannot venture to lean out, and feaſt our eyes with the fine proſpect of the ſea, without ſuffering exceedingly in another ſenſe. The landlord endeavours to comfort us, by aſſuring us that to-morrow's ſun will dry all up.

I begin to have my apprehenſions, that my letters, inſtead

ſtead of acquiring life and ſpirit from our progreſs in this kingdom, have, on the contrary, betrayed of late a great propenſity towards ſtupidity. Heaven forbid, the enfeebling air of Valencia ſhould have ſettled upon my pen! I muſt ſhake it off, and ſtrive to afford you better entertainment.

LETTER XV.

Alicant, December 11, 1775.

WE have been received with the uſual politeneſs by the Britiſh ſubjects reſiding here, whoſe hoſpitality knows no bounds, when any of their wandering countrymen appear to lay claim to it. The factory, which conſiſts of five houſes, lives in a ſtyle of elegance we did not expect to meet with any where out of a capital; every circumſtance attending our reception here, is beyond meaſure agreeable. After ſo warm an acknowledgment of our obligations to the inhabitants, you will naturally ſuppoſe I ſhall launch out in praiſe of the town, and varniſh over every defect; but there you will find yourſelf miſtaken. I confeſs it has neither buildings nor ſtreets to recommend it to notice; though the houſes in general

general are folidly built, with flat roofs, covered with cement; their walls are plaiftered, and every thing as white as the foil of the adjacent country; which fatigues the eye moft cruelly in fun-fhiny weather, that is, almoft every day in the year. Then the duft flies about in whirlwinds; if it rains, there is no poffibility of making one's way through the ftreets without boots, the *Calle-mayor* being the only paved ftreet in the whole town. In the hot months, this place is a very furnace, its form being the beft calculated in the world for intercepting the rays of the fun, and collecting them as in one focus; the mountain behind fhuts out the winds, that, blowing from the cool quarters, might refrefh the atmofphere; but I believe the fea-breeze muft occafionally contribute to the cooling of the air. In fuch mild winter weather as we have felt here, it is impoffible not to be delighted with the climate, and the beauties of fituation that the port of Alicant affords. It ftands on the middle of a narrow neck of land, that runs out into the fea a confiderable way, and almoft comes round in a femi-circular form; in the center of which fhips ride with as much fafety as in a harbour; a rocky mountain rifes directly behind the town; on its fummit is the caftle, now fortified after the modern method, and extended far beyond the limits of the old fortrefs, great part of which was blown up, with a fragment of the rock, in the war with the allies, in the reign of our queen Anne. The Englifh garrifon

garrifon refufed to capitulate, though the French gave them notice of the mine being ready to be fprung. A well that communicated with the mine, gave it fome vent, and prevented the reft of the mountain from being fhivered to pieces by the explofion; however, moft of the officers were blown up, and the remainder of the troops fo ftunned by the fhock, as to be many hours deprived of all power of motion.

Behind the caftle-hill, is a plain fome leagues in circumference, called *Las huertas*; the gardens of Alicant lying along the fea-fhore, furrounded on three fides by very lofty mountains. It is a very beautiful vale, thickly ftudded with villages, villas, farms, and plantations of all kinds of fruit-trees; but in the hot part of the year the air is very unwholefome, and few or none efcape agues or fevers. Here the fine Alicant and Tent wines are made. Only two, of the great number of proprietors of vineyards, make a practice of keeping their wine to a proper age. As the value is enhanced many-fold by keeping, the high price they get for their wines amply repays them for the time they are out of their money. Of the common forts, about five thoufand tun may be the amount, moft of which is deftined for the Bourdeaux merchants.

Water is the great agent, the primum mobile of all productions in this country; every thing languifhes, and foon is parched up, without an ample fupply of it; abundance

dance of rain fecures both a plentiful harveft and a copious vintage. Wherever a fpring breaks out, the king's people feize upon it, and allot to each landholder a proper hour for letting the water upon his grounds. It is of fo much confequence, that the value of a guinea has been paid for an hour extraordinary.

The Englifh factory imports all forts of bale goods, corn, and Newfoundland cod. The articles of exportation are wine and barilla. This laft grows in great quantities along the coaft, efpecially near Carthagena: as I fhall, in all probability, get better intelligence there about it, in its vegetable ftate, I fhall defer entering into any detail at prefent on that head. The merchants here, as they employ agents to tranfact the bufinefs for them, are very little informed of the qualities or peculiarities of the feveral forts of barilla they fhip off. It is brought hither in boats, duty free; afterwards it is packed with rufh-mats, in lumps of about fix hundred weight, which ought to be worth about three or four dollars per hund.; but, as this year has been favourable to the crops, it does not fetch above two and a half.

We have been all the morning in great uneafinefs about Sir T. G.'s valet de chambre, who, till within this hour, was not to be found in any of the places he ufually frequents. His appearance has quieted our apprehenfions; and it feems he has been, from fun-rife till dinner-time, locked up in the facrifty of the great church, curling and friz-

zling

zling the flaxen perriwig of the ftatue of the Virgin, who is to-morrow to be carried in folemn proceffion through the city.

There is a forry kind of an Italian opera here; bad as it is, there is a fomething in Italian mufic, however ill executed, incomparably foft and grateful to ears like ours, fo long fatigued with French fqualling, and the drone of Spanifh *feguidillas*. We were upon the point of being deprived of this amufement, by the wifdom of the clergy, who attributed the want of rain to the influence of that ungodly entertainment; luckily for the poor ftrollers, and for us, there fell a fmart fhower juft as the orders were ready to be iffued out againft any further performance, and as it continued to rain all next day, the church thought no more of the opera.

From Alicant is feen, at nine miles diftance fouth, the ifland of S. Polo, where the Conde de Aranda fettled a colony of Genoefe and others, who formerly inhabited an ifland on the African coaft. The regency of Tunis deftroyed their fettlement, and carried them all into flavery; from which they were redeemed by Spain, and, with the allowance of a piftreen a day, fent to form a new town on this barren ifland. As it yields no productions of any kind, they are obliged to be fupplied from the main land with every neceffary of life; fo that fhould the adminiftrators neglect to lay in a fufficient ftock for their fuftenance, in cafe of tempeftuous weather they muft inevitably

tably perish with hunger and thirst. Even as matters now stand, from their scanty allowance and perpetual confinement, I believe they think themselves no great gainers by being rescued from their slavery.

LETTER XVI.

Carthagena, December 15, 1775.

TO continue the journal of our peregrinations:—We left Alicant on the 12th, and brought away with us some bottles of choice Tent for you. We hope, on our return, to present you with a compleat collection of the best wines in Spain; travelling with such a waggon-load of things, a few bottles more or less are not felt; we are obliged to carry, not only our beds, but bread, wine, meat, oil, and salt, from one great town to another; for we seldom meet with any thing in the inns but the bare walls, and perhaps a few eggs, which they sell at an unconscionable price. If we chance to find a few unbroken chairs, we esteem ourselves uncommonly fortunate; yet it is astonishing how dear travelling is in this country. They ask as much for giving you house-room, and for the *ruydo de casa*, or the noise you make, as would purchase a good a good supper and lodgings in the best inns, in most other parts of Europe. As our health is excellent, and consequently our spirits good, we are easily reconciled to these kinds of hardships. Indeed we no longer look upon them in that light; the mildness of the climate obviates all inconveniences that might accrue from a total want of glass, or even paper, in the windows; or of a door or shutter that can be fastened close enough to keep wind or rain out.

As soon as we arrive at one of these barns, called Ventas, our first care is to set up our beds. The kitchen is generally at one end; the mules stand in the back part, and our apartment is a partition run up against the wall to the street, with a hole or two for light, defended by three or four very useless iron bars, for a pigmy could not squeeze through the window.

Next, our cook takes his stand at the hearth, to warm our broth, which we carry, ready made, in a kettle behind our chaise; and if he can procure fuel and elbow-room, tosses up a hash, or some such campaign dish. Sometimes we are lucky enough to have an opportunity of setting our spit, or broiling a chop upon our gridiron; but these are luxuries we are not to expect above once or twice in the course of a week.

While our repast is preparing, we read, draw, or write, by the light of a long brass lamp. Our supper dispatched, and a bottle of wine placed between us, we enjoy

joy an hour's merry chat, to give the fervants time to fup, and then we retire to bed, where we lie very fnug till the dawn of day calls us up, to our ufual tafk of four or five leagues before dinner, and about three in the afternoon. The continual tinkling of the bells of the mules was very irkfome to us at firft, but we are now fo well accuftomed to thefe chimes, that I believe we fhall not be able to go to fleep without them, when we return to France.

We ftopped at Elche, a large town belonging to the duke of Arcos, built on the fkirts of a wood, or rather foreft, of palm-trees, where the dates hanging on all fides in clufters of an orange colour, and the men fwinging on bafs ropes to gather them, formed a very curious and agreeable fcene. The palms are old and lofty; their number is faid to exceed two hundred thoufand. Many of the trees have their branches bound up to a point, and covered with mats to prevent the fun and wind from getting to them. In procefs of time the branches become quite white, and are then cut off, and fent by fhip-loads from Alicant to Genoa, and other parts of Italy, for the grand proceffions of Palm-Sunday; an uncommon fpecies of traffic.

The country round this town is very chearful, and fo are the environs of Orihuela. They are indebted for their fertility to the abundance and proper diftribution of water. In dry years, every field that has not fome

fpring

spring or aqueduct, to furnish it with repeated rigations, is sure to fail in its crop. There is a Spanish proverb in favour of the last-mentioned city; *Si llove, aytrigo en Orihuela, y si no llove aytrigo in Orihuela*: " If it rains, there is plenty of wheat in Orihuela, and if it does not rain, there is still plenty of wheat in Orihuela." Indeed we found its bread excellent, and it has the reputation of producing the best corn in Spain. It is a bishop's see, pretty large, and well enough built, at the foot of a ridge of bare rocks, near the head of a very fruitful *vega* or vale. Near it are avenues of Peric-pepper-tree, or *Schinus molle*, loaded with bunches of a handsome rose-coloured fruit; the people of the country call it *Tiravientos*, probably from some wind-expelling quality. From hence we proceeded along the skirts of the rocks, up into the celebrated vale of Murcia, far superior, in the variety and richness of its culture, to any plain we had hitherto travelled through. Although we were then in the heart of winter, its general appearance was a bright green, the colour of the young corn, flax, lucerne, pulse, and orange-groves. As this vale is not too extensive, but most agreeably bounded on both sides by mountains, the insipid sameness that cloys the eye in most flat countries, however well cultivated, is not perceptible here.

The city of Murcia is neither large nor handsome. The *Segura*, a muddy river, which divides it into two unequal parts, though it contributes nothing to the embellishment

bellishment of the town, claims the merit of creating, by means of its waters, the surprizing fertility of the plain. Hundreds of small drains convey them to the inclosures; and, in spite of the effects of the scorching rays of the sun, preserve the vegetable system fresh and succulent.

The walks about the place are trifling; the streets so full of black stagnated water, as to be almost unpassable. The only thing we found worth seeing was the cathedral, a large massive pile.

Round one part of it is a chain, cut in stone, with a great deal of truth and ease. The steeple, though unfinished, is lofty, and intended, I presume, to exhibit specimens of every one of the five orders of architecture. You may ride up to the top by a passage that goes gradually winding round the tower. From it we had a full view of the town and country; but at this season of the year, the landscape was not decked out in all its beauty, and the bare brown mountains appear too near to please. The names and banners of the Jews, that have been burnt in this town by the inquisition, are stuck up in the church like so many trophies won in the day of victory from some mighty foe.

From Murcia we struck directly across the vale, into the chain of mountains on the south side of the town, and the rugged bed of a torrent was all the road we found. You cannot conceive a more shocking one. The naked

naked clayey cliffs that hemmed us in on each side, were very unpleasant.

As soon as we emerged from this ditch, and surmounted a very greasy, marly height, we found before us a plain, almost without bounds, and absolutely without a tree. A ridge of mountains separates it from the sea-shore. Our muleteers pointed out to us the break in it, where the island of Escombrera closes in the harbour of Carthagena. A cluster of islands to the left, appear as if they had been struck off the mountain by some furious earthquake, and tumbled headlong into the sea. Most of the plain is sown with barilla.

We dined at the door of a most pitiful *venta*, where we found only one man, sent out by the magistrates of Carthagena to wait upon travellers, as the inn-keeper and all his family had been lately carried to prison, on account of a woman, who had been murdered and thrown into a pond behind his house, in which transaction they were suspected of being, at least, accessaries.

We arrived early at Carthagena; for the story of the murder had operated powerfully on the minds of our muleteers, who drove very fast over the plain, to get in before night. We are lodged at the Golden Eagle, kept by a Frenchman, the best cook, in the best inn we have met with in Spain.

LETTER XVII.

Carthagena, December 17, 1775.

I AM in a very bad difpofition for writing, for we are juft returned from the arfenal, where every feeling of our humanity has been put to the torture. Heaven forbid I fhould communicate to you any part of the difagreeable fenfations the fight of fo many of my fellow-creatures in mifery has excited in my foul! but I fhall dwell upon the fubject no longer than will be neceffary to inform you of the plain matter of fact. A letter from Barcelona procured us an order from the governor for feeing the docks and magazines of this port, one of the moft confiderable of the Spanifh dominions.

This arfenal is a fpacious fquare, fouth-weft of the town, under the mountains; forty pieces of cannon defend its approach from the fea; but on the land-fide it is without defence. We only faw one feventy-gun fhip on the ftocks, and a rotten hulk heaved down to be repaired, which fcarce feemed worth the time and expence beftowed upon it. Mr. Turner, an Englifhman, is the head builder. The timber for fhip-building lies in ponds, behind a long range of magazines for ftores, oppofite which the men of war are moored in a wet dock, each
before

before the door of its own magazine. We were told that every one of thefe ftore-houfes contained all things requifite for the compleat equipment of a fhip of war; but, from the flight furvey I took in walking through, I dare venture to affirm, that there is not at prefent, in the whole yard, a fufficient quantity of every article to fit out a frigate. The new ropery, and the forges where they put frefh touch-holes into old cannon, are eftablifhed upon an extenfive plan, but there is little activity in either.

The government of this yard is now in the hands of the officers of the navy, having been lately taken out of thofe of the civil intendants. Upon the whole, the making of thefe docks, and their actual management, have been, and ftill are, conducted after the moft prodigal manner; and either from the vaft demands of the late expedition, or from neglect in the adminiftrators, there is now fo inconfiderable an affortment of arms and ftores, that, were it not for its celebrity, it would fcarce deferve a minute's attention from a curious traveller. Yet the Spaniards are very jealous, and appear uneafy when ftrangers vifit it; perhaps from a confcioufnefs of there being nothing in it. There was no perfuading them that we travelled merely for pleafure, with no finifter views.

The fhips are heaved down in a dry dock, which, by reafon of the back water, and the fprings that ooze through the marfhy foil, would never be clear of water, were it not for feveral fire-engines continually going, and for the great pump, which is plied without intermiffion by Spanifh criminals and Barbary flaves. Of the former, they have eight hundred; of the latter, fix hundred: moft of thefe wretches are kept at it fixteen hours out of the twenty-four, by four hours at a time; fome work only twelve, and moft of the Moors only eight hours. It is the hardeft labour in the world: ten men are fet to each pump, to the amount of about an hundred, in the room above ground, and as many in a kind of dungeon below. In fummer-time, fcarce a day paffes without fome of them dropping down dead at their work; and even at this cool feafon of the year, we have met every day fome of them carrying to the hofpital. The defpair that feizes them is fo outrageous, that if they can get within reach of a weapon, there are many inftances of their having plunged it into their own breaft, or that of fome perfon near them, which anfwers the fame purpofe, a fpeedy deliverance from all their woes by death. As we were looking at them, a dirty little keeper ftruck a fine tall Moor over the head, for leaving his pump to beg of us. The Algerine darted a look of indignation at his tyrant, and refumed his tafk, without faying a word or fhrinking from the blow.

On our leaving this houfe of forrow, we met feveral ftrings of galley-flaves, going to relieve thofe at work, or to fetch their provifions. The Moors had an M on the

fackcloth

fackcloth that covers them, and the whole gang were lively pictures of malady and defpair. The king allows them a piftreen a day, but I am afraid they are defrauded of their allowance; for we faw them making their dinner upon black bread, and horfe-beans boiled in faltwater. We are returned quite melancholy from this fcene of woe. The only reflection that diminifhes our compaffion, is, the atrocioufnefs of the crimes that have brought the Chriftians to the chain; none are here that have not deferved death in fifty fhapes. One boy, of fifteen years old, is here for the murder of his father and mother; and either murder, facrilege, or fome fuch enormous and horrible offences, have been perpetrated by almoft all thofe condemned for life to this punifhment. The feverity exercifed over the Moorifh captives, is not fo eafily reconciled to the principles of humanity, and the meek doctrine of Chriftianity. Retaliation does not feem a fufficient plea.

Since I wrote the foregoing part of my letter, we have been upon a more agreeable party, which has helped to diffipate the gloomy impreffions of the morning. The governor gave us leave to take a boat and row round the harbour. Some gentlemen of our acquaintance were fo obliging as to accompany us, and explain the fituation and intent of each particular place and fortification.

The port of Carthagena is the compleateft I ever faw, formed by the hand of Nature in the figure of a heart.

The

The island of Escombrera blocks up the entrance, and shelters it from the violence of wind and waves. High, bare mountains rise very steep, from the water-edge, on the east and west. On the north, a narrow, low ridge of hills, on which the city stands, shuts out the view of the inland country. We first rowed by the arsenal, and under the mountains on the right hand, the deepest and safest position in the whole bay, where a large fleet may lie in the utmost security, out of the sight of all ships that may be at sea, or even in the narrow part of the entrance of the harbour. There are at present two frigates and four chebecs in port. As we came along-side of the St. Joseph, the commodore, she fired a gun, which our steersman informed us was the signal for weighing anchor and getting under sail, orders being come from court for them to leave Carthagena this day. As we were desirous of learning a little of the method and skill of the Spanish seamen, we desired our master (who, from having been long employed in the service of the English merchants, has contracted the habit of looking upon himself as an Englishman) to lie upon his oars and remain along-side, that we might have the pleasure of seeing the men of war move out. The old sailor laughed heartily at our request, and, after reminding us that we were not at Portsmouth, nor these ships English men of war, bade his men row away, as he was very certain none of the vessels would be ready to depart for three days at least,

and

and that the gun was fired merely in compliance with the letter of the orders.

On our approach to the mouth of the harbour, we got out of the calm, ſtill water we had hitherto glided upon, and began to be toſſed about with great violence. The day grew cold, and the ſky looking lowering towards the ſea, we ſtruck directly acroſs the paſſage, in order to return to the town by the eaſt ſide of the bay. This entrance is much wider than I had any idea of; the forts on the rocks, on each promontory, ſeem to be too far diſtant from the middle to do any damage to an enemy that might think it neceſſary to puſh through; but without a ſkilful pilot, I doubt a ſtranger would pay dear for his temerity; for directly in the center of the haven, in a line between the mouth and the mole-gate, lies a ledge of rocks, only five feet under water, without any breakers or rippling near it.

The eaſt ſide of this port is much ſhallower than the weſt ſide, and the anchorage is looſe and ſandy. Veſſels have been frequently forced from their anchors, and daſhed to pieces againſt the rocks, by the ſtorms from the ſouth-weſt. However, with good cables, I was aſſured there is no great danger to be apprehended. In any other part of the harbour, the waters are perfectly dormant, never ruffled by wind or tides. There is ſo little agitation in them, that, during the ſtay of the many hundreds of veſſels deſtined for the Algerine expedition, they became

came abfolutely putrid and infectious, from the filth thrown out of the fhips. Juft as we landed on the pitiful platform called the mole, we had an opportunity of knowing the exact fpot where the rocks lie. An Englifh merchantman coming in at a great rate before the wind, but unfortunately without a pilot, ftruck upon the ledge, and was not got off without fome damage.

We are now going to the play, where we are not to expect any fcenes, as it is a working-day; and the actors come out from behind a bit of red curtain hung acrofs the ftage, and never move far from it, as a file of prompters are drawn up behind, whofe fhadows and motions are not unlike that kind of entertainment called *Italian fhades*. Though there are three regiments here in garrifon, befides engineers and naval officers, you can fcarce imagine any thing fo dull as this town. Except the wretched comedy, and the coffee-houfe, there is not the leaft life or amufement going forward. This city is large, but has very few good ftreets, and ftill fewer grand or remarkable buildings. The hofpital is a large fquare houfe, round two courts, three ftories high towards the fea, and only one towards the land: the architecture, and method of laying out the plan, are good; but the ftone is of fo foft and friable a contexture, that the fea air has corroded it, and made it crumble away more than half: there is no probability of any care being taken to repair the injury.

Farther

Farther east, at the foot of the summer-evening walk, is a small church, erected in honour of St. James, the patron of Spain, who is piously believed to have landed here, when he came from Palestine to convert this country to Christianity.

LETTER XVIII.

Carthagena, December 18, 1775.

I HAVE been busy all morning walking about the fields near the town, in search of specimens of the various plants, that produce the false and true barilla; but the season of the year is unfavourable to my researches, and I have only been able to meet with two sorts. Mr. James Macdonnel, a young gentleman lately settled in business here, has been so obliging as to furnish me with some notes on that head, which contain the result of many observations made on these plants in their vegetable state, and on the different modes of cultivating and preparing them for sale. The following pages convey the substance of his memorandums.

There are four plants, which in the early part of their growth bear so strong a resemblance to each other, as would deceive any but the farmers, and very nice observers. Thefe four are, *barilla, gazul* (or, as fome call it, *algazul) foza,* and *falicornia* or *falicor.* They are all burnt to afhes, but are applied to different ufes, as being poffeffed of different qualities. Some of the roguifh farmers mix more or lefs of the three laft with the firft; and it requires a compleat knowledge of the colour, tafte, and fmell of the afhes, to be able to detect their knavery.

The 1ft, Barilla, is fown afrefh every year. The greateft height it grows to above ground is four inches: each root pufhes out a vaft number of little ftalks, which again are fubdivided into fmaller fprigs, refembling famphire, and all together form a large, fpreading, tufted bufh. The colour is bright green; as the plant advances towards maturity, this colour dies away, till it comes to a dull green tinged with brown.

The 2d, Gazul, bears the greateft affinity to barilla, both in quality and appearance; the principal difference confifts in its growing on a ftill drier, falter earth, confequently it is impregnated with a ftronger falt. It does not rife above two inches out of the ground, fpreading out into little tufts. Its fprigs are much flatter, and more pulpy, than thofe of barilla, and are ftill more like famphire. It is fown but once in three, four, or five years, according to the foil.

The 3d, Soza, when of the fame fize, has the fame appearance

pearance as gazul, but in time grows much larger, as its natural foil is a ſtrong ſalt-marſh; where it is to be found in large tufts of ſprigs, treble the ſize of barilla, and of a bright green colour, which it retains to the laſt.

The 4th, Salicor, has a ſtalk of a green colour, inclining to red, which laſt becomes by degrees the colour of the whole plant. From the beginning it grows upright, and much reſembles a buſh of young roſemary. Its natural ſoil is that on the declivities of hills, near ſalt-marſhes, or on the edges of the ſmall drains or channels cut by the huſbandmen for the purpoſe of watering the fields: before it has acquired its full growth, it is very like the barilla of thoſe ſeaſons in which the ground has been dunged before ſowing. In thoſe years of manuring, barilla, contrary to its nature, comes up with a tinge of red; and when burnt, falls far ſhort of its wonted goodneſs, being bitter, more impregnated with ſalts than it ſhould be, emitting a diſagreeable ſcent if held near the noſe, and raiſing a bliſter if applied for a few minutes to the tongue. The other three ſpecies always have that effect. Barilla contains leſs ſalts than the others; when burnt, it runs into a maſs reſembling a ſpungy ſtone, with a faint caſt of blue.

Algazul, after burning, comes as near barilla in its outward appearance, as it does while growing in its vegetable form; but if broken, the inſide is of a much deeper and more glossy blue. Soza and Salicor are darker, and almost black within, of a heavier consistence, with very little or no sign of spunginess.

All these ashes contain a strong alkali; but barilla the best and purest, though not in the greatest quantity. Upon this principle, it is the fittest for making glass, and bleaching linen; the others are used in making soap: each of them would whiten linen, but all, except barilla, would burn it. A good crop of barilla impoverishes the land to such a degree, that it cannot bear good barilla a second season, being quite exhausted. To avoid this inconvenience, the richer farmers lay manure upon the ground, and let it lie fallow for a season; at the end of which, it is sown afresh without danger, as the weeds that have sprung up in the year of rest, have carried off all the pernicious effects of the dung. A proper succession of crops is thus secured by manuring and fallowing different parts of the farm, each in its turn. The poorer tribe of cultivators cannot pursue the same method, for want of capital, and are therefore under the necessity of sowing their lands immediately after manuring, which yields them a profit just sufficient to afford a present scanty maintenance, though the quality and price of their barilla be but trifling.

The method used in making barilla, is the same as that we follow in the north of England, in burning kelp. The plant, as soon as ripe, is plucked up and laid in heaps,

heaps, then set on fire; the salt juices run out below, into a hole made in the ground, where they consolidate into a black vitrified lump, which is left about a fortnight to cool. An acre may give about a tun. I was told, that there is a species of *Scarabaeus*, or beetle, that burrows in the root of the barilla, and there deposits its eggs, which foxes are so fond of as to dig up the plant to come at this favourite morsel. To gratify this appetite, they would in one night lay waste a whole plantation, if the peasants did not keep a strict watch with guns to destroy or drive them away. Nevertheless, I cannot depend enough upon my information, to vouch for its authenticity.

Not far from Carthagena, is a place called Almazaron, where they gather a fine red earth called Almagra, used in the manufactures of Saint Ildephonso, for polishing looking-glasses. In Seville, it is worked up with the tobacco, to give it a colour, fix its volatility, and communicate to it that softness, which constitutes the principal merit of Spanish snuff.

LETTER

LETTER XIX.

Ifnallos, 7 at Night, December 24, 1775.

WE are juft arrived at this difmal ruinous village of mud walls, after the hardeft day's labour of our whole journey, benighted, our baggage-vehicle broken to pieces, and every bone about us aching. We have been fourteen hours on the road without unharneffing the mules. I have walked many miles to-day, which has tired my legs; but at leaft my fpirits are lefs jaded than they would have been had I remained locked up in the chaife, through the dangerous paffages and dreadful precipices of this day. I am happy to hear that from hence to Cadiz is almoft all level road, and, if it does not rain, not very bad; if there fhould fall a great quantity of rain, I doubt we may come to ftick in the clays of Andalufia. One cook is hard at work below ftairs, making us a difh of fomething warm to cheer our drooping hearts; with that help, a bottle of wine, and a tolerable clean room, we hope foon to drive away all remembrance of our diftreffes and fatigues.

On the 19th, we left Carthagena, and for two long days travelled up the plain, 'till the two ridges of mountains, that run on each fide of it, unite at its head.

The firſt part of this plain is very naked, but well cultivated, the laſt two-thirds are as compleat a defart as any in the fands of Africa; not a bufh, tree, or houfe, to be feen in all the vaft expanfe of level ground; the mountains are as bare as the low lands. The want of water, productive of a want of inhabitants, accounts for this prodigious defolation; for the foil feems very fit for tillage. One of the days we dined at Lorea, a large town at the foot of the hills. I faw nothing in it to make a note of, but the drefs of a gipfy, daughter to the innkeeper. Her hair was tied in a club, with a bunch of fcarlet ribbons; large drops hung from her ears; and on her breaſt fhe wore a load of relics and hallowed metals; the fleeves of her gown were faſtened together behind by a long blue ribbon, that hung to the ground. I could not prevail upon her to explain the ufe of this laſt piece of ornament.

On the 21ſt, the fcene changed, but did not improve upon us; the dry bed of a torrent was our highway for half the day, and ſteep barren mountains for the remainder. This proved the firſt day of difagreeable weather we had met with on the road fince we left France. It blew a perfect hurricane, and rained very heavily, with a fharp biting wind.

The next morning brought us back funfhine and genial warmth; the road grew mountainous, and more difguſtingly bare, except for a mile or two, while we paſſed through

an

an uneven country pretty well tilled, and planted with large bufhy evergreen oaks, exactly in the manner of fome of our Englifh parks. We faw this day many vultures on wing, but they never came within reach of our guns. I can give you no information concerning the town of Baça, as we entered it after it was dark, and left it before break of day. It ftands quite in a bottom, furrounded by high mountains, over which we, next morning, found the paffage both difficult and frightful. Not the leaft agreeable patch of country on the heights, except fome poor remains of ancient forefts of evergreen oaks. We dined at a venta near fome mountains, where we were told of mines of gold having been wrought in days of yore, but now long loft and forgotten; the little brook that runs down from them abounds in many metallic particles, which appeared to the eye lead and copper. Much *gypfum*, or plaifter-ftone, is alfo to be found in this torrent.

Yefterday afternoon, we had nothing but rapid afcents and defcents, rendered incredibly greafy and fatiguing by the heavy rain of the foregoing night. Guadix, an epifcopal fee, is exactly fituated in the fame kind of gully as Baça; a narrow valley worn down by the river. The clay-hills, that encompafs it on every fide, are the moft extraordinary in nature; they are very high, and wafhed into broken maffes, refembling fpires, towers, and mifhapen rocks. Whole villages are dug in them, the

windows

windows of which appear like pigeon, or rather marten holes. The paſſage through is remarkably ſingular, winding for half a mile between two huge rugged walls of earth, without the leaſt mixture of rock or gravel.

The Cueſta yerma, which with the utmoſt difficulty we climbed up this morning, is perhaps not to be matched for badneſs on any carriage-road in the world. All our mules yoked together were ſcarce able to wrench either of the carriages out of the narrow paſs between the rocks, or drag them up the almoſt perpendicular parts of this abominable mountain. After this happy deliverance from our well-grounded fears of paſſing the whole day, and perhaps night, in fruitleſs endeavours to extricate ourſelves, we travelled along a high level country, winding round the mountains of Granada. The wind was very loud, but the air warm and pleaſant, though the ſnow lay in view along the top of that high ridge of mountains called, from their covering of ſnow, *ſierra nevada*.

Thus, methinks, I have brought you very fairly as far as myſelf on our dreary journey; and am of opinion, that neither the beauties of nature, nor thoſe of art, to be met with in this kingdom, can be deemed an equivalent for the tediouſneſs of travelling, the badneſs of the roads, or the abominable accommodations of the inns: certain it is, that no man has as yet undertaken this tour a ſecond time

time for pleasure; and, if my advice be listened to, no body will ever attempt it once.

Granada, December 25.

Our baggage being put upon a cart this morning, we proceeded down a valley, and over some heath and forest land, till we came in view of the plain and city of Granada.—Beautiful beyond expression even in its winter weeds, what must it be when decked out in all the gaudy colours of spring? You must not expect an account of it for some days, as I intend getting all possible intelligence, turning over all my books, and examining every place, before I venture to describe this city, its palace, and environs.

LETTER XX.

THE Moorish kingdom of Granada consisted of those parts of Spain that lie in the south-east corner of the peninsula, and at its most flourishing period never exceeded seventy leagues in length from east to west, and twenty-five in breadth from north to south. Its historians have laboured hard to prove, that it had separate monarchs soon after the Moorish conquest of Spain; but it is more than probable, that this country did not become a distinct sovereignty, while the Caliphs of the East retained any authority in Europe. By degrees, the weakness of the other Mahometan potentates, who could afford no succour against the common enemy; the coalition of the Christian kingdoms under one or two powerful heads; and, more than all, their own civil discords and deadly feuds, had, long before its final overthrow, reduced the kingdom of Granada to little more than the Alpuxaras mountains and the capital city.

The Granadine antiquaries, with Pedraza at their head, insist that Granada was a colony of the Phœnicians, known to the Romans by the name of Illiberia. They allege, in support of their system, that the walls of the most ancient of its inclosures, which was afterwards called the Alcaçaba, are of a different sort of masonry from those of the Romans and Saracens, and similar to such remains of antiquity as are universally acknowledged to be the work of the Phœnicians. The spot where this mode of building is most conspicuous, is, the *Hetna-roman*, a tower where the stones are very long and narrow, laid regularly upon beds of cement of equal thickness with the stones. It is now of little consequence to endeavour to discover the founders of this city, and an analysis of the volumes published on these chimerical topics,

topics, would but ill repay the time loft in writing and reading fuch a diſſertation.

Another argument, that has afforded much entertainment to many doctors profoundly ſkilled in etymologies, is, the meaning, date, and origin, of the name of Granada. Some writers make out the derivation by compounding the word *Nata*, which they ſet down as the name of Count Julian's daughter [7], with the word *Gar*, a cave, where ſhe retired after the battle of Xeres: others will have it to come from the abundance of corn *(Grano)*: and ſome again from *Nata*, a goddeſs of the Aborigines: others, with an appearance of probability, aſcribe the origin of the name to the pleaſantneſs and fertility of its environs, a word very like it, in the Phœnician language, meaning *fruitful* and *agreeable*. The Romans expreſſed the fame ſignification by the title of *municipium floren-*

[7] It is the common opinion (though not ſufficiently warranted by authentic teſtimonies) that Rodrigo, laſt king of the Goths, raviſhed the daughter of Julian, governor of Africa. The father, enraged at ſuch an injury, made a treaty with the Saracens, whom he induced to croſs the Straits and invade Spain. Muſa, lieutenant of the Caliph Walid, ſent over Tarif with a ſmall force to try his ſtrength. There being great appearance of ſucceſs, Tarif received a conſiderable reinforcement, and attacked the Goths near Xeres de la frontera. The Goths were defeated, their king killed, and the Gothic empire annihilated in 712. Muſa, and his immediate ſucceſſors, completed the conqueſt of all Spain, except the mountains of Oviedo, where Pelayo afterwards formed a principality, the parent of all the other Spaniſh kingdoms.

tinum

tinum illiberitanum. The Arabs called it *Roman*; the Jews *Rimmón*: and there are authors that derive it from *Granatum*, a pomegranate, brought from Africa, and first planted near this place. Many affirm it to be called so from the resemblance its position bears to that fruit when ripe; the two hills to represent the bursting skin, and the houses crowded into the intermediate valley, the pips. This is a very favourite opinion, and seems to be adopted by the nation, which gives a split pomegranate for its arms, and places it upon every gate or ornamented post in the streets and public walks.

Granada stands on two hills, at the foot of the *Sierra nevada*, where two small rivers join their waters. One of them, the Dauro, sometimes washes down gold; the other, the Xenil, virgin silver; but it was not possible for me to procure any specimens of either, on account of the severe prohibition issued out by government against all searchers after mines and minerals. The ancient palace of the *Alhambra*, and the *Torre vermeja*, crown the double summit of the hill between the rivers; the other hill, north of the Dauro, is covered with the *Albaycin* and *Alcaçaba*. The remainder of the city extends along the skirts of the plain in a semicircular form. The Vega, or plain, is eight leagues long, and four broad; a gentle slope of beautiful hillocks bound the horizon on all sides, except that of the Sierra nevada, and to the northwest, where it is terminated by the bare top of the *Sierra Elvira*,

Elvira, or *Sierra de los infantes*. This mountain was so named from the death of the princes of Castille, Peter and John, who perished here, through excess of heat and thirst, in a battle against the Moors, 1319.

The country about Granada was so alluring, the situation so striking, and the salubrity of its air so universally celebrated, that the victorious Saracens soon were induced to turn their arms that way. It was taken by the forces of Tarif in 715, the ninety-fifth year of the Hegira [g]. As long as Spain remained subject to the viceroys of the Caliphs of the family of the Ommiades, Granada does not appear to have undergone any great revolution, although now and then an ambitious governor might make an attempt towards independency. The first that brought this design to bear, and rendered the crown hereditary in his family, was Mehemed Alhamar, governor of Arjone, who began his reign in 1236.

Mehemet Alhamar.

1236. This first king became tributary to S[t]. Ferdinand, king of Castille, and paid him one moiety of all his revenues, which half amounted to one hundred and seventy thousand pieces of gold: he even assisted that prince in his conquest of Seville.

1273. The second king was his son Muley Mehemed Abdallah, who is said to have begun the Alhambra.

[g] The flight of Mahomet, which happened in the night between the 15th and 16th of July, in the year 622.

1302.

1302. 3. *Mehemed Abenalhamar* the blind, son to Muley, was dethroned and murdered by his brother. Mehemed had a great passion for building; one of the magnificent monuments he left for the admiration of posterity, was the great mosque included in the Alhambra. The form was most elegant, the inside mosaic, adorned with ingenious devices in sculpture, supported upon lofty pillars with silver bases and capitals. He endowed this pious foundation with revenues arising from the baths, which he had built opposite to it, out of the tribute paid by the Christians and Jews. He also purchased lands, and let them out for the benefit of this mosque.

1310. *Nazer aba algueiusch* murdered his brother, and was himself driven into banishment by his sister's son.

1315. *Ismael ben pharagi abulgualid,* who was murdered by the alcayde of Algeziras, from whom he had forcibly taken a very beautiful female captive.

1326. *Mehemed Abuabdallah,* his son, succeeded. This prince was murdered by his own servants [9], and succeeded by his son.

[9] In a sally which the Christians made during the siege of Baeca, this king of Granada hurled a lance, enriched with precious stones, at a Spanish soldier; who, finding himself grievously wounded, limped away towards the town with the weapon fixed in his body. The Moors rushed forwards to recover the lance, but Mehemed forbade them to molest the poor wretch, and suffered him to carry away the spear to pay for his cure.

1333.

1333. *Jufaf Abuhagiagi.* In 1340, this king, and Abi Haffan, king of Morocco, were defeated in the famous battle of Salado, by Alphonfus the eleventh. From that day Granada declined in power, and gradually dwindled away. The uninterrupted feries of evil fortune that attended this unhappy prince, at length drew upon him the univerfal hatred of his fubjects, one of whom ftabbed him in the ftreet.

1354. His fucceffor was *Mehemed Lago*, a younger brother of Pheragi. He was dethroned by his coufin,

Mehemed Ifmael ben Alhamar. Don Pedro, king of Caftille, having always been intimately connected with Lago, efpoufed the caufe of that exiled prince with great warmth, and made feveral attempts to reinftate him. Ben Alhamar, diffident of his own ftrength, and preffed to it by the entreaties of his counfellors, thought it fafeft to fubmit, and purchafe the friendfhip of Pedro at any rate. With this view, he demanded a fafe conduct, and went to the court of Seville, where he threw himfelf at the feet of the Spanifh monarch, with the immenfe treafures he had brought with him as prefents. That king received him with all apparent refpect and cordiality for a few days, but then he ordered him, and thirty of his moft noble attendants, to be

led

led round the city upon affes, and afterwards to be brought to the field of the Tablada, where, if any credit is to be given to the Spanifh hiftorians, Don Pedro himfelf ran the unfortunate Mehemed through with a lance. His death being made known at Granada, Lago refumed the reins of government without oppofition, and died quietly in 1379.

1379. His fon Mehemed Abouhadjad, was one of the beft kings that ever reigned in Granada. He preferred the folid advantages of peace to all the brilliancy of military glory. Under his wife adminiftration, the kingdom gradually recovered its vigour; commerce and hufbandry gave fpirit and alacrity to every part of the realm, and fpread abundance over the face of the land. His attention to the more important objects of government, did not prevent his fhewing himfelf an earneft promoter and protector of the fine arts. The cities of Granada and Guadix were embellifhed with many noble ftructures during his reign. His affection for the latter was fo confpicuous, that he was furnamed by his people, Mehemed of Guadix. He had the addrefs to maintain peace with the Caftillians, and at his death left a flourifhing, peaceful fucceffion to his fon,

1392. Juzaf Abiabdallah, who was deftroyed by means

of an envenomed shirt, sent as a present by the Sultan of Fez.

1396. Mehemed Balba, second son to Juzaf, seized upon the crown in prejudice of his elder brother, and passed his life in one continual round of disasters. His wars with Castille were invariably unsuccessful. His death was also caused by a poisoned vest. As soon as he found his case desperate, he dispatched an officer to the fort of Salobrena, to kill his brother Juzaf, lest that prince's party should form any obstacle to his son's succeeding to the crown. The Alcayde found the prince playing at chess with an Alfaqui or priest. Juzaf begged hard for two hours respite, which was denied him; at last, with great reluctance, the officer permitted him to finish the game. Before it was ended, a messenger arrived with the news of the death of Mehemed, and of the unanimous election of Juzaf to the crown.

1408. Juzaf Abul Haxex. The most unwearied importunity, and abject submission, were unable to procure him a peace with the Christians. The regent of Castille, D. Ferdinand, being inflexibly bent upon expelling the whole Saracen race out of our continent. At length, Ferdinand was elected king of Aragon, and finding sufficient employment with the affairs of his new kingdom, gave up all thoughts of his Moorish conquests, and listened to the proposals

posals of the king of Granada. A truce was agreed upon, and afterwards a peace concluded, which afforded Juzaf an opportunity of repairing his losses. He wound up the end of his days in tranquillity, and employed them solely in gaining the affections of his people, by a steady pursuit of a most equitable plan of administration. From the time Juzaf became possessed of the royal dignity, he was never known to shew the least sign of resentment against the grandees that had assisted his brother in depriving him of his birth-right and liberty: nay more, he conferred great honours and favours upon many of them, and gave them posts of trust in various capacities. Some of his own party found fault with his lenity, and endeavoured to work him up to the destruction of those noblemen; but Juzaf always made answer, Would you have me, by my cruelty, furnish them with an excuse for having preferred my brother to me? He educated the sons of Mehemed in his palace, and treated them in every respect like his own children.

1423. His eldest son, Mehemed Elazari, or the left-handed, succeeded. He was more remarkable for the strange vicissitudes of his fortune, than for any thing great of his own atchieving: his tyranny and negligence encouraged his cousin-german,

1427. Mehemed El Zugair, or the lesser, to take up

arms againſt him, and drive him out of the kingdom. Two years after Elazari, with the aſſiſtance of the kings of Caſtille and Tunis, retook Granada, and made El Zugair priſoner, whom he put to death in the moſt cruel and ignominious manner that could be deviſed.

1429. Elazari being thus reſtored to his throne, was far from altering his method of proceeding; in conſequence of which, after many defeats in a bloody war againſt the Chriſtians, he was a ſecond time dethroned, and the grandſon of that Mehemed who was killed at Seville, raiſed up in his ſtead.

1432. Juzaf aben Almaoalnayar gave great hopes of his proving a juſt and wiſe monarch; but his death, which happened in the ſixth month of his reign, put an end to all his projects, and Mehemed Elazari, was once more proclaimed king. The people of Granada were now become ſo well accuſtomed to a frequent change of maſters, and ſo very prone to novelty, that it was no longer poſſible for any prince to remain firm in the royal ſeat for any length of time. Accordingly Elazari, that perpetual butt of fortune, was for the third and laſt time deprived of his ſceptre, and ſhut up in a cloſe priſon by his nephew,

1445. Mehemed ben Oſmin, ſurnamed the Tame. In the beginning of his reign, he waged war againſt the

the Chriftians with great fuccefs; but in the year 1452, his good fortune abandoned him, and he met with nothing ever after but croffes and difappointments. The king of Caftille fpirited up againft him a competitor for the crown, Ifmael, his coufin-german; who being admitted into the capital by a party he had previoufly fecured, furprized Mehemed, and threw him into the fame dungeon where their common uncle had already languifhed eight years. Thus ended thefe two princes like puppets, which, after having been made to move upon the ftage the time allotted for reprefentation, are thrown by in a lumber-room, and never thought of more.

1453. Ifmael thus found himfelf in the peaceable poffeffion of a crown, which had been fo often fhifted from head to head, and fo mutilated and curtailed during a long feries of misfortunes, that any fagacious obferver might fafely pronounce the period of its final diffolution to be near at hand. The Chriftians had fo long laid wafte with fire and fword the rich plain of Granada, that Ifmael found that fource of plenty almoft irretrievably loft. To make up in fome degree for this deficiency, he ordered a large tract of foreft to be cleared, and the mountainous lands behind Granada to be levelled, and converted into arable and garden grounds. Earth

was

was even brought from the Vega, to render the hills more fruitful. Great supplies of water were conveyed from the Dauro, by means of aqueducts and conduits, to water those eminences naturally barren and parched up by the sun. These improvements were the support of the Granadines, after their implacable enemies had not only burnt their crops in the plains, but even destroyed their farms, cut down their fruit-trees, rooted up their vines, and changed one of the most delightful spots on earth into a mere naked desart. Upon engaging to pay an annual tribute of twelve thousand ducats, and to deliver every year six hundred Christian captives, or, in case of there being none to releafe, an equal number of Moors (an almost incredible condition, which more than any thing evinces the miserable state of this kingdom) the Moors at last obtained a peace, or rather truce, which even did not extend to that part of the kingdom that is near Jaen.

1475. Muley Mehemed Abilhaſſan succeeded his father Ismael, and was so imprudent as to engage in a war with Castille, which ended only with the ruin of the Muſſulman empire in Spain. The first important conquest of the Spaniards was Alhama, a town famous for its magnificent baths, whither the Moorish princes were wont frequently to retire for their

their health and diversion. In 1484, Abilhassan having put away his wife Ayxa, and taken to his bed Fatima, a Grecian slave, surnamed for her beauty *Zoraya*, or the morning-star, the disgraced Sultana made her escape from the Alhambra, and raised a rebellion in favour of her son Abouabdoulah. The old king was forced to fly for refuge to Malaga, to his brother El Zagal, who soon after gained great glory by a victory he obtained over the grand master of St. Jago. About the same time, the young king was routed and taken prisoner by the Castillians at Lucena, being the first Arabian prince led into captivity by the Christians. Hassan was restored; but Ferdinand of Aragon, husband to Isabella of Castille, set the son at liberty, with a view of fomenting their civil dissensions, and thereby facilitating the conquest of their kingdom. El Zagal, soon quarrelled with the old king, and drove him into exile, where he died soon after, in misery and despair.

Abouabdoulah, or the young king, was the lawful monarch; but his uncle, who had already destroyed one rival, endeavoured to put the other also out of the way by assassination. The plot was discovered, the nephew's party prevailed, and El Zagal, rather than submit to his own relation, from whom he had no right to expect mercy, went over, and delivered up all his possessions to Ferdinand. The Spanish monarch immediately summoned Abouabdoulah to fulfil the conditions of the treaty,

upon

upon which he had obtained his liberty. Thefe were, to deliver up Granada, as foon as Almeria, Guadix, and Baca, fhould be in the hands of the Spaniards. This contingency was now come to pafs. It was not natural to fuppofe the Moor would fubmit tamely to his utter ruin; therefore Ferdinand, who had forefeen his refufal, laid fiege to Granada. After nine months blockade, for the compleating of which he built a new town, called Santa Fé, he obliged the Moorifh king to furrender. Ferdinand and Ifabel made their triumphant entry on the 2d of January 1492. Abouabdoulah, in his way to Purchena, the place appointed for his refidence, ftopped on the hill of Padul, to take a laft farewell look of his beloved Granada. The fight of his city and palace, to which he was then about to bid an eternal adieu, overcame his refolution: he burft into a flood of tears, and, in the anguifh of his foul, broke out into the moft bitter exclamations againft the hardnefs of his fate. The Sultanefs Ayxa, his mother, upbraided him for his weaknefs, in the following terms: "Thou doft well to weep, like a woman, over the lofs of that kingdom, which thou kneweft not how to defend, and die for, like a man."

This prince was the laft Moor that reigned in Spain, where their empire had fubfifted feven hundred and eighty-two years.

Such Moorifh families as remained in Granada after the diffolution of the monarchy, were continually molefted by by zealous priests and bigotted princes. Every article of the capitulation was in its turn eluded, or openly violated, and the Moors reduced to the alternative of renouncing the religion of their ancestors, or of abandoning their native country. The Spanish clergy, not at all satisfied with the outward shew of conversion in those that had embraced the Christian religion, were eager to discern the sincere from the hypocrite, and therefore set spies over them, encouraged all accusations, and cavilled with every part of their dress and behaviour. Thus harrassed, and urged to the very brink of despair, the Moriscos, as they were then called, formed a grand conspiracy, which broke out on Christmas night, in the year 1568. Having placed at their head a young man, descended from their ancient princes, by name Ferdinand de Valor, which he changed to Mehemed Aben Humeya, they rose in arms in most parts of the kingdom of Granada. The revolt began by wreaking the most bloody vengeance on all Christians, especially priests, that fell into their hands. Notwithstanding considerable forces were sent against them, and many furious battles fought between the Spaniards and the insurgents, generally to the disadvantage of the latter, the rebellion continued in great vigour near two years. Aben Humeya, having betrayed an inclination to capitulate, was murdered by his own officers, and a desperate captain, called Abenaboo, elected in his stead. This shadow of royalty soon passed away, and met with the fate of his predeceffor. After his affaffination, the Morifcos fubmitted, and were difperfed all over Spain, the rabble of the two Caftilles being fent to occupy their lands.

In the year 1610, Philip the third iffued out an edict, commanding every perfon of Moorifh extraction, without exception, to retire out of Spain, which rigorous, and extraordinary order was to all appearance punctually obeyed; yet fo late as the year 1724, the inquifition ferretted out, and drove into banifhment, fome confiderable remnants of that unfortunate race.

LETTER XXI.

DRYDEN has built the ground-work of his play, of *The conqueft of Granada*, upon circumftances taken out of a romantic *hiftory of the diffentions between the Zegris and the Abencerrages*, noble Moors of Granada, by Giles Perez. The Spanifh ballad, tranflated in Dr. Percy's relics of ancient poetry, is drawn from the fame force. As Peres is an author read by all ranks of people in this country, his dreams are generally received as undoubted facts, confecrated by tradition; and moft of the tales repeated by the keepers of the palace, &c.

have

have been learnt in his book. Indeed [10] Medina Conti, author of the *Paſſeos de Granada*, pretends to have found an Arabic manuſcript account of theſe times, which corroborates the teſtimony of Peres; but theſe writers are ſuch notorious impoſtors, that little credit can be given to any thing they advance: however, there muſt undoubtedly be ſome foundation for theſe anecdotes, and a previous knowledge of them is rather neceſſary for the perfect underſtanding of the deſcription of the Alhambra; I ſhall therefore preſume ſo far upon your patience, as to ſketch you out an abſtract of the latter part of his hiſtory.

In the days of Boabdil or Abouabdoulah, the laſt king of Granada, the Alabeces, Abencerrages, Zegris, and Gomeles, were the moſt powerful families in that city;

[10] Conti, in order to favour the pretenſions of the church in a great lawſuit, forged deeds and inſcriptions, which he buried in the ground where he knew they would ſhortly be dug up again. Upon their being found, he publiſhed engravings of them, and gave explanations of their unknown characters, making them out to be ſo many authentic proofs and evidences of the aſſertions of the clergy. His impoſture was detected, and he now lies in priſon, without much hope of ever recovering his liberty. I am told he is a moſt learned, ingenious man, profoundly ſkilled in the antiquities of his country. The Morocco ambaſſador, in his way through Granada, purchaſed of this man a copper bracelet of Fatima, which Medina proved, by the Arabic inſcription, and many certificates, to be genuine, and found among the ruins of part of the Alhambra, with other treaſures of the laſt king, who had hid them there in hopes of better days. This famous bracelet turned out afterwards to be the work of Medina's own hands, and made out of an old braſs candleſtick.

they filled moſt of the great employments about court, and ſcarce a brilliant atchievement in war was heard of, that was not performed by the arm of ſome knight of theſe four houſes. High above the reſt towered the Abencerrages, unequalled in gallantry, magnificence, and chivalry. None among the Abencerrages more accompliſhed, more diſtinguiſhed, than Albin Hamet, who for his great wiſdom and valour ſtood deſervedly foremoſt in the liſt of the king's favourites. His power roſe to ſuch a pitch, that it excited the moſt violent envy in the breaſt of the Zegris and Gomeles, who determined to pull him down from this poſt of ſuperior eminence. After concerting many ſchemes for his deſtruction, none appeared to them more effectual than one propoſed by a conſummate villain of the Zegri family. He ſeized an opportunity of being alone with the king, whoſe character was as yet frank and unſuſpicious; aſſuming an air of extreme anguiſh of mind, he obſerved to the prince how very weak his conduct appeared to all wiſe men, by repoſing ſuch unbounded confidence in, and truſting his perſon with, ſuch traitors as the Abencerrages, who were well known to be laying a ſcheme for a general revolt, thereby to deprive Abouabdoulah of his life and crown. Nay more, he, and three men of honour, had ſeen the queen in wanton dalliance with Albin Hamet Abencerrage, behind the lofty cypreſſes in the gardens of the Generaliph, from whence Hamet had returned inſolently crowned with a garland

of

of roses. These calumnies roused all the furies of jealousy in the breast of the credulous monarch, and the destruction of the whole lineage of Abencerrage was planned in the bloody junto. The principal men of the devoted family were, under some pretence or other, summoned one by one to attend the king in the court of lions. No sooner was each unhappy victim admitted within the walls, than he was seized by the Zegris, led to a large alabaster bason in one of the adjoining halls, and there beheaded. Thirty-six of the noblest of the race had already perished, before the treachery was discovered. A page belonging to one of those noblemen, having found means to follow his master in, and to get out again unseen, divulged the secret of this bloody transaction. The treason once known, all Granada was in an instant up in arms, and many desperate combats ensued, which, by the great havock made amongst the most valiant of its chieftains, brought the state to the very brink of ruin. These tumults being appeased by the wisdom of Musa, a bastard brother of the king, a grand council was held, in which Abouabdoulah declared his reasons for the punishment inflicted on the Abencerrages; *viz.* their conspiracy, and the adultery of the queen. He then solemnly pronounced her sentence, which was, to be burnt alive, if within thirty days she did not produce four knights to defend her cause against the four accusers. The queen's relations were upon the point of drawing their scimitars in the
audience-

audience-chamber, and refcuing her from the danger that threatened her; but their fury was checked by the eloquence of Mufa, who obferved to them, they might by violence fave the life of the Sultana, but by no means clear her reputation in the eyes of the world; which would certainly look upon that caufe as unjuft, which refufed to fubmit to the cuftomary trial. The queen was immediately fhut up in the tower of Comares. Many Granadine warriors were ambitious of having the honour of expofing their lives in her quarrel, but none were fo happy as to prove the object of her choice. She had conceived fo high an idea of the Chriftians, from the valour fhe had feen them difplay in a great tournament lately held at Granada, and the treachery of the Zegris had impreffed her with fo defpicable an opinion of Moorifh honour, that fhe was determined to reft her defence upon the gallantry of the Spanifh knights. In hopes of roufing their noble fpirit to action, fhe difpatched a trufty meffenger with a letter to Don Juan de Chacon, lord of Carthagena, entreating him to efpoufe her caufe, and like a true knight, bring with him three brave warriors to ftand her friends on the day appointed. Chacon returned for anfwer, that he fet too high a price upon that honour, not to be punctual to the hour of trial. The fatal day arrived, and all Granada was buried in the deepeft affliction, to find that their beloved queen had been fo remifs as not to have named one of her defenders.

Mufa,

Musa, Azarque, and Almoradi, the judges of the combat, pressed her, in vain, to accept of their swords, or those of several other warriors willing to assert the justness of her cause. The Sultana, relying on the Spanish faith, persisted in her refusal; upon which, the judges conducted her down from the Alhambra, to a scaffold in the great square, hung with black, where they seated themselves on one side. At the sight of this beauty in distress, the whole place resounded with loud cries and lamentations; and it was with difficulty that the spectators could be restrained from attacking her enemies, and rescuing her by main force. Scarce were the judges seated, when twenty trumpets announced the approach of the four accusers, who advanced armed cap-à-piè, mounted on the finest coursers of Andalusia. Over their armour they wore loose vests, with plumes and sashes of a tawny colour. On their shields were painted two bloody swords, and these words: *For the truth we draw them.*—All their kinsmen and adherents accompanied them to their post within the lists. In vain did the crowd cast a longing eye towards the gate through which the champions of injured innocence were to enter; none appeared from eight in the morning to two in the afternoon. The Sultana's courage began to fail her; and, when four valiant Moors presented themselves, to sue for the honour of drawing their swords to vindicate her innocence, she promised to trust her life in their hands, if within two hours the persons

sons she expected should not appear. At that inftant a great noife was heard, and four Turkish horfemen came prancing into the fquare. One of them addreffed the judges, requefting the favour of fpeaking to the Queen; which being granted, he knelt down, and told her aloud, that he and his companions were Turks, come to Spain with the defign of trying their ftrength againft the heroes of Ferdinand's army; but that, hearing of this folemn trial, they had changed their refolution, and were now arrived at Granada, to devote their firft effay of arms in Spain to her fervice, and hoped fhe would approve of them for her champions. As he fpoke, he let drop into her lap the letter fhe had written to Don Juan; by the fight of which, fhe difcovered this feigned Turk to be no other than the lord of Carthagena, who had brought with him, as companions in this dangerous conflict, the duke of Arcos, Don Alonzo de Aguilar, and Don Ferdinand de Cordova. The queen accepted of their propofal; and the judges having folemnly declared her choice, gave orders for the charge to found. The onfet was fierce, and the fight long doubtful. At length, Don Juan overthrew Mahandin Gomel, and the duke flew Alihamet Zegri; Mahandon Gomel fell by the fword of Aguilar, and the laft of all, the arch-traitor Mahomed Zegri, difabled by repeated wounds, and fainting with lofs of blood, funk at the feet of Don Ferdinand; who, fetting his knee on the infidel's breaft, and holding his dagger

to

to his throat, fummoned him to confefs the truth, or die that inftant. "Thou need'ft not add another wound," faid Mahomad, "for the laft will prove fufficient to rid the world of fuch a monfter. Know then, that to revenge myfelf of the Abencerrages, I invented the lye that caufed their deftruction, and the perfecution of the Sultana; whom I here declare free from all ftain or reproach whatfoever, and with my dying breath implore her forgivenefs." The judges came down to receive this depofition of the expiring Zegri, and it was afterwards announced to the people, who expreffed their joy by the loudeft acclamations. The day ended in feftivity and rejoicing. The queen was efcorted back in triumph to the palace, where the penitent Abouabdallah fell at her feet, and with floods of tears endeavoured to atone for his crime; but to no purpofe; for the queen remained inflexible, and, retiring to the houfe of her neareft of kin, refufed to have any further intercourfe with him. The four knights left Granada, without difcovering themfelves to any other perfon; and foon after, the numerous friends and adherents of the Abencerrages abandoned the city, and, by their feceffion into Caftille or Africa, left Abouabdallah deftitute of able officers, and entirely at the mercy of his enemies, who in the courfe of a few months deprived him of his kingdom.

LETTER

LETTER XXII.

WE have got acquainted with a very converfable old Spanifh officer, of a great family, and ftill greater appetite. He has very freely imparted to us all he knows about the prefent as well as ancient ftate of this province, and the comparifons he makes between them, often draws a figh from us all three. His nephew is poffeffed of large lordfhips and eftates in the neighbourhood; which has afforded him many opportunities of coming at good information on a fubject we are very defirous of inveftigating, I mean, whether there exift any remains of Moorifh families in this country, and what is the tradition concerning the manners and cuftoms of that people before their expulfion.

Granada, while governed by its own kings, the laft years excepted, feems to have enjoyed greater affluence and profperity than ever it has done fince it became a province of Spain. Before the conqueft, it was one of the moft compact, well-peopled, opulent kingdoms in the world. Its agriculture was brought to great perfection, its revenues and circulation were immenfe; the public works carried on with great magnificence, and its population not to be credited by any perfon that fees it in its prefent

prefent condition. Nothing but the numerous ruins fcattered over its hills can induce one to believe, that thofe bleak, barren waftes, which make up more than two-thirds of the province, were formerly covered with luxuriant plantations of fruit-trees, abundant harvefts, or noble forefts. Each Moor had his allotment of as much ground as fufficed for his habitation, the maintenance of his family, and the provender of his horfe, which every man was obliged to keep. Thefe fmall freeholds formed the general appearance of the country, before the inceffant inroads and ravages of the Chriftians had driven the Moors to cities, mountains of difficult accefs, or quite away to the coaft of Barbary. The fingle city of Granada contained eighty thoufand families, and frequently fent out armies of thirty thoufand foot, and ten thoufand horfe. An Arabian author fays, that the kings had a conftant ftock of an hundred thoufand horfes for their own ufe, and for mounting their cavalry in time of war, and more than once had muftered two hundred thoufand foldiers in actual pay, for the purpofe of making war upon the Caftillians.

A great deal of filk was produced in the plain, and the hills behind the city afforded corn enough for its confumption. The rich mines of the mountains were opened, and, tho' not wrought with any thing like the fkill of modern miners, yielded fuch a quantity of gold and filver, that both metals were more common in Granada

nada than any country in Europe. I cannot give you a more diſtinct idea of this people, than by tranſlating a paſſage in an Arabic manuſcript, in the library of the Eſcurial, intitled, " The Hiſtory of Granada, by Abi Ab-
" dalah ben Alkalhibi Abſaneni," written in the year of the Hegira 778, which anſwers to the year of Chriſt 1378; Mahomet Lago being then for the ſecond time king of Granada.

It begins by a deſcription of the city and its environs, nearly in the following terms :

" The city of Granada is ſurrounded with moſt ſpa-
" cious gardens, where the trees are ſet ſo thick as to
" reſemble hedges, yet not ſo as to obſtruct the view of
" the beautiful towers of the Alhambra, which glitter
" like ſo many bright ſtars over the green foreſts. The
" plain, ſtretching far and wide, produces ſuch quantities
" of grain and vegetables, that no revenues but thoſe
" of the firſt families in the kingdom are equal to their
" annual produce. Each garden is calculated to bring
" in a neat income of five hundred pieces of gold
" (aurei ") out of which it pays thirty minae " to the
" king. Beyond theſe gardens lie fields of various cul-
" ture, at all ſeaſons of the year clad with the richeſt
" verdure, and loaded with ſome valuable vegetable pro-

" I was not able to obtain from the interpreters of Arabic, any ſatisfactory account of the real value of theſe Granada coins, therefore have left them as I found them in Caſire's Latin tranſlation,

" duction

" duction or other; by this method, a perpetual fucceffion
" of crops is fecured, and a great annual rent is produced,
" which is faid to amount to twenty thoufand aurei.
" Adjoining, you may fee the fumptuous farms belong-
" ing to the royal demefnes, wonderfully agreeable to the
" beholder, from the large quantity of plantations of
" trees, and the variety of the plants. Thefe eftates oc-
" cupy an extent of twenty miles fquare; for the purpofe
" of taking care of and working them, they keep num-
" bers of able-bodied hufbandmen, and choice beafts both
" of draught and burthen. In moft of them are caftles,
" mills, and mofques. Great muft be the profit upon
" thefe royal farms, arifing from confummate fkill in
" hufbandry, affifted by the fertility of the foil, and the
" temperature of the air. Many towns, remarkable for
" the number of their inhabitants and the excellence of
" their productions, lie difperfed round the boundaries of
" thefe crown lands. The plain contains alfo large tracts
" of meadow and pafture, villages and hamlets full of
" people, country-houfes and fmall dwellings belonging
" to one perfon, or to two or three copartners. I have
" heard the names of above three hundred hamlets in the
" environs of Granada: within fight of the city walls
" may be reckoned fifty colleges and places of worfhip,
" and above three hundred water-mills."

He next proceeds to the character of the inhabitants.

" The Granadians are orthodox in religion; of the fect.
" of

" of the Molekites. They pay implicit obedience to the
" mandates of their princes; are patient of labour, and
" above meafure liberal : in perfon comely; of a middle
" ftature, with fmall nofes, clear complexions, and black
" hair: elegant in their language, but rather prolix in
" difcourfe : in differting and difputing, haughty and
" obftinate. The greater number of their families de-
" rive their origin from houfes of Barbary. Their drefs
" is ftriped Perfian or Turkifh robes of the higheft
" prices, either fine woollens, linens, filks, or cottons.
" In winter they wear the *Albornos*, or African cloak ;
" in fummer a loofe white wrapper. The foldiers of
" Spanifh extraction ufe in war a fhort coat of mail,
" light helmet, Arabian horfe-furniture, a leathern buck-
" ler and flender fpear. Thofe born in Africa bear
" very long ftaves, which they call *Amras*, i. e. rope-
" ends. Their dwellings are but flightly built. It is
" very curious to affift at the diverfions of their feftivals;
" for then the young people affemble in fets at the danc-
" ing-houfes, and fing all manner of licentious ballads.
" The citizens of Granada eat the very beft of wheaten
" bread, throughout the year; the poorer fort, and la-
" bourers, are fometimes, in winter-time, obliged to put
" up with barley-bread, which, however, is excellent in
" its kind. They have every fort of fruit in abundance,
" efpecially grapes, of which the quantity eaten is incre-
" dible. The vineyards in the neighbourhood bring in
" fourteen

" fourteen thousand aurei. Immense are the hoards of
" all species of dried fruits, such as figs, raisins, plumbs,
" &c. They have also the secret of preserving grapes
" found and juicy from one season to another.

" Both their gold and silver coin is good, and near to
" purity.

" Many are the amusements and recreations of the
" citizens, when they retire in autumn to their pretty
" villas in the suburbs. They are passionately fond of
" decking themselves out with gems, and ornaments of
" gold and precious stones.

" The women are handsome, but of a stature rather
" below the middle size, so that it is rare to meet with
" a tall one among them: they are very delicate, and
" proud of encouraging a prodigious length of hair;
" their teeth white as the driven snow, and their whole
" person kept perfectly sweet, by the abundant use of
" the most exquisite perfumes; light and airy in their
" gait, of a sprightly acute wit, and smart in conversa-
" tion. In this age, the vanity of the sex has carried the
" art of dressing themselves out with elegance, profusion,
" and magnificence, to such an excess, that it can no
" longer be simply called luxury, but is become absolute
" downright madness."

In Granada, no house was without its pipe of water, and in every street were copious fountains for the public convenience. In short, they neglected no art or inven‐
tion

tion that could contribute towards rendering their lives eafy and voluptuous. I am afraid their urbanity and refinement helped to accelerate their ruin.

You have hitherto been fhewn the brilliant fide of the picture; alas! how different will you find it, when confidered from another point of view, that of its prefent ftate. The glories of Granada have paffed away with its old inhabitants; its ftreets are choaked with filth; its aqueducts crumbled to duft; its woods deftroyed; its territory depopulated; its trade loft; in a word, every thing, except the church and law, in a moft deplorable fituation.

At the time of the expulfion of the Moors, fuch of them as were particularly fkilled in the filk-manufactures, or in the art of conveying and diftributing water to the grounds, were fuffered to remain in the kingdom. Befides thefe, fome were lucky enough to find powerful protectors, who fcreened them from fharing the common fate of their brethren. So late as the year 1726, the Inquifition, with the fanction of government, feized upon three hundred and fixty families, accufed of fecret Mahometifm, and confifcated all their effects, which have been eftimated at twelve millions of crowns: an immenfe fum, of which no account was ever given! The anceftors of thefe people had at their baptifm affumed the furnames of their godfathers, by which means they had the fame appellations as many of the beft families in Spain;

a kind

a kind of relationship that was of great service to them in their misfortune, and probably saved their lives from the fury of the holy office. They were dispersed into distant parts of Spain, where, it is said, that with so much experience and skill in commerce, they soon grew rich again, and no doubt acquired wisdom enough to secure their second acquisitions better than their first. They were the principal merchants and monied men of Granada; their custom was to buy up for ready money all the silk made in the Vega, and sometimes advance the value of it to the landholders before the season. This raw silk they distributed to the manufacturers in the city, whom they supplied with cash for their present maintenance, and were repaid by degrees in wrought silks. All these artificers thrived under their protection, and provided a comfortable subsistence for themselves and their families. The proprietors of land felt the sweets of a ready sale for their commodities; and the annual produce of silk in this province, before the year 1726, seldom fell short of two millions six hundred thousand pounds weight, whereas now it does not exceed one hundred thousand.

The sea-coast of Granada, from Marbella to Motril, afforded formerly large quantities of sugar, which was an article of commerce to Madrid, till within these thirty years. What is now produced, is consumed in the neighbourhood in sweetmeats. From heavy duties which were laid on this branch of trade, and still continue, it is almoſt loſt, there being now only three mills at work, in a declining ſtate. At Motril, and at Toros near Velez, ſugar-canes have been produced nine feet high, and of a proportionable thickneſs. They ſay, the firſt plants were carried from thence to the Weſt Indies, and that the quality and grain of the ſugar is ſtill equal to any imported from thence.

A village in the mountains up the Dauro, is to this day almoſt wholly compoſed of the deſcendants of Moors; but it is not poſſible to know whether they have retained any attachment to the cuſtoms and religion of their anceſtors, or whether they are as good Chriſtians at heart as in outward appearance. You may eaſily diſtinguiſh them from the Caſtillians who were tranſplanted hither, by their round plump faces, and ſmall bright eyes, little noſe, and projecting under jaw. In their deportment, they are extremely humble and ſmooth-tongued; but ſo tenacious of their ready money, that it is with difficulty they can prevail upon themſelves to part with the rents and dues which they cannot well avoid paying. Theſe people, and the progeny of the Moſarabic Chriſtians, who inhabited the country before the conqueſt, are eſteemed a much better race of men, both as to morals and induſtry, than the deſcendants of thoſe vagabonds of Caſtile, who conſtitute the major part of the preſent inhabitants. Many veſtiges of Moorish manners and cuſtoms may ſtill be traced:—when they go in ſummer to bathe,

PIECES OF MOSAIC on the Walls of the Carmen

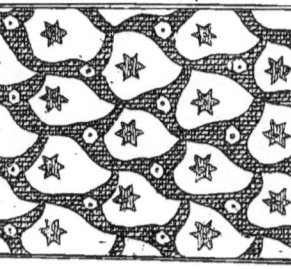
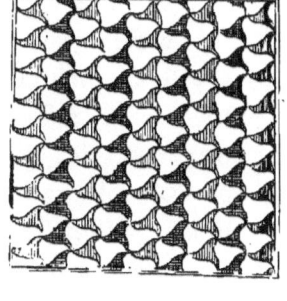

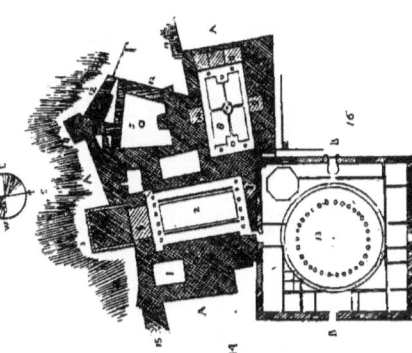

PLAN OF THE PALACES of Charles the Fifth, and of the Moorish Kings in the Alhambra of Granada.

References

A. Moorish Part.
B. Part built by Charles V.
1. Chapel & Governor's House
2. Commune.
3. Torre de Comares.
4. Tocador of the Sultana
5. Garden of Lindaraxa
6. Hall of Embassadors.
7. Gallery of communication.
8. Court of the Lions.
9. Hall of the Abencerrages.
10. Torre das Hermanas.
11. Hall of the Pictures.
12. Additions by ye Emperor.
13. Circular Portico.
14. Court of the Cisterns.
15. Court of the Church or Old Mosque.

bathe, at the end of a plentiful harveft, or on receiving a piece of good news, they are wont to fet up the moft hideous yells and outcries imaginable. I was affured, that whenever any failors belonging to the Maltefe fhips ftray up from Malaga, the populace of Granada, hearing them fpeak Arabic, and feeing them dreffed in a kind of Moorifh habit, follow them up and down the ftreets, and pay them extraordinary refpect.

LETTER XXIII.

AFTER the tedious preamble of three long letters, it is high time to bring you to the palace of the Alhambra.

This ancient fortrefs, and refidence of the Mahometan monarchs of Granada, derives its name from the red colour of the materials that it was originally built with, Alhambra fignifying a red houfe. Moft of the fovereigns took a delight in adding new buildings to the old towers, now called *Torres de la campana*, or in embellifhing what had been joined by their predeceffors. The pleafantnefs of the fituation, and purity of its air, induced the Emperor Charles the fifth to begin a magnificent edifice on the ruins of the offices of the old palace, and it is thought, he intended to fix his chief abode here; but his volatile temper, continual wars, and frequent abfences from Spain, made him give up all thoughts of Granada, long before he had finifhed the plan. It ftands between the rivers, on a very high hill, that projects into the plain, and overlooks all the city; the road up to it is through a narrow ftreet, called *Calle de los Gomeles*, from a great family among the Moors. This brings you through a maffive gate, built by the Emperor, into the outward inclofure of the Alhambra. You then continue to afcend by a very fteep avenue of elms, which foon encreafes to a wood, interfected in many directions by wild, neglected walks, where ftreams of clear water, finding their paffage obftructed by the rubbifh of their old channels, fpread over the whole road. A large fountain adorns the platform near the top of the hill. The water, diverted from its proper conduits, has been fuffered to run at random for fuch a length of time, that it has deftroyed moft of the fculpture and embellifhments, which were in a very good tafte. Here you turn fhort to the left, and come under the walls of the inner inclofure. Its appearance is that of an old town, exhibiting a long range of high battlemented walls, interrupted at regular diftances by large lofty fquare towers. Thefe have one or two arched windows near the top, and a precipitate flope from the bottom into a dry ditch. The whole is built with round irregular pebbles, mixed with cement and gravel. Some

parts

GATES OF THE ALHAMBRA.

PUERTA DE LOS SIETE SUELOS

PUERTA DEL JUICIO

parts are covered and smoothed over with a thick coat of plaister; in other places, mortar has been laid in between the stones, leaving as much of them uncovered as came to the level; then the trowel has been carefully drawn round, forming about them triangles, half-moons, &c. Just before you, stands the present principal entrance into the castle, a square tower built by the king Jusaf Abuhagiagi, in 1348, as an inscription informs us: from its being the place where justice was summarily administered, it was styled *the Gate of Judgment*. You pass through it under several arches (each of which is more than a full semicircle, resting upon a small impost, the ends of the bow being brought towards each other in the form of a horseshoe.) On the key-stone of the outward arch, is sculptured the figure of an arm, the symbol of strength and dominion: on that of the next arch is a key embossed, the armorial ensign of the Andalusian Moors. Above it, the wall of this partition is covered with a beautiful blue and gold mosaic, in the middle of which they have placed an image of the Virgin Mary. As this is not a gate ever used for carriages, the passage winds through several turns, full of images, indulgences, and altars, before you get through, out into a narrow street, between a row of shabby barracks on the right, and on the left the castle wall, supposed to be built by the Phœnicians. I examined the work very narrowly, and found it consisted of a layer of cement one or two inches thick, upon which

which is placed flatwise a stone of the same thickness, chisselled on the face into a kind of a chequered design. This is the regular method employed from top to bottom. This lane ends in the great square, or *Plaza de los Algibes*, so named from the ancient cisterns, that undermine it from end to end, and are constantly fed by a supply of running water. The prospect from the parapet-wall is wonderfully grand, over the vale of Dauro, the Albaycin, and down the Vega. On the very brow of the hill, hanging over the city, stand the *towers of the bell*, a groupe of high square buildings, which now serve for prisons. Below them, on the south-side, on a slip of terrace, is the governor's garden, a very pleasant walk, full of fine orange and cypress trees, and myrtle hedges, but quite abandoned. The view it commands is incomparable. Two large vases enamelled with gold and azure foliages and characters are the only ornaments left: these were taken out of the vaults under the royal apartments. On the right hand of the Plaza de los Algibes, is a solitary gateway, formerly the entrance into some of the outward quadrangles thrown down by Charles the fifth, to make room for his superb palace, which stands facing the *Torres de la campana*. This edifice is a perfect square of two hundred Spanish feet; it has two orders of pilasters, Doric and Ionic, upon a rustic base. The whole measures sixty-two feet from the top of the upper entablement to the ground. Three of the

fronts

fronts are free from all other buildings; the fourth (that to the north) is joined and connected with the ancient palace of the Moorish kings. It was never finished, which is much to be regretted by all lovers of the fine arts, for there are few edifices more deserving of their admiration. The architect was Alonzo Verruguete, a native of Paredes de Navas, near Valladolid. In this work he has discovered a most transcendent genius, grandeur of style, and elegance and chastity of design. How different from all that has been done for a century past in this kingdom! The doors are designed in a great manner; the bass-reliefs, figures, festoons, medallions, &c. are of excellent invention and execution; the ornaments of the cornices, windows, and capitals, are delicate, and suitable to the general effect. On the pedestals of the columns, that support the entablement of the great door, are reliefs on dark marble, that for polish might pass for bronze at a little distance; the Doric door in the south side, called El Zanguenete, pleased me greatly, as there is something simply elegant in the taste, and new in the ornamental part; the pediment is filled with a scroll thrown with great ease, on which is inscribed *Plusoutre*, the motto of the Emperor, which he never failed introducing into every public work he undertook. You come, through an oblong vestibule, into the court which forms the center of the palace. It is an

exact

exact circle, of one hundred and forty-four feet diameter, round which runs a Doric colonnade, or portico, of thirty-two columns, supporting an upper gallery of an equal number of pillars, of the Ionic order. They are all of them of one entire block of reddish marble. The portico is nineteen feet wide, and serves as a communication with the stair-case, and the intended apartments, which are disposed round the court in various forms and proportions. The roof of the gallery is crumbling away very fast, and many of the columns are much damaged. The apartments never had any other covering than the sky; and nothing but the matchless temperature of the climate could have saved this beautiful work, so many years, from total ruin. The magnificence, the unity of this whole pile, but, above all, the elegance of the circular court, quite transported me with pleasure, on the first view, and I have ever since found my admiration encrease in proportion to the number of my visits.

Adjoining (to the north) stands a huge heap of as ugly buildings as can well be seen, all huddled together, seemingly without the least intention of forming *one* habitation out of them. The walls are entirely unornamented, all gravel and pebbles, daubed over with plaister by a very coarse hand; yet this is the palace of the Moorish kings of Granada, indisputably the most curious place within, that exists in Spain, perhaps in Europe. In many

GREAT BATH OF THE ALAMBRA.

many countries, you may fee excellent modern as well as ancient architecture, both entire and in ruins; but nothing to be met with any where else can convey an idea of this edifice, except you take it from the decorations of an opera, or the tales of the Genii. I therefore look upon it to stand alone in its kind, and consequently think no excuse necessary, previous to my entering upon the dry detail I intend giving you of it.

Passing round the corner of the Emperor's palace, you are admitted at a plain unornamented door in a corner. On my first visit, I confess, I was struck with amazement, as I stept over the threshold, to find myself on a sudden transported into a species of fairy-land. The first place you come to, is the court called the *communa*, or *del mesucar*, that is the *common baths*: An oblong square, with a deep bason of clear water in the middle; two flights of marble steps leading down to the bottom; on each side a parterre of flowers, and a row of orange-trees. Round the court runs a peryftile paved with marble; the arches bear upon very flight pillars, in proportions and style different from all the regular orders of architecture. The ceilings and walls are incrustated with fretwork in stucco, so minute and intricate, that the most patient draughtsman would find it difficult to follow it, unless he made himself master of the general plan. This would facilitate the operation exceedingly, for all this work is frequently and regularly repeated at certain distances, and has been executed by means of square moulds applied succeffively, and the parts joined together with the utmost nicety. In every division are Arabic sentences of different lengths, most of them expressive of the following meanings, " There is no conqueror but God;" or, " Obedience and honour to our Lord Abouabdallah." The ceilings are gilt or painted, and time has caused no diminution in the freshness of their colours, though constantly exposed to the air. The lower part of the walls is mosaic, disposed in fantastic knots and festoons. A work so new to me, so exquisitely finished, and so different from all I had ever seen, afforded me the most agreeable sensations, which, I assure you, redoubled every step I took in this magic ground. The porches at the ends are more like grotto-work, than any thing else I can compare them to. That on the right hand opens into an octagon vault, under the Emperor's palace, and forms a perfect whispering-gallery, meant to be a communication between the offices of both houses.

Opposite to the door of the communa through which you enter, is another, leading into the *Quarto de los leones*, or apartment of the lions, which is an oblong court, one hundred feet in length, and fifty in breadth, environed with a colonade seven feet broad on the sides, and ten at the end. Two porticos or cabinets, about fifteen feet square, project into the court at the two extremities. The square is paved with coloured tiles; the colonade

with

of GRANADA.

Court of the LIONS in the ALHAMBRA or MOORISH PALACE of GRANADA

179

t up
posed
small
rabic
od."
re of
rned.
and
irre-
ps of
lth of
nches
eiling
com-
the
n the
xceed
each
rence
id to
You
ll as
ela-
epre-
the
ents.
fur-
nded

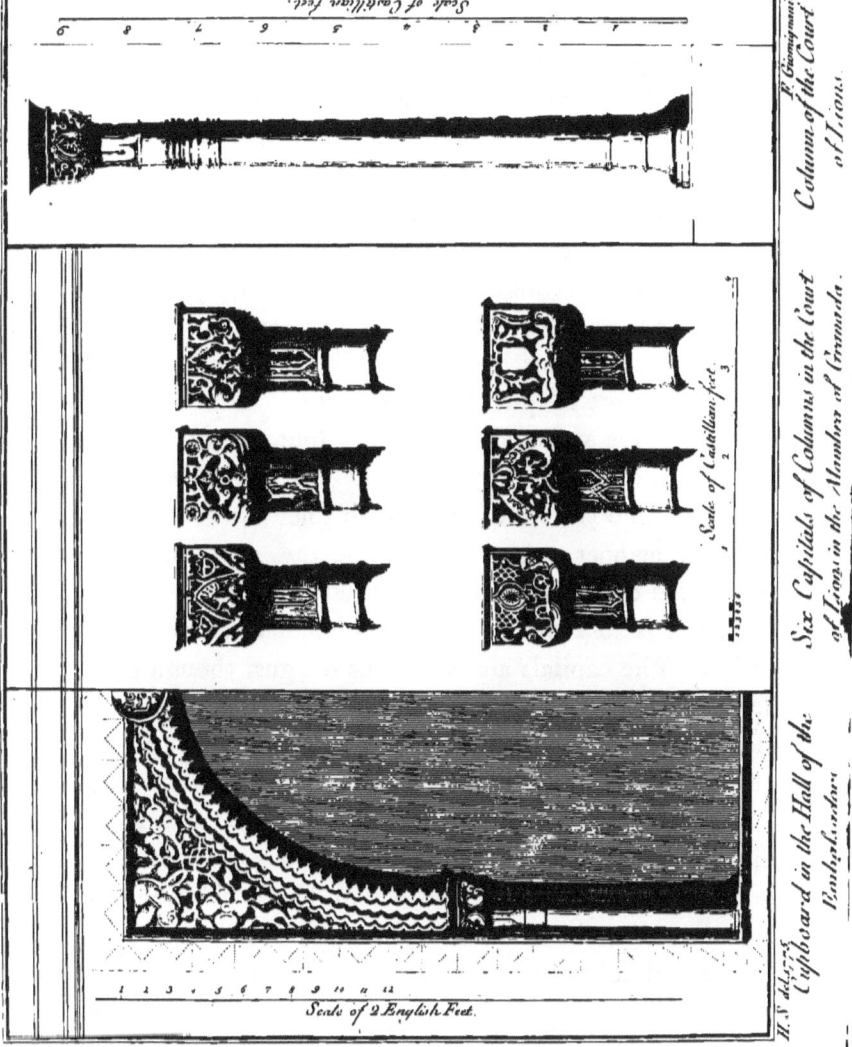

with white marble. The walls are covered five feet up from the ground with blue and yellow tiles, difpofed chequerwife. Above and below is a border of fmall efcutcheons, enamelled blue and gold, with an Arabic motto on a bend, fignifying, " No conqueror but God." The columns that fupport the roof and gallery are of white marble, very flender, and fantaftically adorned. They are nine feet high, including bafe and capital, and eight inches and an half diameter. They are very irregularly placed, fometimes fingly, at others in groups of three, but more frequently two together. The width of the horfe-fhoe arches above them is four feet two inches for the large ones, and three for the fmaller. The ceiling of the portico is finifhed in a much finer and more complicated manner, than that of the *communa*, and the ftucco laid on the walls with inimitable delicacy; in the ceiling it is fo artfully frofted and handled, as to exceed belief. The capitals are of various defigns, though each defign is repeated feveral times in the circumference of the court, but not the leaft attention has been paid to placing them regularly or oppofite to each other. You will form a much clearer idea of their ftyle, as well as difpofitions, from the drawings, than from the moft elaborate defcription I can pen. Not the fmalleft reprefentation of animal life can be difcovered amidft the varieties of foliages, grotefques, and ftrange ornaments. About each arch is a large fquare of arabefques, furrounded

rounded with a rim of characters, that are generally quotations from the Koran. Over the pillars is another square of delightful filligree work. Higher up is a wooden rim, or kind of cornice, as much enriched with carving as the stucco that covers the part underneath. Over this projects a roof of red tiles, the only thing that disfigures this beautiful square. This ugly covering is modern, put on by order of Mr. Wall, the late prime minister, who a few years ago gave the Alhambra a thorough repair. In Moorish times the building was covered with large painted and glazed tiles, of which some few are still to be seen. In the center of the court are twelve ill-made lions muzzled, their fore-parts smooth, their hind-parts rough, which bear upon their backs an enormous bason, out of which a lesser rises. While the pipes were kept in good order, a great volume of water was thrown up, that, falling down into the basons, passed through the beasts, and issued out of their mouths into a large reservoir, where it communicated by channels with the jet d'eaus in the apartments. This fountain is of white marble, embellished with many festoons, and Arabic distichs, thus translated:

" Seest thou not how the water flows copiously like
" the Nile?"
" This resembles a sea washing over its shores, threat-
" ening shipwreck to the mariner."
" This water runs abundantly, to give drink to the lions."
" Terrible

"Terrible as the lion is our king in the day of battle."

"The Nile gives glory to the king, and the lofty mountains proclaim it."

"This garden is fertile in delights; God takes care that no noxious animal shall approach it."

"The fair princess that walks in this garden, covered with pearls, augments its beauty so much, that thou may'st doubt whether it be a fountain that flows, or the tears of her admirers [12]."

Passing along the colonade, and keeping on the south side, you come to a circular room used by the men as a place for drinking coffee and sorbets in. A fountain in the middle refreshed the apartment in summer. The form of this hall, the elegance of its cupola, the chearful distribution of light from above, and the exquisite manner in which the stucco is designed, painted, and finished, exceed all my powers of description. Every thing in it inspires the most pleasing, voluptuous ideas: yet in this sweet retreat they pretend that Abouabdoulah assembled the Abencerrages, and caused their heads to be struck off into the fountain. Our guide, with a look expressive of implicit faith, pointed out to us the stains of their blood in the white marble slabs; which is nothing more than the reddish marks of iron-water in the quarry,

[12] This passage is very obscure in the Latin translation. I have endeavoured to make something of it, but it still remains a forced conceit.

or perhaps the effect of being long expofed to the air. Continuing your walk round, you are next brought to a couple of rooms at the head of the court, which are fuppofed to have been tribunals, or audience-chambers. In the ceiling are three hiftorical paintings, executed with much ftrength, but great ftiffnefs in the figures and countenances. One of them feems to be a cavalcade; the other the entrance of fome princefs; and the third a divan. When thefe were painted, and what they are meant to reprefent, I could not make out; but our *Cicerone* naturally adapted them to the hiftory of the Sultana and her four Chriftian knights. If they are reprefentations of that doubtful ftory, they muft have been painted in the Emperor's time, or a little before, for it cannot be fuppofed that Abouabdoulah would wifh to perpetuate the memory of a tranfaction in which he bore fo very weak and difhonourable a part. And befides, the anathema denounced by the Koran againft all reprefentations of living creatures, renders it next to impoffible that thefe pieces fhould have exifted previous to the conqueft. The lions of the great fountain may be brought as an argument againft my laft reafon; and indeed they fhew that the Granadine princes, as well as fome of the oriental caliphs, who put their own effigy on their coin, ventured now and then to place themfelves above the letter of the law. Be this as it will, if the antiquity of thefe pictures can be proved to go as far back as the reign of Ferdinand,

ENTRANCE of the TORRE de las dos HERMANAS in the ALHAMBRA.

dinand, or at least the beginning of that of Charles, which I take to be no very difficult matter to make out, I should have much greater respect for the authority of Giles Peres than many think him entitled to. It can scarce be supposed that the events of the reign of Abouabdoulah could be so totally forgotten so soon after, that a painter should dare to invent a trial and combat, at which many still living in Granada might have assisted as spectators.

Opposite to the *Sala de los Abencerrages* is the entrance into the *Torre de las dos hermanas*, or the tower of the two sisters, so named from two very beautiful pieces of marble laid as flags in the pavement. This gate exceeds all the rest in profusion of ornaments and in beauty of prospect, which it affords through a range of apartments, where a multitude of arches terminate in a large window open to the country. In a gleam of sunshine, the variety of tints and lights thrown upon this enfilade are uncommonly rich. I employed much time in making an exact drawing of it from the fountain; and hope it will help you to comprehend what I am labouring to explain by my narrative. The first hall is the concert-room, where the women sate; the musicians played above in four balconies. In the middle is a jet d'eau. The marble pavement I take to be equal to the finest existing, for the size of the flags, and evenness of the colour. The two sisters, which give name to the

room,

room, are flabs that meafure fifteen feet by feven and a half, without flaw or ftain. The walls, up to a certain height, are mofaic, and above are divided into very neat compartments of ftucco, all of one defign, which is alfo followed in many of the adjacent halls and galleries. The ceiling is a fretted cove. To preferve this vaulted roof, as well as fome of the other principal cupolas, the outward walls of the towers are raifed ten feet above the top of the dome, and fupport another roof over all, by which means no damage can ever be caufed by wet weather, or exceffive heat and cold. From this hall you pafs round the little myrtle-garden of Lindaraxa, into an additional building made to the eaft end by Charles V. The rooms are fmall and low: his dear motto, *Plus outre*, appears on every beam. This leads to a little tower, projecting from the line of the north wall, called *El tocador*, or the dreffing-room of the fultana. It is a fmall fquare cabinet, in the middle of an open gallery, from which it receives light by a door and three windows. The look-out charming. In one corner is a large marble flag, drilled full of holes, through which the fmoke of perfumes afcended from furnaces below; and here, it is prefumed, the Moorifh queen was wont to fit to fumigate and fweeten her perfon. The emperor caufed this little pretty room to be painted with reprefentations of his wars, and a great variety of grotefques, which appear to be copies, or at leaft imitations, of thofe in the

the loggie of the Vatican. They have been shamefully abused by idle scribblers; what remains shews them to be the work of able artists. From hence you go through a long passage to the hall of ambassadors, which is magnificently decorated with innumerable varieties of mosaics, and the mottos of all the kings of Granada. This long narrow antichamber opens into the *communa* on the left hand, and on the right into the great audience-hall in the tower of *Comares*, a noble apartment, thirty-six feet square, thirty-six high up to the cornice, and eighteen from thence to the center of the cupola. The walls on three sides are fifteen feet thick, on the other nine; the lower range of windows thirteen feet high. The whole hall is inlaid with mosaic of many colours, disposed in intricate knots, stars, and other figures. In every part are repeated certain Arabic sentences, the principal of which are the following:

" The counsel of God and a speedy increase, and give " joy to true believers."

" Praise to God, and to his vicegerent Nazar, who gave " this empire, and to our king Abouabdoulah, to whom " be peace, elevation, and glory."

> N. B. Nazar is an appellation of eminence, and supposed to mean the famous Emirmoumelin Jacob Almanzar.

" There is no God but God."

" Valour, success, and duration to our king Abul-" haghagh,

"haghagh, king of the Moors; God guide his ftate and elevate his power!"

"Praife be to God, for I enliven this dwelling of princes with my beauty, and with my crown. I ftrike firm root; I have fountains of pureft water, and handfome apartments; my inhabitants are lords of mighty puiffance. May God, who guides his people, protect me, for I attend to the fayings of the holy! I am thus adorned by the hand and liberality of Abulhaghagh, who is a bright moon that cafts forth his light over the face of heaven."

Thefe infcriptions, and many others difperfed over the palace, prove that there is very little of it remaining that is not the work of Abulhaghagh, or of Abouabdoulah.

Having thus completed the tour of the upper apartments, which are upon a level with the offices of the new palace, you defcend to the lower floor, which confifted of bedchambers and fummer-rooms: the backftairs and paffages, that facilitated the intercourfe between them, are without number. The moft remarkable room below is the king's bedchamber, which communicated, by means of a gallery, with the upper ftory. The beds were placed in two alcoves, upon a raifed pavement of blue and white tiles; but as it has been repaired by Philip V. who paffed fome time here, I cannot fay how it may have been in former times. A fountain played in the middle, to refrefh the apartment in hot weather.

weather. Behind the alcoves are small doors, that conduct you to the royal baths. These consist in one small closet with marble cisterns for washing children, two rooms for grown-up persons, and vaults for boilers and furnaces, that supplied the baths with water, and the stoves with vapours. The troughs are formed of large slabs of white marble; the walls are beautified with party-coloured earthen ware; light is admitted by holes in the coved cieling.

Hard by is a whispering-gallery, and a kind of labyrinth, said to have been made for the diversion of the women and children.

One of the passages of communication is fenced off with a strong iron grate, and called the prison of the sultana; but it seems more probable that it was put up to prevent any body from climbing up into the women's quarter.

Under the council-room is a long slip, called the king's study; and adjoining to it are several vaults, said to be the place of burial of the royal family. In the year 1574, four sepulchres were opened, but, as they contained nothing but bones and ashes, were immediately closed again.

I shall finish this description of the Alhambra, by observing how admirably every thing was planned and calculated for rendering this palace the most voluptuous of all retirements; what plentiful supplies of water were brought to refresh it in the hot months of summer; what a free circulation of air was contrived, by the judicious disposition of doors and windows; what shady gardens of aromatic trees; what noble views over the beautiful hills and fertile plains! No wonder the Moors regretted Granada; no wonder they still offer up prayers to God every Friday for the recovery of this city, which they esteem a terrestrial paradise.

LETTER XXIV.

Granada, December 30, 1779.

AFTER the Alhambra, I am afraid the rest of the city will go down but poorly: indeed there is little worth seeing here.

The Alameda, along the banks of the Xenil, is as pleasant a walk as any in Spain, but the river has seldom water enough to enliven the prospect with a reflected landscape. The hill rises boldly, to back the avenue, with orange-groves, cypress-alleys, and clusters of houses, grouped upon the waving line of its sides and summit. This, and another drive beyond the river, are the chief places of resort for people on foot or in coaches; and the

beauty

beauty of Granada is no where more striking than from these points of view. The more distant parts of the hill are rather bare, and hollowed out into caverns, inhabited by a tawny, ill-favoured tribe, who have either excavated the mountain, or found it ready scooped out to their hands by the ancient possessors of the country. In winter, these grottos are so warm, that they sleep in them without cloaths or covering to the bed; and in summer they are so cool as to be dangerous for such persons as come suddenly out of the heat of the external atmosphere.

The environs of the town are charming even now. Every body tells us, that in summer Granada is a delicious abode, never too cold nor too hot, refreshed by numberless streams, and perfumed by all the sweets wafted by the breeze from the gardens that lie scattered over the declivities of the neighbouring hills. Nothing can be more agreeable, in the mild sunshiny afternoons which we enjoy here, though at Christmas, than the walks along the heights of the Alhambra. There is always a great concourse of people sitting on the grass, basking in the sun, and diverting themselves, as if it were a fair. Venders of cakes, toys, and liquors, call their wares through the crowd. The women come to shew themselves in their holiday finery, drest out in black silk petticoats and veils. In that habit every woman has something uncommonly alluring. Here indeed the sex is

really

really handsome in any dress; their complexions are fairer, their skins clearer, and their cheeks glow with a brighter tinge than any faces we have met with in our journey down the coast. The distance of Granada from the sea-ports has probably preserved it from that general infection of the odious disease, which rages with such virulence in all the trading towns. The surprizing purity of its air must also greatly contribute towards the freshness of their looks. In many houses, a current of water passes in an uncovered channel through bedchambers where people sleep, winter and summer, without its having the least bad effect upon their health. Fruit and butchers meat remain in the Alhambra an unusual length of time without taint or putrefaction.

The walls and gates of the town, very few parts excepted, are demolished or built up, and the city is open on all sides. Most of the streets are narrow and dirty. To the lanes and alleys the common people retire to perform the most filthy of nature's functions; but they do it with much decency, having by long practice acquired great expertness in casting their cloak like a net, so as to fall exactly round at a proper distance from the body. Though it is common enough to find them squatted down in the streets, you never see any body make water publicly, for when pressed, they always retire behind a door, into an entry, or to some secret corner.

The Rambla is a very broad, long street, leading to

the great walk: a lofty church, and some public buildings, give this street an air of grandeur not common in a Spanish city. Most of the small houses are Moorish built, or coarse imitations of that manner, the modern masons decorating their walls with uncouth copies of Saracenic mosaics. I believe there is scarce a house in Granada that has not over its door, in large red characters, the words, *Ave Maria purissima sin pecado concebida*; which is the *cri de guerre* of the Franciscan friars, who are the heads of the party that maintain the conception of the Virgin Mary to have been performed without her participating of the stain of original sin. This is a favourite tenet in Spain, strengthened and confirmed by the institution of the new order of knighthood of Carlos Tercero, by the vows of the ancient military orders, and by the oath administered to all candidates for degrees. At their reception they swear to defend, by word and deed, the doctrine of the immaculate conception. The Dominicans are the grand antagonists of the Conceptionists.

The market-place is spacious, but its buildings are horridly ugly. They are Moorish, and from top to bottom seem to be nothing but rows of large windows, divided by narrow brick pilasters. The shambles are a building apart, and clean enough. All meat bought in them must be weighed before a sitting committee of magistrates, before the buyer is suffered to carry home his purchase. One of our servants was yesterday hurried to jail, through ignorance of this regulation. An alguazil, coming up behind him, feized on his catering bafket: this abrupt mode of proceeding was repulfed by a violent blow on the chaps with a fhoulder of mutton, which brought the Spaniard to the ground. Our hero was marching off triumphant, when the pride of victory getting the better of his prudence, he fuffered himfelf to be furprized by a detachment of alguazils, who lodged him in prifon, till our banker waited upon the magiftrates, and procured his difcharge.

The outfides of the churches are painted in a theatrical tafte, and their infides fet off with a profufion of marbles, brought from the neighbouring mountains: the dark green, from the Sierra Nevada, is the moft valuable. Tables of an extraordinary fize have been lately cut of that marble, for the infant Don Lewis; but as the roads have been fince quite deftroyed by the torrents, the future carriage of fuch large blocks from the mountain will be attended with great expence and trouble. There are alfo many handfome brown marbles and alabafters, diverfified with an infinite number of fhades and tints. One whole ftreet of artificers is employed in making little boxes, bracelets, necklaces, and other knick-knacks, of fuch materials, which they retail cheap enough. It is ufual in gentlemen's houfes to frame fine fpecimens of marble, and hang them up in the apartments by way of ornament.

The cathedral, which, in point of architecture, stands very high in the opinion of the Granadines, is an assemblage of three churches. The first is a clumsy parish-church; the second, a large chapel, erected by Ferdinand V. at that unfortunate æra of the arts, when all the lightness and beautiful caprice of the Saracenic taste was laid aside, to make room for an unwieldy, preposterous mode of building, and a few years before the magnificence, elegance, and purity of Grecian architecture came again to be understood, relished, and copied. Both within and without, this chapel is incumbered with the weight of its own ill-proportioned ornaments. Ferdinand and Isabella repose before the altar, under a large marble monument full of figures and grotesques, in a pretty good style; which proves what a surprizing revolution the arts had undergone since the time of building the chapel. The two catholic monarchs lie by the side of each other; and adjoining, on a similar tomb, are stretched out the effigies of Philip the Fair, of Austria, their son-in-law, and of Joan their daughter, his wife. Over the great door is the emblem of the united monarchies, a bundle of arrows tied together, and clutched in the talons of a single-headed eagle.

From the chapel you pass into the main church, begun in the reign of Charles V. but not yet quite finished. It has the advantage of receiving abundance of light in every part; but the architect, who has essayed every order of architecture both on the outside and inside of the church, has combined and disposed them in so heavy and confused a manner, that they produce none of that grand effect which results from the well-proportioned parts of one *whole*, when placed in perfect harmony with each other; such as fills the eye with one great object, and affords the senses a repose and satisfaction, undisturbed by the irregular predominance of any of the component members. Here they have carried the extravagance of fancy to such a pitch, that at one altar they have turned a set of twisted columns of beautiful marble topsy-turvy, and placed the smaller end on the base: the uncouthness of the appearance corresponds with the absurdity of the idea. The high altar is insulated, after the Roman fashion, under a very lofty dome, which would be entitled to the admiration of connoisseurs, had they taken less pains to load the arches, and the angles of the cupola, with statues, pictures, and festoons. The area round its basis, with the fine iron railing, and marble pavement, makes a great shew. I observed no very good paintings over any of the altars; but read an order, hung up in one of the iles, which thunders out the pain of the greater excommunication against all such as walk here for their pleasure, or converse with women in any of the chapels. Lest this anathema should not restrain the idle and the amorous, the spiritual court has added to it a fine of four ducats for each offence.

The

The church of St. John of God is richly ornamented, and so are many others in Granada; but I saw none that did much credit to their architects, few of whom seem to have comprehended or admired the principles upon which Verruguete proceeded in building the new palace in the Alhambra.

The amphitheatre for bull-feasts is built with stone, and passes for one of the best in Spain.

The court of chancery sits in a new building, of a disagreeable style, heavy and disjointed. There are some medallions, and pillars of fine marble, in the main front. This court of judicature (of which species there is but another in the kingdom, established at Valladolid) comprehends within its jurisdiction more than half Spain, extending to the very neighbourhood of Madrid. Appeals lie to it from all the audiences and lower courts, and from it to the council of Castille only. Before the condemnation has been ratified here, no inferior judge is authorized to execute the sentence of death upon a criminal, under the pain of forfeiting five hundred maravedis, a sum so trifling, according to the present value of money, that it is not likely to deter a resolute officer of justice from punishing an offender without delay.

This tribunal draws a swarm of lawyers to the place, who absorb its riches, and are the only people that live with any degree of luxury or affluence. They soon consume the little wealth a farmer or tradesman may have scraped.

scraped together, by involving him in some law-suit or other, out of which he cannot extricate himself, as long as he has a farthing left to pay his attorney with. This, and many other kinds of oppression, have reduced Granada to a state of great poverty and despondency. Commerce is very feebly carried on, without encouragement or protection; the crops of the fertile Vega diminish annually; population gradually decreases. The city does not contain more than fifty thousand inhabitants, of which number about eighteen thousand only are useful working hands; the surplus is made up of lawyers, clergymen, children, and beggars. There are not less than a thousand sturdy, able-bodied rascals, that live by alms and conventual donations. We this morning saw a whole regiment of them drawing off in great order from the gate of the Carthusians, where they had been to receive a luncheon of bread and a platter of porridge apiece. Many of them afterwards adjourned to a shop, where several persons were playing publicly at dice.

The play-house differs in some respects from those we have seen in other parts of the kingdom: the men occupy all the ground-floor, and the women sit very high up, in a crazy kind of gallery. The fire of the flints and steels was so quick among the men, who were all preparing to smoke, or smoking, that it looked like soldiers going through their exercise. They gave us one day a strange farce, which it was impossible to make any thing of; it was

was all metamorphofis, a continual change of cloaths and character; at laft out came a Capuchin friar, mounted on an afs, who, after many grimaces and buffooneries, coupled the other actors in the bands of holy wedlock.

LETTER XXV.

Granada, January 1, 1776.

YESTERDAY morning we took a ftroll behind the Alhambra, paffing below the *Puerta de 'los fiete fuelos*, which was formerly the great entrance. This gate has been long blocked up, and the feven ftories of vaults, from which it derived its name, filled with rubbifh. A little farther on, the wall turns to the north-eaft, where the towers are very high. Part of the hill, which is a ftrong-cemented gravel, has been cut through, to make a dry ditch before them. A fingle arch croffes it, and conveys into the palace a copious fupply of water. The path down this folitary, gloomy hollow, is rugged, and broken by the wafte waters. About the middle is a very low poftern, through which the court paffed, when it chofe to retire to the fpring palace, which ftands on a hill to the right.

Nearer

Nearer the Dauro, the water has burft all its conduits, and broken the gravel-bank into a tremendous precipice. Here we defcended into the charming vale of Dauro, where we remarked the remnants of a Moorifh bridge and tower, that appear to have fupported a gallery of communication between the Alhambra and Albaycin. The view from the little green bank near the river, tho' a confined one, is unfpeakably beautiful; at the bottom, where the cathedral and other fteeples rife in a group, in the narrow reach, the little ftream winds its way into the heart of the city. To the fouth, the fine verdant flopes are crowned with the turrets of the Alhambra, the hanging woods and gardens of the Generaliph, and the banks of the Sierra del Sol: on the north, are the Albaycin, innumerable gardens and orchards, and caverns full of inhabitants. We found our mules waiting for us here, and proceeded up the river, a very pleafant ride, between villas and convents, romantically fituated, mills and water-falls, gardens, and plantations of fruit-trees, and thickets of filberts. We turned off to the fouthward, by the ruins of a fmall aqueduct, and came back over the mountain, on the top of which is a long ridge of ftones, faid to be the remains of the ancient Illiberia. It has more the appearance of a park-wall, or line of circumvallation. On the point that overlooks the Alhambra, ftood formerly the fort of the Sun, or Saint Helena, under which run three canals, cut in the rock, one above the other,

other, which serve to convey water to the city, from the mountains, springs, and the river. Some large reservoirs, of Moorish, or perhaps more ancient origin, still subsist below, in perfect preservation. The water of the largest is very limpid, and it was never known to be dry. Historians relate a very singular proof of the abundance of its springs and supplies, though none can be discerned to boil up in the bason. When D. John of Austria marched a body of troops of five thousand men into the Alpuxaras mountains, against the Moriscos, at the hottest season of the year, he halted at this reservoir, to allow them time to quench their burning thirst. They drank and wasted as much of its water as they chose, yet there could not be perceived the least diminution in the original quantity contained in the pond. We stopped at the Generaliph, which was the residence of the sultan in April and May: it now belongs to the Conde de Campotejar, a Genoese nobleman, of the name of Grimaldi, descended in the female line from the royal family of Granada. The remains of the building are scarce worth looking at; for the noblest halls, and best finished work, are almost entirely demolished. The things yet existing, that claim attention, are the following: the double hedge of royal myrtle, above fifteen feet high; a row of cypresses of prodigious height and bulk — the servant pointed out a little recess behind them, where the sultana was accused of having committed adultery with Abencerrage;—great

abundance

abundance of water running through all the little courts, but the grand jet d'eaus are no longer kept in repair.

This day, being the anniverfary of the furrender of Granada to Ferdinand and Ifabella, was òbferved as a great feftival, and day of rejoicing. Two or three feeble cracks from the cannon of the palace announced the feaft to the populace, who flocked to the hill to pay their annual vifit to the Moorifh palace, which is this day open to all comers that can pay an acknowledgment to the governor's fervant. He accounts to his mafter for thefe perquifites, which in fome years amount to five hundred pezzettas. The prefent alcalde, or governor, refides in a fmall corner of the palace, where the emperor had made his chapel, and from a little window fuperintends the bufinefs, counting the heads that pafs the threfhold, and calculating the fum they may have taxed themfelves at. He lives quite retired in his caftle, and employs his many leifure hours, not in profound fpeculations or learned refearches, but in emptying as many bottles of wine as the only arm he has left (for he has loft one) has fteadinefs to pour into his glafs.

We entered the Alhambra with the crowd, and took a laft farewell of that charming fpot, where we have paffed many delicious hours every day during our ftay in Granada.

LETTER

LETTER XXVI.

Antequera, January 8, 1776.

THE second day of this new year, we set out from Granada, by the way of the Vega, in which we saw neither vines nor mulberry-trees, but all arable lands, which, near the city, let at about a *doblon* the fanega for the upper grounds, and in the low, well-watered parts, at a *doblon de à ocho*: some spots, that are proper for growing water-melons, run up to near six doblons a year. The fanega contains 31,700 square feet. Copiousness of water fertilizes these plains; but in rainy weather the roads are not passable. We came for dinner to the Soto de Roma, where we had already paid a visit. This was originally a hunting-seat for Charles V. since occasionally inhabited by his successors, and now granted for life to Lieutenant-general Richard Wall, late prime minister of Spain. It was quite in ruins when he came to live here: he has rebuilt part of it, cleaned it, and fitted up the house with elegant English furniture, in the style of one of our villas. The waters of four rivers meet here, and cause frequent inundations in winter. In summer the air is very unwholesome,

wholesome, as the woods and ditches at that season abound with reptiles and vermin of all sorts. The foreſt round it contains about four thouſand acres, and was reſerved to the crown by Ferdinand the Catholic, when he divided the conquered country among his followers. Elm, poplar, and ſome oak, are the kind of trees that grow here in any quantity: they are cut down for repairs of the eſtate, and for the ſervice of the royal arſenals. Mr. Wall has drained moſt of the woods, opened pleaſant drives throughout, filled up the naked ſpots with plantations of uſeful timber trees, and thinned the old quarters with great judgment. This is almoſt the only place in Spain where pheaſants thrive and multiply. In the beginning of ſpring, at the end of autumn, and during the winter months, this is a very agreeable rural habitation. Mr. Wall reſides at the Soto from October to May; he then goes to Aranjuez, to attend the court for a month; after which he comes for the ſummer to the city of Granada. The king has given up to him all the revenues ariſing from theſe demeſnes, and they are laid out in improving and beautifying the place, which Mr. Wall ſeems to underſtand perfectly well. He has every thing within himſelf: his own flocks, herds, and poultry, ſupply his table with meat proviſions; the woods furniſh it with game, the rivers with fiſh, and the kitchen-garden with

every

every kind of vegetable. He is now in his eighty-third year, a man of a spare, neat make, active, and fond of exercise, of a fair complexion, and engaging countenance. He rises betimes, walks several hours a day, superintends his workmen, and, though he sees but little company, takes the greatest care to have every thing that is excellent in its kind served up at his table, where his behaviour is as easy and chearful as if he were only thirty years of age; not the smallest grain of ministerial reserve or affectation: he is free and communicative in his conversation, which he renders infinitely agreeable, by seasoning it with a variety of lively anecdotes of events and persons, which so long a life of public employment has furnished him with in great abundance. He is fond of talking, but acquits himself so well of the task, that the most loquacious must listen with patience and pleasure to his discourse, always heightened with mirth and good-humour. Courts and ministers he treats with the ridicule they, for the most part, deserve. A man who has passed so many years behind the curtain, must often reflect with contempt on the futile, absurd springs, that set in motion the grand political machine. It was with the greatest regret that we took leave of this most amiable statesman [11],

[11] Mr. Wall died in the beginning of 1778.

and purſued our journey to Loja, a large town on the Xenil, where we got in juſt in time to eſcape a moſt terrible ſtorm of thunder and lightning, followed by a very heavy ſhower.

The next morning we ſaw all the mountains covered with ſnow. This ſtorm ſoaked ſo deep into the fat, greaſy ſoil, that it was not without very extraordinary efforts that our mules dragged us up the ſteep hills. The country between Loxa and this place is very hilly, except an extenſive plain in this neighbourhood. We paſſed through ſome very fine woods of evergreen oak.

Antequera is a large ſtraggling town, at the extremity of the plain, ſituated on ſeveral hillocks in a nook of the mountains.

On the 5th inſtant we hired a guide, and ſet out on horſeback for Malaga, by the mountain road, which is a ride of about ſeven leagues, whereas it requires a couple of days to go round in a carriage. At a ſhort league from Antequera we came to the foot of the Eſcaruela, an almoſt perpendicular rocky mountain, which we aſcended by a very dangerous winding path. A fellow employed to keep the mule-track in repair, lives in a hut half way up, and ſells brandy to travellers, who very often ſtand in great need of a cordial in this cold region of the air. Having gained the ſummit, we traverſed a plain encircled by ſhaggy rocks, and

and then rode for some hours up and down a chain of high wild mountains. We then descended gradually to lower hills in cultivation. The vines are planted in rows, without props: the intervals are ploughed with oxen once a year, and the shoots pruned, which is almost all the dressing they require. These are the outskirts of the high-country vineyards, which produce the wine we drink in England by the name of Mountain.

We next got down to still lower land, where we found the almond-trees white with blossoms, and the hedges full of periwinkle, myrtle, marigold, oleander, cistus, honeysuckles, and many other flowers in full blow. We dined upon some cold meat, at the door of a venta, in the shade, for the sun was too powerful to sit in. An itinerant beggar made no difficulty, though it was Friday, of partaking of what we could spare from our repast; and in return for our kindness, rolled up a little minced tobacco in a piece of white paper, put it in his mouth, to try if the roll was properly constructed, and then presented it, ready lighted, to my friend S. T. as the most polite acknowledgment he could make.

After dinner, we jogged on over hills and dales, along very narrow paths, to the playa or plain of Malaga, at which city we arrived about four o'clock;

and

and here met our miquelet, whom we had difpatched from Granada acrofs the mountains with a letter. He had paffed a fevere night in the Sierra during the great ftorm, and was very near being imprifoned on his arrival, for being the bearer of a letter, which nobody is allowed to carry in Spain without leave from the poft-office.

Malaga ftands in the very corner of the plain, which is quite bare of wood, except the little that grows about the country-houfes; the naked craggy mountains hang over the fhore, and fcarce leave room for the city. A Moorifh caftle, on the fharp point of a rock, commands every part of it. This fituation renders Malaga moft infufferably hot for eight months in the year. I was affured it was hardly poffible to breathe in it in fummer. The port and road feem fafe enough, but will be much improved, when the new mole is carried out its full intended length into the fea. The folid manner in which it is built, by rolling large maffes of rock into the water, to form a foundation for the wall of the pier, infures an almoft eternal duration to the work, but at the fame time makes it difficult to compute the number of years it will require to complete the undertaking. The fea has loft ground here, on account of the fand hurried down from the mountains by a neighbouring river, and accumulated annually along the
fhore.

shore. The Darsena, or docks where the Moors kept their gallies, are still remaining on the wharf, and now serve as warehouses. The streets are narrow: some squares are of a good size; but I do not recollect any very remarkable building, except the cathedral, which is indeed a stupendous pile, begun by Philip II. while married to Mary queen of England. Their united arms are still to be seen over the door. Two gentlemen, who said they had measured both churches, assured me this cathedral was as large as that of St. Paul's in London; but I am not convinced of the exactness of their measurement. The church of Malaga may be as wide, but I cannot think it near as long. No doubt a Protestant church appears larger within than a Roman Catholic one of the same dimensions, as the latter is incumbered with pictures, tapestry, altars, &c. The outside of this edifice is crowded with columns and embellishments. The two belfreys are already of a prodigious height, and an order or two more are yet to be added. Its interior appearance is pleasing and majestic.

The bishop's palace, in the same square, loaded with frivolous ornaments, is a large building, but looks insignificant so near the other. Its prelate enjoys an income of £.16,000 sterling.

General O'Connor, an old Irish officer, is governor of this

this province, and refides at Malaga. Brute beafts are his delight, and all his apartments are ftuffed with bears, dogs, cats, and monkies, to the great terror and annoyance of his vifitors.

There are about fourteen foreign houfes fettled in trade at Malaga, who export five thoufand butts of wine a year, of which the average price is from ten to thirty pounds a butt. Till within the laft fifteen years, the quantity fent off was ten thoufand butts; but, as no difference is made in England, in the duties, between old and new wine, the exporter grew carelefs in the quality of the wine fent, and the demand for it fell one half. The grapes, of which the choiceft raifins are made, (a capital branch of commerce here) are half cut off the ftem, and left four days to dry and candy in the fun. If preffed, they would make a rich white wine. The raifins dried upon the coaft of Valencia are of an inferior quality, being dipped in a lye of lees of wine and afhes.

Yefterday I took a long walk into the Vega, and after enjoying the fight and perfumes of the orange-groves near every villa, was very much furprized to perceive in a farmer's yard a large bufh of yellow rofes in full beauty. This exceeded all idea I before had of the warmth of the climate, and earlinefs of its fpring. In the evening we affifted at a very bad Italian

lian opera. In the middle of a song, all the actors and audience dropped upon their knees at the sound of a sacring bell, which let them know that the host was passing by. In a few minutes the singer resumed his amorous ditty.

We returned this afternoon from Malaga by the same road. The great variety of flowers blown since we had passed, made the mountain ride very agreeable, till we were overtaken by a storm of wind and rain that has not yet abated any of its violence.

Between Malaga and Gibraltar are twelve sugar-mills, where they have wrought time out of mind. The tradition is, that the sugar-cane was first brought into Spain by the Arabs.

Being now upon the point of taking leave of this eastern coast of Spain, which we have seldom lost sight of for these three months, it might be proper to introduce some general remarks upon the inhabitants and country; but I really have not presumption enough to attempt it, as I am conscious that the disposition of a people, their habitual character, customs, and manners, are not to be learnt without a long stay among them, and without becoming in some sort a messmate and familiar acquaintance of theirs. With all due respect for the Spanish nation, I don't wish to sacrifice the time such a study would require, as I apprehend I should

should not be very amply rewarded for my pains. The peasantry seems very poor, and frugal in their diet: bread steeped in oil, and occasionally seasoned with vinegar, is the common food of the country-people from Barcelona to Malaga.

LETTER XXVII.

Puerto Santa Maria, January 13, 1776.

ON the 9th instant, on leaving Antequera, we were stopt by a river much swelled by the late rain, and lost a great many hours in seeking a road to the distant bridge. This was a real disaster to us, as, by retarding us half a day, it broke the chain of our stages, and laid us under the disagreeable necessity of stopping each ensuing night at a very bad inn, the good ones being placed at our dining distances. From Antequera to Pedrera the country is champaign and pleasant; some large lakes appearing between us and the mountains, and now and then some forest-land and olive-plantations, serving to enliven the prospect.

About Ossuna, a large stinking town, we observed a
great

great many crosses set up along the road-side, to mark the places, as we were informed, where murders had been committed: but I very much doubt that piece of intelligence. Before we came into Spain, we had been so much alarmed by all we had heard of the number of banditti in the kingdom, and the danger of passing from one province to another, that we thought we could not take too many precautions, and accordingly made ample provisions of arms and ammunition; but having seldom heard any mention of robbers since we came into the country, our apprehensions have insensibly worn off, and we walk unarmed along the roads, about the villages, and in the bye-paths, without the least fear, or indeed reason to fear. In Catalonia and Valencia, where a regular police is established for apprehending thieves and preventing robberies, travellers go without arms; further south, I have observed that no horseman, muleteer, or ass-driver, is without his gun or sabre slung at the pommel of his saddle. Whether this implies any real danger, or only an ancient custom, I cannot pretend to determine. Whatever risks a single passenger may be supposed to run in a cross road, and unfrequented waste, I am very certain that a caravan like ours need be under no apprehensions of attack.

At Ossuna we found we were come to the country of large.

large white hats, few of the men wearing any other. The environs of the town are handsome; gentle eminences covered with young corn, and large olive-yards on the declivities.

On the 11th, a beautiful park-like country, where the swells are covered with forests of pines and cork-trees, or rows of olive-trees. The intermediate vallies in pasture, full of herds of brood mares feeding at large. That afternoon we came to a flat heath of rushes and palmetos, where we saw great flights of vultures, storks, and plover. We passed the night in a most infamous *posada* at Molares; the place so wretched as to afford no wine. No innkeeper is allowed to sell liquor, and the wine-houses are generally near the inn; but in this miserable hamlet there was no such thing.

On the 12th, boundless heaths and arable grounds; on the former innumerable herds of cattle; on the latter we saw no less than twenty-four ploughs at work in the same field, each drawn by a pair of oxen. We had now fairly entered the rich plains of Andalusia, where we found the roads cruelly spoiled by the wet weather, and our wheels almost buried in the stiff clay. At Alcanterilla is a bridge of two arches, over a deep runner, guarded by an old Moorish tower at each end. The lower part of the bridge is Roman, as it is very easy to discern by the regular rustic cut of the stones,

stones, and the words AVGVST....PONTEM, the remains of an inscription, between the arches. A little beyond a place called Cabecas we met the first travelling coach we had seen on the road since we left Barcelona.

Farm-houses are disperfed about this country, as they are with us in England. The harvest is gotten in by the Galliegos, that travel from Galicia to affist those provinces, where the inhabitants are too lazy or too few in number to gather the riches which Nature, almost unfolicited, throws before them with profusion. The excessive badness of the highway obliged us to drive through the lands, which in their year of fallow run up into the thickest and strongest crops of French honeysuckle I ever beheld. Were this province properly peopled there would be no bounds to its produce, for the soil is inexhaustible, so eminently rich, that through all this luxuriancy of vegetation the wheels penetrated many inches into the loam. To balance these advantages, it must be confessed that the crops in Andalusia are very precarious, for if a sudden glare of sunshine succeeds too rapidly to a morning fog, the whole country is blighted.

We passed by the lake of Lebrixa, a handsome piece of water, surrounded by sloping grounds, and regular plantations of olive-trees.

Xeres

Xeres is a large town, with winding ſtreets, and horrible kennels of black ſtagnated water; as the wheel broke the cruſt upon them, there aroſe an almoſt ſuffocating ſtench. The hills about the town are pretty, and the views towards Cadiz very pleaſing. Some poets have placed the Elyſian fields in this neighbourhood, and pretended that the Guadalete was Lethe or the river of oblivion. If ſo, they had never ſeen the place, or it has undergone ſtrange alterations ſince their days; for this paradiſe is now an immenſe marſhy flat, through which a narrow river, much reſembling thoſe in the Lincolnſhire fens, winds its courſe to the ſea: not a ſtick of wood to be ſeen near it. We are to paſs this Lethe to-morrow, and, leſt the influence ſhould operate upon me, I think it adviſable to end my letter with aſſuring you, while I yet remember the ties and friendſhip of this upper world, that I am your's affectionately.

Cadiz, January 14.

Our carriages were ſent off this morning, ſeven leagues round, by the bridge of Suaço, which joins the iſland of Leon to the main land of Spain; and we hired a bark, and fell down the Guadalete. Port St. Mary's is a long town, pleaſantly ſituated on the river ſide. The bar at the mouth of the river is often very dangerous;

gerous; our mafter made a collection among us for the fouls of fuch as have perifhed there. The view of the bay, fhipping, and city ftretching into the ocean, is one of the moft beautiful in the world. The paffage, which is about nine miles broad, took us two hours, as the wind failed us, but it may be done in lefs than half the time.

LETTER XXVIII.

Cadiz, January 30, 1776.

I SCARCE hope to fee a fair day again, for we have had nothing but rain fince our arrival. The fea has been very boifterous, and feveral fhips have been caft away along the coaft. Yefterday two men coming to town with provifions were fwept off the ifthmus by a fudden fwell of the waves, and never heard of more.

Cadiz occupies the whole furface of the weftern extremity of the ifle of Leon, which is compofed of two large circular parts, joined together by a very narrow bank of fand, forming all together the figure of a chain-fhot. At the fouth-eaft end, the ancient bridge of Suaço,

Suaço, thrown over a deep channel or river, affords a communication between the ifland and the continent; a ftrong line of works defends the city from all approaches along the ifthmus; and, to render them ftill more difficult, all the gardens and little villas on the beach were in 1762 cleared away, and a dreary, fandy glacis left in their room, fo that now there is fcarce a tree on the whole ifland. They expected an attack from the Englifh during the laft war; but it would be madnefs in an enemy to attempt it on this fide; and a by-ftander is apt to think an immenfe fum of money has been lavifhed on thefe fortifications without any apparent neceffity; but the Spaniards are warranted in their caution by the authority of hiftory, from which we learn that the earl of Effex ftormed Cadiz in 1596, by an affault on the land-quarter.

Except the *Calle Ancha*, all the ftreets are narrow, ill-paved, and infufferably ftinking. They are all drawn in ftrait lines, and moft of them interfect each other at right angles. The fwarms of rats that in the nights run about the ftreets are innumerable; whole droves of them pafs and repafs continually, and thefe their midnight revels are extremely troublefome to fuch as walk late. The houfes are lofty, with each a veftibule, which being left open till night, ferve paffengers to retire to; this cuftom, which prevails throughout Spain,

renders

renders thefe places exceedingly offenfive. In the middle of the houfe is a court like a deep well, under which is generally a ciftern, the breeding-place of gnats and mofquitos; the ground-floors are warehoufes, the firft ftories compting-houfe or kitchen, and the principal apartment up two pair of ftairs. The roofs are flat, covered with an impenetrable cement, and few are without a *mirador* or turret for the purpofe of commanding a view of the fea. Round the parapet-wall at top are placed rows of fquare pillars, meant either for ornament according to fome traditional mode of decoration, or to fix awnings to, that fuch as fit there for the benefit of the fea-breeze may be fheltered from the rays of the fun; but the moft common ufe made of them, is to faften ropes for drying linen upon. High above all thefe pinnacles, which give Cadiz a moft fingular appearance, ftands the tower of fignals: here flags are hung out on the firft fight of a fail, marking the fize of the fhip, the nation it belongs to, and, if a Spanifh Indiaman, the port of the Indies it comes from. The fhips are acquainted with the proper fignals to be made, and thefe are repeated by the watchmen of the tower: as painted lifts are in every houfe, perfons concerned in commerce foon learn the marks.

The city is divided into twenty-four quarters, under the infpection of as many commiffioners of police, and its population is reckoned at one hundred and forty thoufand inhabitants, of which twelve thoufand are French, and at leaft as many more Italians.

The fquare of Saint Antonio is large, and tolerably handfome, and there are a few fmaller openings of no great note. The public walk, or Alameda, is pleafant in the evening: it is fenced off the coach-road by a marble rail. The fea-air prevents the trees from thriving, and deftroys all hopes of future fhade.

From the Alameda, continuing your walk weftwards, you come to the Campofanto, a large efplanade, the only airing-place for coaches; it turns round moft part of the weft and fouth fides of the ifland, but the buildings are ftraggling and ugly; the only edifice of any fhew is the new orphan-houfe; oppofite to it is the fortrefs of Saint Sebaftian, built on a neck of land running out into the fea. The round tower at the extremity is fuppofed to have faved the city, in the great earthquake of 1755, from being fwept away by the fury of the waves. The building proved fufficiently folid to withftand the fhock, and break the immenfe volume of water that threatened deftruction to the whole ifland. In the narrow part of the ifthmus the furge beat over with amazing impetuofity, and bore down all before it; among the reft, the grandfon of the famous tragic-poet Racine, who ftrove in vain to
escape,

escape, by urging his horse to the utmost of his speed.

On Saint Sebastian's feast, a kind of wake or fair is held in the fort; an astonishing number of people then passing and repassing, on a string of wooden bridges laid from rock to rock, makes a very lively moving picture.

From hence to the wooden circus where they exhibit the bull-feasts, you keep turning to the left close above the sea, which on all this side dashes over large ledges of rock; the shore seems here absolutely inaccessible. This part of the walk is dirty, and infected with all manner of nasty smells, for here the whole filth of the town is brought, to be tumbled through a hole in the wall, into the sea. It might puzzle an observer, what cause to ascribe this piece of management to, whether to the great distance from garden or tillage grounds, which renders the carriage of the dung too expensive; or to the laziness of the citizens, who are glad to rid themselves, with the least possible trouble, of the obligation laid upon them of removing that dirt, which they had rather were left to rot under their noses. As water-carriage must be cheap, I am inclined to attribute this waste to the latter cause.

On this shore stands the cathedral, a work of great expence,

expence, but carried on with so little vigour, that it is difficult to guess at the term of years it will require to bring it to perfection; I think fifty have already elapsed since the first stone was laid, and the roof is not yet half finished. The vaults are executed with great solidity. The arches, that spring from the clustered pilasters to support the roof of the church, are very bold; the minute sculpture bestowed upon them seems superfluous, as all the effect will be lost from their great height, and from the shade that will be thrown upon them by the filling up of the interstices. From the sea, the present top of the church resembles the carcase of some huge monster cast upon its side, rearing its gigantic blanched ribs high above the buildings of the city. The outward casings are to be of white marble, the bars of the windows of bronze; but I fear the work will be coarsely done, if one may draw an inference from the sample of a small chapel, where the squares are so loosely jointed and ill fitted, that in a few years the facing will be quite spoilt. It is unfair to prejudge a piece of architecture in such an imperfect state, but I apprehend the style of this will be crowded and heavy.

Next, crossing before the land-gate and barracks, a superb edifice for strength, convenience, and cleanliness, you come down to the ramparts that defend the city

city on the side of the bay. If the prospect to the ocean is solemn, that towards the main land is animated in the highest degree; the men of war ride in the eastern bosom of the bay; lower down the merchantmen are spread far and near; and close to the town an incredible number of barks, of various shapes and sizes, cover the surface of the water, some moored and some in motion, carrying goods to and fro. The opposite shore of Spain is studded with white houses, and enlivened by the towns of Saint Mary's, Port-real, and others, behind which, eastward, on a ridge of hills, stands Medina Sidonia, and further back rise the mountains of Granada. Westward, Rota closes the horizon, near which was anciently the island and city of Tartessus, now covered by the sea, but at low-water some part of the ruins are still to be discerned.

In a large bastion, jutting out into the bay, they have built the custom-house, the first story of which is level with the walk upon the walls. When it was resolved to erect a building so necessary to this great emporium of trade, the marquis di Squillace gave orders that no expence should be spared, and the most intelligent architects employed, in order to erect a monument, which by its taste and magnificence might excite the admiration of posterity; the result of these
precautions

precautions proved a piece of vile architecture, compofed of the worſt of materials.

Don't expect from me a long, ſcientific detail of the operations of commerce in this port; ſo much has been written on the ſubject by perſons verſed in theſe matters, that, as it would be impertinent to repeat their obſervations *verbatim*, ſo it would be ridiculous in me, who am not initiated in the myſteries of trade, nor long reſident in the place, to attempt to add any thing to their accounts; all I have to obſerve amounts to this, that of late years the Spaniards have entered with more ſpirit into the concerns of the flota [14] than they did formerly; and that there have been ſome egregious breaches of that ſo-much-celebrated punctilio of honour, which, added to the immenſe profits expected from the riſk, induces foreigners to truſt their property upon this venture, with no other ſecurity than the bare word of a Spaniſh ſupercargo. Not along ago, one of theſe, upon his landing at Vera Cruz, made a declaration before the governor, that the cargo entered and ſhipped in his name was not his own, but belonged to a French houſe. Matters turned out rather contrary to his expectations;

[14] The flota is a fleet of large ſhips (fourteen this year) which carry out the goods of Europe to the ports of America, and bring back the produce of Mexico, Peru, and other kingdoms of the new world,

for the governor threw him into gaol, where he still remains; but I believe the French owners give up their merchandize for lost.

The stir here is prodigious during the last months of the stay of the flota. The packers possess the art of pressing goods in great perfection; but, as they pay the freight according to the cubic palms of each bale, they are apt to squeeze down the cloths and linens so very close and hard, as sometimes to render them unfit for use. The exportation of French luxuries in dress is enormous; Lyons furnishes most of them; England sends out bale-goods; Brittany and the north, linens.

As the king exacts four per cent. on all gold and silver coin exported, and punishes very severely all delinquents taken in the fact, the smugglers have long followed a very simple but sure method of defrauding him of his duty:—A man well known in the town comes to any merchant that he thinks may want to make a remittance of dollars, and proposes to send the sum wanted on board such a ship, at two and a half per cent. the smuggler to advance the money, and to be repaid upon producing the captain of the ship's receipt. As the officer at the gates is commonly one of the confederates, this practice has been long carried on with tolerable security; but since the late coinage, the profits upon running money are scarce equivalent to the risks of having the ship confiscated, and all concerned in the transaction sent for life to the African presidios.

Great interest is made to protract the departure of the flota beyond the day fixed for its sailing, that all the goods expected may have time to arrive; and in this case, as in most others, money properly distributed seldom fails of producing the desired effect.

Every commercial nation has a consul resident at Cadiz; those of England and France are the only ones not allowed to have any concern in trade.

This small, populous, and well-inclosed city has the misfortune of being under worse regulations of police than any place in Europe. All this winter, street-robberies and house-breakings have been frequent, and no effectual steps taken to prevent the disorder. I have heard that the Conde de Xerena Bucarelli, the governor, has made a vow to shed no blood during his regency; this cruel clemency has given such spirit to the operations of the robbers, that they have had the audaciousness to paste up an advertisement in the streets, cautioning all people whatever to avoid resistance, and to submit quietly to be rifled, that their plunderers may not be reduced to the disagreeable necessity of employing the poniard. A very little diligence, with the assistance of so strong a garrison, would restore the public safety in a short time; but, as a burgher always
accompanies

accompanies the patrol, the military cannot act but under his direction, and he will never hurt or moleft any of his countrymen or neighbours, for the fake of preferving the lives and property of ftrangers: indeed, if a native be apprehended for the moft enormous offence againft the laws of his country, it is next to impoffible to procure a fentence againft him; for, as long as he has a groat in the world to fpend in prifon, or a friend to folicit in his favour, the *alcade* or judge will never bring him to trial; and when at laft his purfe is drained, and his crimes proved againft him, it is ten to one they can get no body to make a gallows to hang him upon. A foldier is foon difpatched, if he falls under the fame predicament. Burglaries have been committed, and large fums of money carried out of compting-houfes, the thieves taken and lodged in gaol, yet the owners have not been able to recover any part of the cafh; which the gentlemen of the robe and the culprit have fpent in caroufing together. Nay, one villain, in an attempt to carry part of his prize out of the gates, in order to take fhipping for the Indies, being ftopt, and the money feized as contraband, the perfon who had been robbed could not prevail upon the governor to reftore his property to him, notwithftanding the cleareft proofs of the robbery. Take notice, that in cafes of confifcation,

fifcation, one half of the feizure goes to the informer, the other to the governor. However, this moft glaring piece of injuftice could not be tamely fubmitted to, and the caufe was laid before the council of Caftille, where it is ftill depending. In lefs confiderable loffes, the beft way is to fit down contented with your misfortune, and take better care for the future, as it would coft you double the fum loft, were you to purfue any of the methods pointed out by the law for redrefs.

The way of life here is not very brilliant. The different nàtions keep much among themfelves. The French houfes follow rather a gayer plan than the others. Our countrymen fettled here, live in a very hofpitable, focial ftyle, and are always happy to contribute every thing in their power towards rendering the place agreeable to fuch travellers as vifit their city. Indeed this is a tribute of praife our gratitude will ever prompt us to pay to the Britifh merchants eftablifhed beyond feas, having in many parts of Europe had occafion to experience their friendly difpofition.

At this time of the year neither the meat nor the fifh is excellent. The bottom of the bay being muddy, and the fifhermen not venturing from the coaft, the quality of the fifh brought to market is not fo firm and good as might be expected; at fome feafons the oyfters
taken

taken here are rank poifon; the water of the ifland is bad, and what moft families drink comes from Port Saint Mary.

The ufual afternoon amufements in winter are, a faunter on the Alameda, and the theatres. The Spanifh play, which exhibits but a poor fet of actors, begins about four; the Italian opera, not much better provided, about feven; and the French houfe opens rather earlier, and ends fooner, by which means the company may partake of great part of each of the entertainments in the fame evening. The laft-mentioned theatre is upon a very grand footing, fupported by the voluntary fubfcriptions of the French merchants fettled here. As the out-goings exceed the profits, they begin to be fick of fo heavy a load, and it is likely their ftage will be given up, upon the expiration of the term for which the factory entered into engagements with the actors.

LETTER XXIX.

Gibraltar, March 9, 1776.

THE end of the carnival at Cadiz differed very little from the beginning; no public balls or mafquerades being allowed; the only marks of the feftivity of fhrove-tide, were the pailfulls of water which the women in the balconies poured upon the men in flouched hats and cloaks that paffed within their reach. There were, however, many affemblies and balls of a lower clafs, where the fandango was danced *a la ley*, that is, in all the perfection it is capable of. Among the gipfies there is another dance, called the *Manguindoy*, fo lafcivious and indecent, that it is prohibited under fevere penalties; the tune is quite fimple, little more than a conftant return of the fame fet of notes; this, as well as the fandango, is faid to have been imported from the Havannah, being both of negro breed. I have been told, that upon the coaft of Africa they exhibit a variety of ftrange dances, pretty fimilar to thefe. Whatever may have been the birth-place of the fandango, it is now fo thoroughly naturalized in Spain, that every Spaniard may be faid to be born with it in his head and heels;

I have

I have seen a child of three years of age dance it to the mother's singing, with steps and turns scarce to be credited in an infant of that age. Towards the close of the great balls given heretofore in the theatre, when all the company appeared drooping with fatigue and overpowered with sleep, it was a constant trick of the fidlers to strike up the fandango. In an instant, as if roused from the slumbers of enchantment by the magic touch of a fairy's wand, every body started up, and the whole house resounded with the uproar of clapping of hands, footing, jumping, and snapping of fingers.

As I have mentioned the gitanos, or gipsies, who swarm in this province more than in any other part of the realm, I think it a proper place to note down some particulars relative to this singular sept, who have kept themselves separate from the rest of mankind ever since their first appearance recorded in history. Their origin remains a problem, not to be satisfactorily solved, and I doubt whether the gitanos themselves have any secret tradition that might lead to a discovery of what they really were in the beginning, or from what country they came. The received opinion sets them down for Egyptians, and makes them out to be the descendants of those vagabond votaries of Isis, who appeared to have exercised in ancient Rome pretty much the same profession as that followed by the present gipsies, viz.

fortune-

fortune-telling, ſtrolling up and down, and pilfering. Few of them employ themſelves in works of huſbandry or handicraft; indeed the Spaniards would not work with them. Except a ſmall number that follow the trade of blackſmiths or vintners, moſt of the men are makers of little iron rings, and other trifles, rather to prevent their being laid hold of as vagrants than really as a means of ſubſiſtance. Several of them travel about as carriers and pedlars, but none enliſt as ſoldiers or ſailors, or bind themſelves as ſervants. Though they conform to the Roman catholic mode of worſhip, they are looked upon in the light of unbelievers; but I never could meet with any body that pretended to ſay what their private faith and religion might be: all the gipſies I have converſed with, aſſured me of their ſound catholiciſm; and I have ſeen the medal of Nueſtra Señora del Carmel ſewed on the ſleeves of ſeveral of their women. They ſeldom venture upon any crimes that might endanger their lives; petty-larceny is the utmoſt extent of their roguery. Their men are tall, well built, and ſwarthy, with a bad ſcowling eye, and a kind of favourite lock of hair left to grow down before their ears, which rather increaſes the gloomineſs of their features: their women are nimble, and ſupple-jointed; when young, they are generally handſome, with very fine black eyes; when old, they become the worſt-favoured

voured hags in nature. Their ears and necks are loaded with trinkets and baubles, and moſt of them wear a large patch on each temple. Both ſexes are remarkably expert at dancing, and ſing the wild ſeguidillas with a peculiar turn of humour or tenderneſs, according to the ſubject. The preſent king had thoughts of baniſhing the whole race out of his dominions; but I believe the project is dropt, as the gipſies are rather an uſeleſs than a miſchievous people. Their abode in the country, or their expulſion, ſeems a matter of little conſequence, for the loſs would not be ſeverely felt, except in the apparent diminution of population; as they are of little or no ſervice in the ſtate, neither cultivating its lands, forwarding its manufactures and commerce, conveying its productions to foreign parts, or fighting its battles. Perhaps they render themſelves neceſſary to the amuſement of the common people, out of whoſe ſimplicity they work themſelves a maintenance.

The weather being tolerably ſettled, we ſet out on horſeback from Cadiz, about a fortnight ago, taking with us our beds and proviſions, a precaution of great conſequence in this journey. We left Cadiz in the afternoon, travelling along the ſandy iſthmus to the Iſla, a town of a ſingle ſtreet, that leads down to the bridge and redoubt of Suaço, where we got once more upon the main land. Soon after we ſtruck off the great Xeres road,

road, into a flat marshy country, interfected by numberless drains and ponds for making falt, of which we faw many large heaps. This commodity is made with fo little trouble, and fold to fo fmall an advantage, that the makers don't think it worth their while to fet up sheds, or build magazines, but prefer running the rifk of lofing half of it by the wet. Pafling through a great mill, acrofs many bridges and creeks, and through a very fine wood of pines, we arrived by moonlight at Chiclana, the Clapham or Hampstead of the merchants of Cadiz. It is a large well-built town, upon a navigable river, that winds through the low lands into the bay. After Easter, all is mirth and jollity here, for it is then crowded with families that retire hither to divert themfelves, and to rub off the dull ruft of Lent. The houfes are exact copies of thofe of Cadiz, and the streets very near as offenfive to the fmell; but the environs are charming, and beautifully rural.

The next morning we were out very early, expecting a long laborious ride. After a troublefome afcent up fome greafy hills, we paffed through a noble pine wood, into an immenfe expanfe of heath-land, fpeckled with an incredible variety of flowers, moft of them unknown to me in their natural uncultivated ftate. I here faw a great many of the fmall red and yellow tulip, which, I am told, is the only fpecies indigenous in Europe, and many beautiful kinds of the orchis, some representing bees and flies so naturally as to deceive at first sight.

On our right we left Conil, once famous for its tunny-fishery, which of late has dwindled away to nothing. We had afterwards an hilly corn country to pass, where the peasants, at work weeding the fields, amused themselves with giving us a volley of abuse, which to us was utterly unintelligible, but was no doubt very witty, as every speech the orator of the crew made raised loud peals of laughter in his companions. Their mirth was a little disturbed by a piece of humour of our Catalans, who, setting their sharp three-cornered hats up perpendicular on their heads, in imitation of horns, and sticking out their fingers, began to whistle with might and main. The Andalusians did not seem to relish the joke, and after some silence, set a scolding at us in a very angry tone of voice, which lasted as long as we were within hearing.

From these bare heights, we descended into a narrow vale, which almost encompasses the mountain that the town of Vegel stands upon. Seven picturesque aqueducts, or rather divisions of one, convey a fine supply of water from the hills to seven mills belonging to the Duke of Medina Sidonia. Each mill is placed at a considerable distance below the other, the seventh stands quite in the level at the bottom. Nothing can be prettier than thefe terraces, and little falls of water. Round each dwelling is a fweet orange-grove. The hedges along the fteep fides of the road are thick fet with lauruftinus, now in flower, and many other handfome plants. The loweft part of the valley is a delightful fpot, full of orchards and gardens, refrefhed by innumerable ftreams of clear water running through the meadows into a deep river, which falls into the fea a few miles below.

We intended to have dined at the foot of the mountain of Vegel, but the hovel, called an inn, was fo intolerably nafty, and the appearance of the fky feemed fo much to threaten us with a dark, rainy evening, that we determined to pafs by, and content ourfelves with eating a morfel on horfeback, as we jogged on. We croffed the river on an ancient Roman bridge, plain and folid, and then mounted a very fteep fandy bank, on the top of which I found a ledge of mouldering rocks, full of *oftracites* and *pectinites*, fome in a hard natural ftate, others fo foft as to crumble to duft under the finger. The road lay afterwards through a foreft of cork-trees, and the latter part of the day along a wet open pafture country. After being thirteen hours on horfeback, with a drizzling rain upon us half the time, we were glad to ftop at *Los Cortijos* about eight at night.

Here

Here had formerly been a venta, but all we could find was the cabin of a retailer of tobacco. This miserable dwelling consisted of one room, not well enough thatched to prevent the rain from beating through, and yet too close to let out the smoke of a few sticks burning in the middle of the house. The landlord, his wife, and children, occupied one end of the habitation, and abandoned the remainder to us, who were seven in number, squeezed into the space of a few feet square. The smoke grew so powerful, and the company so streightened for room, that after supper I retired across a kind of yard, to a manger in the stable, where I lay down, wrapped up in my cloak, upon the straw, and got a very comfortable nap till day-break, when we proceeded on our journey.

We travelled through a large tract of wet pastures, full of herds of cattle, with here and there a wretched hut for the herdsmen. After a long dreary ride over the hills that encircle these plains, we entered the woodlands, where we found the roads so wet and stony, that our baggage-mules were more than once laid fast. This forest extends many miles, during which we saw but one house; and that being white, and placed at the head of a lawn, environed with hanging woods, made a most romantic appearance. The prospects in these wildernesses are delightful, and we should have found the ride through them charming, had our attention been lefs engaged by the continual apprehenfions we were under of our horfes falling in the deep broken roads. High mountains, and bold rocky cliffs, hang on every fide over the groves; the timber trees are oak and cork, the underwood, fhrubs of numberlefs kinds, growing with the greateft vigour and luxuriancy; fuch as the lauruftinus, arbutus, brooms, citifus, forb, maftick-tree, privet, phylirea, ciftus, oleander, pomegranate, bay, laurel, myrtle, butcher's broom, wild pear, heath at leaft fifteen feet high, &c. but the moft remarkable is the rhododendron ponticum, with large purple flowers; it grows by the edge of the torrents that tumble down through the woods, and is a plant of fingular beauty.

Upon leaving the thickets, we had a fine view of the rock of Gibraltar and the coaft of Africa, a very grand marine fcene. We then came to a rich vale of cornland, and a pretty meandring river, which we croffed twice near *Los Barios*, a fmall hamlet. From thence we found all the country marfhy by the fide of the bay of Gibraltar, or bare and hilly near San Roque, a large village on the top of a hill, overlooking the whole bay. Here the Spanifh governor of the lines refides.

The next day we waited upon Don Joachim de Mendoza, the governor, who gave us the neceffary paffports.

By

By his perfuasion, we depofited what cafh we had in the hands of his fecretary, as it is forbidden to take above a crown apiece out of the Spanifh territory. This proved a very fuperfluous caution, for we paffed unfearched through the lines, and might have carried out of the Spanifh bounds as much gold as we pleafed. The lines are a fortification, that runs acrofs the ifthmus which feparates Gibraltar from the continent. A regiment of infantry, feveral batteries, and a fort at each end, defend this barrier of the Spanifh monarchy. It is about half an hour's ride from the land-gate of the Englifh garrifon.

The moft extraordinary fortrefs and mountain, from which I date my letter, have been fo often defcribed by particular hiftories, prints, and drawings, that I fhall not take up your leifure with needlefs repetitions. The views publifhed by Major Macé are exact, and convey a very good idea of the four different faces of the mountain. Since the time of their publication, general Boyd has compleated the roads up the hill in every neceffary direction : a carriage may now go up to the fignal-houfe, which before feemed a place where none but goats could climb up to.

The hofpitality of the governor, officers, and inhabitants; the buftle, military mufic, and parade; the fine appearance of the troops; the variety of tongues fpoken

and.

and of dreſſes worn here, are themes I could enlarge upon for whole pages. After ſo long a journey through the ſtill waſtes and ſilent ſtupid towns of Spain, where every thing bears the marks of languor and indolence, we were at firſt quite flurried and confounded with the hurry in the garriſon, the perpetual noiſe of cannon, and the reports of the ſoldiers going through their firing exerciſe. In the firſt nights we were ſtartled with the frequent paſſing of the parole, which runs like a train of fire round the line of fortifications. It ſeemed ſtrange to hear our native language ſpoken in the ſtreets, to read it under the ſigns, and to meet ſo many Engliſh faces. I ſhould have forgotten how far I was from home, had I not been reminded of the latitude by the brilliant clearneſs of the deep blue ſky, and the ſight of the African mountains, whoſe ſnowy tops, and even the objects at their feet, are very diſtinctly ſeen by the naked eye. You may difcern all the buildings in Ceuta, and even in Tangier the houſes may be diſtinguiſhed in a clear day. We indulged the honeſt pride of Engliſhmen, in admiring the tall, handſome figures, and ſpirited, martial preſence of the ſoldiers, and in drawing very comfortable parallels between them and the dirty melancholy dwarfs we had ſeen mounting guard in the Spaniſh garriſons.

We are now waiting for a fair wind to carry us over

to

to Tetuan or to Tangiers. The boat-loads of fresh oranges brought over almost every morning from the coast of Barbary, and tumbled out into the streets, increase the eagerness we have long felt for that expedition: but the wind is very cruel, and I begin to have my fears about the possibility of it. The Barbary oranges are exquisite, but, as the summer advances, are apt to grow too luscious, though they preserve their juiciness.

Gibraltar, March 11.

We are wind-bound, but remain in hourly expectation of sailing to Africa. Our *settee*, or bark, and baggage, are ready, and we ourselves on the watch for an easterly breeze. Yesterday the wind came about to the east, and in a trice the bay was covered with Dutch men of war, and all sorts of merchantmen, crowding sail to get through the Gut before the wind should change: above fifty sail came from the Mediterranean, round Europa Point, but in less than an hour the wind shifted to its old corner again, and every one of them was driven back into the bay, or behind the rock, where they may beat about for weeks against wind and current. Never was there known so long a continuance of westerly winds at this time of the year.

Gibraltar,

Gibraltar, March 13.

Laſt night all the Jews were in maſquerade, dancing and merry-making; a fine contraſt with the gloominefs of Lent, a few miles to the north of us. This place may literally be ſtyled the Paradiſe of that diſperſed nation; for here they ſeem to be at home, carry on a great retail trade, and ſupply the garriſon with many common articles of conſumption. They are Barbary Jews, a comely race of men, and much better featured than their Portugueſe or German brethren. Their dreſs differs from that of the common Moors in nothing but the cap, which the latter wear red, the Jews black, though here they venture frequently to put on red ones.

All religions ſeem welcome to this town, and meet without animoſity, as on ſome neutral ground. The Spaniſh church is ſerved by a jolly prieſt, who, beſides very ample emoluments and caſualties, receives from the Engliſh government a ſtipend of fifty pounds: with this income he gives balls and entertainments to his pariſhioners, and lives in a very jovial manner. He ſeems perfectly well pleaſed with his Proteſtant neighbours, and quite reconciled to ſeeing the Cordelier convent converted into the reſidence of an Engliſh governor.

The Barbary beef, furnished on contract by the Moors, is excellent, and the fish taken in the bay is the best I have tasted since I left Bourdeaux.

The mountain abounds with partridges, which breed in peace, and pass their lives undisturbed, as no body is allowed to shoot within the garrison. The young officers take the diversion of fox-hunting on the Spanish hills, where there is abundance of foxes, but little running: the great number of holes among the rocks prevents the game from being kept going, after the first burst.

That beautiful bird, the whoopoop, or March cock, is common on the mountain; and high up are herds of large monkies, but I never was lucky enough to get a sight of them.

On the east side, in the most broken part of the precipices, is a *stratum* of bones of all sizes, belonging to various animals and fowls, enchased in an incrustation of a reddish calcarious rock.

LETTER XXX.

Seville, April 8, 1776.

ALAS! all our fchemes upon Africa came to nothing: the inflexible weft wind continued blowing with uninterrupted fury, till the time fixed for our ftay at Gibraltar was elapfed. At firft we intended to crofs over to Tetuan, and there hire horfes or mules to carry us over land to Tangiers, which would have afforded us an opportunity of feeing a good deal of the country: but this project was dropped, in confequence of an order iffued out by the emperor of Morocco, prohibiting all Chriftians from approaching, or even looking upon the holy city of Tetuan, where fome Englifh had lately committed an outrage upon the Moorifh women. Being difappointed in our firft plan, we pitched upon that of running over to Tangiers, and from thence making an excurfion into the inland parts. Both thefe hopes were defeated by the contrary winds, and we were under the neceffity of giving up fo favourite a point, which, you may believe, was a moft fenfible mortification to us both.

We returned to Cadiz by our former route, fome trifling deviations excepted; one of which was, to vifit the

the almost imperceptible remains of the city of Carteia, where Cneius, son of Pompey the Great, took refuge after the battle of Munda. These ruins, of which scarce any thing but part of a wall is to be seen, stand on a r sing ground at the mouth of a little river, which falls into the north-west corner of the bay. Writers have blundered strangely about the situation of this town, some placing it at Algeçiras, or Old Gibraltar, and others so far off as Tariff. The rubbish, and the quantity of its own coins found here, which are common enough among the Jews of Gibraltar, leave no room to doubt of the truth of the tradition which fixes it upon this spot. In passing the woods beyond *Los Varios*, we raised a prodigious eagle of the golden kind : our servants, who went before, took it for a boy muffled up in a yellowish cloak, and were so surprized when it took wing, that we could not prevail upon the man who carried the blunderbuss to fire at it, till it was got out of reach. Its colour was a dusky yellow shaded with green, its head very smooth and dark ; about the belly it was of a muddy brown.

At nightfall we came to a farm-house belonging to the duke of Medina Sidonia, where the servants, in the absence of the master farmer, refused to give us leave to pass the night. One of our men being dispatched into the field, brought the farmer with him, very much out of humour at his houfe being made an inn of, and fully determined to pack us off about our bufinefs, as he fufpected us to be little better than rogues and fmugglers; indeed the appearance of our meffenger was not unfavourable to that opinion. S. G* exhibited a fet of ftern features, with a thick black beard; an old laced hat fiercely cocked hanging over his eyes; a military jacket, acrofs which was flung a fcimitar and a pair of piftols; dirty leather fpatterdafhes, a hoarfe voice, ftrange language, and foreign accent. All this together could hardly, in fuch a country, convey the idea of any thing but a captain of banditti. When the farmer entered his court-yard, and faw fuch a formidable fet of armed men in poffeffion of his caftle, he thought it advifeable to alter his tone, and be very civil. We accepted his offer of a new barn or granary, where we pitched our tents, fupped, and flept very comfortably, having previoufly ftuffed with ftraw the holes which had been left in the wall for the free ingrefs and egrefs of the pigeons.

Thefe farms are very extenfive, and entirely unconnected with their neighbours. Each farm has its own baker, who twice a week diftributes a certain quota of bread to each houfe-fervant, herdfman, plough-boy, and fhepherd. The plain about the houfe is a deep rich foil, the pafturage luxuriant, but in many places over-run with

with weeds and rank grafs; a muddy rivulet winds through the flats, and is often a very troublefome pafs for travellers.

We met with nothing remarkable on the road to Vegel; ftorks, whoopoops, and a fox, were the only living creatures we faw. The fun grew fo extremely powerful, that we were glad to pafs the noon-tide hours under a large tree before the door of one of the *fiete molinos*, by the fide of a brook. The miller and his neighbours were very civil, and furnifhed us with a table, chairs, glaffes, and every thing neceffary for our repaft, one of the moft delicious I ever made. The old and young formed a circle round us, while we devoured our cold ham and turkey. As I perceived one of the young fellows fmile and look very arch, I told him I hoped he was not fcandalized at our eating meat in Lent, as we were allowed that liberty, as travellers. " No, no," replied he, " not I indeed; for I know you belong to a happy " fet of people, with whom *to-day* is always the *holiday*; " and to-morrow the *vigil* and *faft*." His joke made us laugh, and fet all his companions in a roar: in the height of our mirth and good-humour, a little old woman ventured to afk a tafte of a bumper of Malaga, which being the bottom of a bottle I had given my man to drink, he endeavoured to put her off, with telling her that it was the wine of the Moors, confequently ungodly,

ungodly, and fuch as a zealous Spaniard would think himfelf poifoned were he to put it to his lips; however the old dame begged fhe might tafte it out of curiofity, and having once got the glafs into her hands, fwallowed every drop of the wine at one gulp, to the great aftonifhment of poor S. G***; to comfort him, fhe affured him fhe fhould have a better opinion of the Moors as long as fhe lived, fince they made and drank fuch excellent liquor.

In about three hours ride we got to Chiclana, and next day hired a bark to carry us to Cadiz. The rowing down the river was very pleafant, as by its continual winding we kept in fight of the pretty hill of Chiclana, till we paffed through the arches of the bridge of Suaço into the bay. The channel through the fhallows is very narrow and crooked. The king's dockyards at the Caraccas lie near the entrance; and farther down is the Trocadero, or magazines and docks for merchantmen. The approach to the city was beautiful; but the flownefs of our motion, retarded by contrary winds and currents, made us heartily fick of our water party.

On the 3d of April we left Cadiz, and in lefs than an hour landed at Port Saint Mary, where we were received and entertained for three days by general count Alexander O'Reilly, with every poffible demonftration
of

of politeneſs and cordiality. This gentleman has been of late ſo much talked of, that I was eager to ſeize the opportunity of paſſing ſome time with him. To attempt to draw his character is far above my powers, or thoſe of any three days' acquaintance. It would be unfair and preſumptuous to decide upon the merits or demerits of any man on ſuch ſlight grounds. He appears to be very active, intelligent, and ſevere, in the poſt of inſpector-general of the Spaniſh infantry, an employment of great buſineſs. I believe him ſkilled in tactics; to have read a great deal in his more advanced time of life (for I don't imagine his education furniſhed him with any great ſtock of learning;) to have ſeen with a penetrating eye, and to have ſtudied profoundly the characters and weakneſſes of men. His intrepidity in facing, and ſteadineſs in conquering, all difficulties, that may lie in his way to preferment, are ſufficiently known and variouſly deſcanted upon: his memory is prodigious; his judgment of men and things quick and preciſe, perhaps too peremptory. He has much ready wit at command, eſpecially when he has a mind to turn the laugh againſt any particular perſon, in which caſe he is accuſed of often carrying the joke too far; and I don't know but he may owe ſome of his many enemies to the ridicule he has ſometimes thrown upon them. Some think him rather too fond of talking, and of making himſelf the ſubject of his

his discourse, but they must acknowledge he speaks with great eloquence in a variety of languages. His countenance and figure are rather comely; but a wound in his knee causes him to limp, an imperfection which has afforded his enemies great scope for raillery: the king's fondness for him bears him up against all their efforts to ruin him; his majesty, who thinks himself indebted to O'Reilly for his life, in the sedition of Madrid [15], supports him with inflexible constancy. When the new road was making to the palace of the Pardo, a little, ugly ever-green oak was found to stand in the line marked out for the highway. This tree, by its oddity and solitary position, had attracted the notice and gained the favour of the king, who forbade the engineers to meddle with it. In spite of all the remonstrances of the minister and surveyors, the oak still remains standing in the middle of the road; the king often shews it to his courtiers, and, observing with a smile, that it has no friend but himself, calls it O'Reilly.

The only morning we had free from rain, we employed in a ride to Sanlucar, to see the mouth of the Guadalquiver, the ancient Bætis, where the fleets of Spain were wont to rendezvous, before Cadiz was made the

[15] He rode into the crowd of rioters, and shot a fellow dead that had taken up a stone and was going to throw it at the king.

staple

staple for Indian goods, and before the bar at the mouth became so considerable as to impede the navigation of large vessels.

The ground rises very beautifully west of Saint Mary's; it is a perfect garden: spring, which is now in full vigour, and every hedge and bush covered with flowers, rendered our jaunt delightful. The kermes or holme-oak is in great beauty, quite on fire with the scarlet gall-nuts of the little insect which produces the false cochineal. Near the Guadalquivir, the country is arable, with few inclosures. In times of remote antiquity Sanlucar was called Fanum Luciferi. It was once the port of Seville, and at the seasons for the arrival or departure of the fleets, the most stirring place in Europe: at present it is a neat, quiet town, without much business. The small ships that carry on its trade, lie half a league farther up in the Ansa, where the Indian flota used to moor. The river is wide and very rough at the bar; the opposite shore so dead a flat, that it is difficult to distinguish it from the water. I sauntered along the Playa de Sanlucar, without meeting a soul: how changed from what it was in the days of Cervantes; when it was crowded with the busy and the idle, the honest and the profligate.

On Friday evening we came to Xeres. I was much surprized to hear, from good authority, that this city contains

contains no lefs than forty thoufand inhabitants, of which a twentieth part are ecclefiaftics. We went next morning to the monaftery of Carthufian monks, a few miles off, remarkable for its breed of horfes, and for a very fine view over the plains towards the bay and fhipping of Cadiz. The day was fultry, and I could with pleafure have lolled it out in the prior's garden, under the fhade of a noble lemon-tree, refrefhed by the foft perfumes afcending on every fide from the neighbouring orchards.

This convent, founded in 1482 by Alvaris de Valleto, a citizen of Xeres, is grand, and well laid out: water is conveyed into every public hall and private cell. We were difappointed of the principal end of our journey, which was to fee their fine ftallions, but they were all out in the country at the covering-ftables. The earth, in the cemetries of Xeres, has the quality of preferving corpfes incorrupted for years and ages.

Upon leaving Xeres, we found the roads much the worfe for the heavy rains; and two days were fpent in travelling a few miles through ftiff, deep clays, where we expected to ftick faft every inftant, as the wheels were clogged to a great height. We faw fome buftards in thefe plains.

This morning we arrived in Seville, which appears to great advantage from the hills, at the diftance of a couple

ple of miles. The foil upon the heights is fandy, planted with pine-trees and vines, inclofed with hedges of various kinds of fhrubs, among which there is a great quantity of yellow jafmine. Round the city is a great plain of corn-lands, paftures, and gardens; the Guadalquivir, which runs through it, is very fubject to overflow its banks, and lay all the adjacent country under water; the lowlands by the river fide are common, and two years cropped with corn, the third left to run up into grafs.

When we entered the city, our muleteers were obliged to ride as poftillions on the foremoft mules, to comply with the orders of the magiftrates for preventing ftoppages and accidents in the ftreets, which are uncommonly crooked and narrow.

LETTER XXXI.

Seville, April 9, 1776.

WE arrived yesterday morning in this capital of Andalusia; and as soon as we had dined and drest ourselves, walked out with no particular object in view, but merely to stroll through the streets, by way of making ourselves acquainted with the city; chance led us into the court of the Alcazar, or royal palace, and the centry directed us to a gallery, which he said would bring us to the gardens. You have often heard me launch out in praise of some hanging-gardens in Italy, so refreshing and voluptuous in the summer evenings; this of the Alcazar is exactly such another; several parterres, surrounded by galleries and terraces, intersected by myrtle hedges and jasmine bowers, and perfumed by clumps of orange-trees, have also the advantage of abundance of water. A large party of sprightly damsels and young men that were walking here, were much indebted to us for making the water-works play, by means of a small bribe to the keeper. Nothing can be more delicious than these sprinklings in a hot day; all the flowers seemed to acquire new vigour, the

the odours, exhaled from the orange, citron, and lemon-trees, grew more poignant, more balfamic, and the company ten times more alive than they were; it was a true April fhower. We fauntered near two hours in the groves, till we were quite in extafy with fweets. 'Tis a moft heavenly refidence in fpring; and I fhould think the fummer heats might be tempered and rendered fupportable enough, by the profufion of water that they enjoy at Seville.

Philip the Fifth refided here many years, and paffed his time in drawing with the fmoke of a candle on deal boards, or angling for tench in a little refervoir.

On our firft entrance into the palace, which is a *pafticcio* of Saracenic, Conventual, and Grecian architecture, I was much taken with the principal front of the inner-court; a piece of as good Morifco work as any I had yet feen. Having read that the Moors built one part of this palace, I concluded I was admiring fomething as old as the Mahometan kings of Seville; but upon clofer examination was not a little furprized to find *lions*, *caftles*, and other armorial enfigns of Caftille and Leon, interwoven with the Arabefque foliages; and ftill more fo, to fee, in large Gothic characters, an infcription informing me, that thefe edifices were built in the fourteenth century, by the moft mighty king of Caftille and Leon, Don Pedro.

Within

Within this portico is a court ninety-three feet by fixty-nine: it is flagged with marble, and furrounded with a colonnade of white marble columns of the Corinthian order, elegantly proportioned, and well executed; the walls behind are covered with grotefque defigns in the Moorifh tafte: Charles the Fifth has contrived to foift his eagle and his *plus oultre* into every corner. The great hall adjoining, called the *Media naranja*, or half-orange, from the form of its cupola, is richly gilt and ftuccoed in the fame manner. Here I own, my little knowledge of architecture was fairly nonpluffed; I was convinced that the portion of the fabric, called by the travel-writers the *Moorifh part*, was the work of Peter the Cruel, who might eafily procure fkilful artifts from the kings of Granada, with whom he was connected moft part of his reign; but there was no accounting for the Corinthian pillars, unlefs I fuppofed them to have belonged to fome Roman edifice, deftroyed for the fake of fupplying materials for the palace, or to have been placed by the emperor under the old gallery, in lieu of others in a barbarous ftyle or ruinous ftate. Next to the court of the lions in the Alhambra, this fquare is the moft pleafing piece of Arabic building I have met with, though in delicacy of defign and execution, the ornaments of the Sevillian are much inferior to thofe of the Granadine palace.

Near

Near the western entrance was formerly to be seen a stone seat, with its canopy supported by four pillars, all now destroyed. Here that severe judge, Don Pedro, sat to decide causes, and give sentence upon malefactors. His justice was so very inflexible, that in those days of feudal anarchy, it was looked upon in the light of wanton cruelty and tyranny; perhaps that unfortunate monarch owes to the hatred of those he meant to reduce to order, much of the obloquy which has been so plentifully bestowed upon him by historians, who have painted him to us as a tyrant so bloody, so wicked, as almost to exceed the bounds of probability. In Andalusia, where he fixed his residence, and seemed most to delight, his memory is not held in the same abhorrence. The Sevillian writers speak of him very differently; and instead of his usual appellation of *Pedro el cruel*, distinguish him by that of *El Justiciero*. It is certain that his bastard-brother and murderer, Henry of Transtamare, was guilty of crimes full as atrocious as any of those imputed to Don Pedro; but as he destroyed him, his family, and adherents, the friends of the new spurious race of monarchs were left at full liberty to blacken the characters of the adverse party, without fear of being called to an account for calumny, or even contradicted. Truth is now out of our reach; and for want of proper proofs to the contrary, we must sit down contented with

what

what hiftory has left us, and allow Don Pedro to have been one of the moft inhuman butchers that ever difgraced a throne.

We devoted this morning to an excurfion in fearch of the ruins of Italica, where Trajan, Hadrian, and Theodofius the Great, are fuppofed to have been born; a fearch it may moft properly be called, for we wandered a long league wide of the mark, but had no reafon to be forry for the miftake, whatever our Catalan runningfootman might think of the matter. We took too much to the left, after croffing the river on the bridge of boats, and ftrayed along the walls of a convent, where the monks were felling the lemons of their gardens through a hole in the wall. The wind was rather brifk, and wafted fuch perfumes from the orange-groves, as almoft lulled us to fleep; the meadows and cornfields that we rode through were delightful, as rich and luxuriant as any I ever faw in Flanders. On our right hand a range of orange-gardens perfumed the breeze before it reached us; and on the left the Guadalquivir ran winding through the plain. Our foft reveries were difturbed by a full ftop, that our runner Chriftoval made at a gully, where a brook falls into a river. It could only be paffed on foot, as there was no bridge but a few yawning planks, on which our horfes, however willing, could not pretend to find a footing; this obliged us to difmount, dismount, and send our horses round half a league to join us at the ruins of Italica, which we thought appeared very conspicuous upon a hill before us. The sun was hot, but the spirit of antiquarianism gave us strength and courage to climb up to the platform of Saint John de Alfarache. After sitting awhile to take breath under some arborjudas in full flower, we proceeded to explore every corner of the crown of the hill; it is almost square, inclosed with the ruins of vast towers and bulwarks, built of cemented mud and pebbles. From the knowledge I had acquired of the different modes of building, since I came into the south of Spain, I ventured to pronounce, that if this was Italica, the Moors had built upon the site, and antiquaries were grosly mistaken when they talked of Roman edifices and amphitheatres; not but what I thought the situation such, as the judicious Romans might have preferred to that of Hispalis, the present Seville, both for beauty and strength. The view from it over that city, the course of the river, and the rich plain, are worth more than the labour it cost us to get so high: at this blooming season of the year, when every thing is in full vegetation, green and fresh, I don't remember to have seen a finer country.

An old peasant set my heart at ease (for I confess I was a little out of humour, as every disappointed virtuoso virtuofo would have been) by informing us that this was a Moorifh caftle, [16] and that Sevilla Vieja, or old Seville (the name they give to Italica) was a little beyond a great church of Hieronymites, a league to the north in the fkirts of the plain. Our error once difcovered, we trotted away through the flats to that convent, and there picked up a fellow without fhirt or ftockings, with a patched cloak, white hat, and long black beard; which gentleman undertook to fhew us the antiquities.

Of the ancient colony of Italica, fuppofed to have been compofed by Scipio of his veteran foldiers, fcarce the leaft veftige remains. It is faid the Moors deftroyed it, not to have a rival fo near Seville, where they intended to fix the feat of their empire; but I doubt this is the mere furmife of fome modern hiftorian. I could not pofitively afcertain it, but from a view of the ground, am apt to believe it was built in imitation of Rome, on feven hills, and that the river Bœtis ran at the foot of them. By accidental obftructions and banks of fand, accumulated in a long feries of inundations, the river may have been driven from its ancient bed, and forced more into the heart of the plain, where it

[16] After the lofs of Seville, the Moors are faid to have remained fome time at Alfarache, under the government of a kind of king.

now takes its courfe. Such an event as this would account for the ruin of fo confiderable a city as Italica; and without fuppofing that the Saracens were at the pains of demolifhing it, would afford fufficient caufe for giving the preference to Seville, which ftands upon the Guadalquivir.

On the fummit of the firft hill are fome ruinous brick walls, called *El Palacio*, not in the leaft remarkable. The peafants that were here at work in the olive-yards, told us, that underneath there had formerly been found columns of filver and brafs; but as they were bewitched by fome magician, nobody was ever able to draw them up; and now-a-days, not a foul has the courage even to dig for them, as they have all the reafon in the world to believe, that the conjurer would twift their heads off for attempting it. This is a popular fuperftition, which I have found to be common to moft countries, wherever any great remains of vaults and ancient edifices are to be feen.

On the moft diftant eminence are confiderable ruins of an amphitheatre, built with pebbles, and brick arches; moft probably the marble cafing has been carried away, or deftroyed by burning to lime. The form is a moft perfect oval; the arena meafures, as near as the corn would allow me to be exact, one hundred yards in its greateft length, and fixty in its greateft breadth;

some of the vomitoria, cells, and passages, are yet discernible, but scarce any traces of the seats; however I made out twenty rows, two feet six inches wide, and two feet high; each step of the stairs of communication is one foot high and one wide. This amphitheatre is now more like Stonehenge than a regular Roman edifice [17].

Not far from it is a fine pool of water, in a large vault under the hill; which I take to be the remains of some aqueduct, as the water is too warm to be near the spring head.

Being very hot and hungry, we made the best of our way home through large plantations of orange-trees, which here grow to the size of moderate timber trees; the fruit is much more pleasing to the eye, if less so to the palate, than the oranges of Portugal, as the rich blood-colour is admirably contrasted with the bright tint of the leaves.

[17] The corporation of Seville, having occasion for stones to embank the river, which, by its frequent inundations, caused great damage to the city, ordered the amphitheatre of Italica to be knocked down. Many hands were employed to batter the walls, and to blow up with gunpowder such parts as resisted the pick-ax. By these means they procured sufficient materials for their embankment; but, as if the Guadalquivir meant to revenge the cause of taste upon these barbarians, the very first flood swept away the whole fabrick.

LETTER

LETTER XXXII.

Seville, April 11, 1776.

SEVILLE is fuppofed to have been founded by the Phenicians, who gave it the name of Hifpalis: the Romans called it Julia; in after-ages the old name returned, and after a variety of corruptions, feems to have been revived in the modern appellation of Sebilla, or Sevilla, for the Spaniards ufe both indifcriminately.

Under the Roman government, it was embellifhed with many magnificent buildings, deftined for purpofes of public utility and amufement; but I believe the very ruins of thofe edifices have long ago difappeared.

The Gothic kings refided here before they removed their court to Toledo.

Mufa, the Saracen viceroy, took Seville by ftorm, foon after the victory obtained at Xeres over king Rodrigo.

In the general confufion that enfued upon the down-fal of the kingdom of Cordova, in 1027, Seville became an independent fovereignty, which was annihilated by the violence of the African prince Jufef Almoravides, who came into Spain in 1097.

Ferdinand

Ferdinand the third, king of Castille, (who, in consideration of his great success against the Mahometans, as well as for his sanctity, was canonized after his death, and is still honoured as a saint of the first rank) took Cordova, and many other important places, from the enfeebled, disunited Mussulmen; drove them from post to post, till he reduced the bounds of their empire to a very confined corner of the peninsula; after a year's siege he forced Seville to open its gates to him, and acknowledge his sway. Three hundred thousand Moors are said to have left the city upon the capitulation, and to have carried their arms and industry to such countries, as were still obedient to the law of Mahomet. It is difficult to conceive how Seville could continue to be a great and populous town after such an emigration; yet we find it in a few years enlarged, adorned with new buildings, the chief of which was the cathedral, and long enjoying the rank of one of the most considerable cities in Spain.

Its most brilliant epocha was soon after the discovery of America, when all the new-found treasures were poured into Europe from the fleets that returned from the new hemisphere into the Guadalquivir, and made Seville the magazine of its invaluable productions. The sovereign frequently honoured this place with his presence; merchants from all parts flocked hither to open houses

houses of commerce, or to provide themselves with goods for foreign markets; the sailors and adventurers of the Indian fleets rendezvoused here, and with wanton prodigality lavished the wealth, which they had acquired in America. Then indeed was the time, when the Spaniard cried out in the fullness of his heart, *Quien no a visto Sevilla, no a visto meravilla* [18]. Its court was then the most splendid in Europe; its streets were thronged with an immense concourse of people; its river was crowded with ships, and its keys covered with bales of precious merchandize. Great were the buildings begun, and still vaster the projects for future ones. Its prosperity seemed proof against the fickleness of fortune; but in the course of a very few years, it fell from the highest pitch of grandeur to solitude and poverty, by the danger and embarrassments in the navigation of the Guadalquivir. The superior excellence of the port of Cadiz, induced government to order the Galeons to be stationed there for the time to come.

The shape of Seville is circular, without any great rising in the whole space. The walls seem of Moorish construction, or of the ages which immediately followed the dissolution of the Saracen empire; as I guess by their form and materials. The ditch is filled up in

[18] He that has not seen Seville, has not seen the wonder of the world.

many places. The circumference of the walls is not more than five miles and an half. The fuburb of Triana, on the weſt ſide of the river, is as large as many towns, but remarkable for nothing but its gloomy Gothic caſtle, where, in 1482, the inquiſition formed its firſt eſtabliſhment in Spain.

The ſtreets of Seville are crooked, dirty, and ſo narrow, that in moſt of them two coaches find it difficult to paſs a-breaſt. The wideſt and handſomeſt place is the Alameda, or great walk of old elms, in the heart of the city ; it is ſix hundred yards by one hundred and fifty, decorated with three fountains, and the ſtatues of Hercules, the reputed founder, and Julius Cæſar, the reſtorer of Seville.

Moſt of the churches are built and ornamented in ſo barbarous a ſtyle, that I had not the patience to examine them ; the cathedral, the capuchins, and the charidad, are the only ſacred edifices really intereſting ; the firſt by its antiquity, ſize, and reputation ; the two latter by the chef-d'œuvres of Murillo.

The cathedral is more cried up than I think it deſerves ; it is by no means equal to York minſter, for lightneſs, elegance, and Gothic delicacy. The cluſtered pillars are too thick, the ailes too narrow, and the choir, by being placed in the center, ſpoils the whole coup d'œil, and renders the reſt of the church little better than

a heap

a heap of long paſſages. The ornamental parts, commonly ſaid to be after the Gothic manner, ſeem rather to be clumſy imitations of the models left by the Moors. Not one of the great entrances or porches is finiſhed; and to disfigure the whole pile, a long range of buildings, in the modern ſtyle, has been added on to the old part.

Don Sancho the Brave began this church, near the cloſe of the thirteenth century; and John the Second finiſhed it about an hundred years after. Its length within is four hundred and twenty feet; its breadth two hundred and ſeventy-three; and its greateſt height one hundred and twenty-ſix. The circumference of each cluſter of pillars is forty-two feet. It has nine doors, eighty windows, and eighty altars, at which five hundred maſſes are ſaid every day. The pavement is brick, but they are now new-laying it with marble. The great gate of the cloyſters, (the only remains of the moſque) is a piece of handſome Mooriſh architecture. The large orange-trees that ſhade the fountains in the middle of the cloyſters, make them a moſt agreeable walk. At one angle ſtands the Giralda, or belfry, a tower three hundred and fifty feet high, and fifty ſquare: the Moors erected it about the year 1000: the Chriſtians have added two ſtories, and a prodigious weathercock, which, altogether, agree much better with the ancient building than patchwork is wont to do: the sculpture of the Saracenic part, which is two hundred feet high, is in a much simpler taste than their artists were accustomed to display in public works. The effect of this tower rising far above every edifice in Seville, is extremely noble. Tradition relates, that to form a solid foundation for it, the Moors made a deep hole, into which they cast all the marble and stone monuments of the Romans that could be found: when repairs have been necessary, and the ground has been opened near the bottom, many broken ornaments and inscriptions have been discovered. The whole work is brick and mortar; a winding stair-case is contrived within, so easy and wide, as to admit of two horsemen riding a-breast, above half way up. For some purpose, unknown to us, the architect has made the solid masonry in the upper half, just as thick again as that in the lower, though on the outside the belfry is all the way of the same dimensions.

Murillo has adorned the charidad and capuchins with several most valuable pictures, which may be ranked among his very best performances; his manner puts me much in mind of Guercino: the design of his hands and arms is generally faulty, as he gives them rather too great a length; there is such expression, such truth of colouring, and intelligence, in the composition of his
groupes,

groupes, that a trifling defect of that kind is eafily overlooked.

In the firft of thofe churches, Saint Elizabeth, queen of Hungary, curing fome lepers, and other difeafed perfons, by anointing them with holy oil, is an admirable picture; there is an old woman, and a boy under the hand of the faint, full of truth, character, and expreffion. In the reprefentation of Mofes ftriking the rock, are feveral excellent figures, and a very beautiful white horfe.

In the church of the capuchins, out of many of his pictures, which hang in every chapel on each fide, thofe that gave me moft pleafure, were a Saint Anthony of Padua, holding the infant Jefus on a book; a friar embracing Chrift crucified, who ftoops from the crofs, and brings down an arm to prefs the faint's fhoulder; an adoration of the fhepherds; and Saint Thomas of Villanova, archbifhop of Valencia, diftributing alms at his palace-gate; which laft I like the beft of the whole collection.

In our way to this church, which ftands without the walls, we looked into many others; but found nothing particular in any, except in one, a lift of the books lately condemned by the inquifition; among many others we faw the famous *Fray Gerundio* by father Ifla; fome common French books relative to geography; fome of Voltaire's late publications; and the political hiftory of the European fettlements, by Raynal, prohibited not only as favouring of deifm and infidelity, but alfo as containing many paffages derogatory to the glory of the Spanifh nation.

We returned by the great road round the walls, paffing near the gate and tower where Saint Hermenegild was put to death by order of his father Leovigild, king of the Goths, for deferting arianifm, and for raifing an unfuccefsful rebellion againft him.

Further on we walked under the Caños de Carmona, or the great aqueduct; which is efteemed by the Sevillian hiftorians, one of the moft wonderful monuments of antiquity exifting in the univerfe. We were much difappointed to find none of that beauty or grandeur they talk fo much of; on the contrary, it is rather ugly, its arches unequal, the architecture neglected, and its direction very crooked. The conduit is fo leaky, that a rivulet is formed of the wafte water. Authors are divided in their opinions concerning this aqueduct; whether to look upon it as a Roman, or as a Moorifh work. I believe it was originally planned and built by the former; but the innumerable repairs it has undergone have almoft obliterated every trace of their manner: however, what it wants in fhew, it certainly makes up for in utility; it conveys a very abundant fupply of
water

water, several leagues from a place called Alcalá. The rocks are there bored, in various directions, an immense length of way under ground, in order to intercept every little runner, and collect so considerable a stream as to turn several mills, and bring such a volume of water down to Seville, that almost every house in town has the benefit of it; except those of the quarters, which are supplied by the pipes from the fountain of the archbishop.

We re-entered the city at the new gate, which forms an elegant termination to a handsome street of regular houses one story high, behind the Alcazar. The snuff manufactory is situated in this street: for the more convenient carrying on this lucrative branch of commerce, Ferdinand the Sixth erected a most magnificent, roomy palace, in a grand but rather heavy style of architecture. It was finished in 1756. One thousand men are employed constantly, at the rate of six or four reals per diem, for about nine hours work. One hundred and eighty mules work twenty-eight mills or machines for grinding and mixing the tobacco with the red earth of Almazarron; the excessive adulteration with this earth, practised of late years by the directors, has occasioned a prodigious falling off in the exportation of this commodity, and unless they alter their method, the trade will soon be confined to Spain and its dominions; the northern markets have long refused to take any off their hands.

hands. The leaves of the tobacco are imported from Cuba and the Brafils; the beft fnuff is called *Grance*. Thirty-two reals a pound is the current price of the fnuff, but none is allowed to be fold by retail in the manufactory. We vifited every part of the houfe, at the hazard of being fuffocated; in one room we found four hundred and fixty men fitting at work, making *cigarros* [19], and tying them up in bunches worth four reals a-piece, for each of which they are paid for their labour four quartos. The officer that attended us, told us that the neat profits of laft year, upon all the fnuff and tobacco fold out at the office, amounted to more than fix millions of dollars.

Near the cathedral is the *Lonja*, or exchange, formerly a place of great refort, but now, being deferted by merchants, it is appropriated to other ufes; I believe, to the holding of fome inferior courts of juftice. The building is fquare, its ftyle plain and noble, and it remains a monument of the good tafte of the Spaniards at that brilliant period of their hiftory, which takes in the reign of Charles the Fifth, and of his fon Philip. The Lonja was erected in 1583, upon a defign of Juan de Herrera.

[19] Thefe are little rolls of tobacco, which the Spaniards fmoke without a pipe.

Olavides,

Olavides, the prefent Intendant, is faid to have great fchemes for the embellifhment of Seville; but as he is likewife director of all the new colonies in the Sierra Morena, and not upon the moft folid footing at court, I doubt he has more projects in hand and in idea, than he can poffibly bring to bear, during the time he may probably remain in power [20].

His prefent operation, is to embank with a ftrong brick wall, the bed of the river above the town, thereby to turn off the impetuous currents, that have fo often burft their way into the very heart of the city. Along the banks he has planted avenues of an ever-green tree, very like a poplar. It was brought from South America, and is called *Sapota*.

The great hofpital de la Sangre, and the college of Sant Elmo, founded for a marine fchool, are more remarkable for their fize than for any other merit; the other buildings are little worthy of notice. The police of this city is very fevere, but perhaps not uniformly and impartially fo. My man has been a day and a night in prifon, only for carrying my piftols through the ftreets to the gunfmith's. There has been as much writing as would do for a moderate fuit in chancery,

[20] In 1776 he was taken up and imprifoned in the dungeons of the inquifition, where he will probably end his days.

but it seems to be cheap enough, as I believe the value of a guinea will procure his releafe, and pay the fees as well as the expences of the procedures.

LETTER XXXIII.

Eccija, April 12, 1778.

HAVING feen every thing in Seville that was recommended to our notice, we left it yefterday, and came to lie at Carmona; the road is through a perfect foreft of olive-trees, which are much hacked and pruned, and fet at the regular diftance of twenty-feven feet afunder.

Carmona is a large town, ftanding boldly on a high hill. Its caftle, in ruins, covers a vaft extent of ground, and contains many buildings that ferved for palace and fortrefs to Don Pedro the Cruel, and his family. He placed his main hope in the ftrength of this caftle, and in the faithful attachment of Don Martin Lopes de Cordova, grand-mafter of the order of Calatrava, to whofe care he entrufted his fons Sancho and Diego, whom he had had by a lady he had taken to his bed,

after

after the death of his famous miſtreſs, Maria de Padilla. Henry of Tranſtamare, after the defeat and murder of Pedro in the plains of Montiel, laid ſiege to Carmona, took it by capitulation, together with the children and treaſures of the late king, and baſely breaking his word of honour, cauſed Lopez to be beheaded for his obſtinate reſiſtance.

Like every place in this province, Carmona makes a figure in Roman hiſtory, and has many remains of their walls, inſcriptions, &c. to ſhew as proofs of its ancient importance. The country about it is hilly and champaign, but far from unpleaſant, as it is all green, and has ſome wood and water in different parts of the view.

We dined to-day at the ſolitary venta of Monclova, and rode on hither to get a ſight of the town, but it proved farther off than we imagined, and it was dark before we got in. We were obliged to leave the carriage with our baggage at Carmona, to get the axletree mended, and hitherto we have had no tidings of it, ſo ſhall lie down in our cloaths on a few chairs.

The road from Seville hither, is better than any I have ſeen in Spain, ſome of the new road near Barcelona excepted; it is all gravel, which not being the ſoil of the country, muſt have been brought from a great diſtance, and has ſubſiſted in all probability, unaltered and unrepaired ſince the Moors were driven out of Andaluſiá;

Andalusiá; it is raised above the level of the fields, and commonly runs in a direct line from west to east. As there are no visible remains of pavement, I rather attribute it to the Saracens than to the Romans, although both nations are known to have attended particularly to the highways of this province, and to have made several causeways and roads of communication between the great towns.

We passed through La Luisiana, a tract of land lately put into cultivation by a colony of Germans, who have their habitations not far from the side of the highway, placed at regular distances of two or three hundred yards, all built after one simple model, with an allotment of corn-land round the house: this is the most western of the new settlements.

Eccija seems prettily situated upon the river Xenil, and to have some pleasant walks, and an astonishing number of steeples.

Cordova, April 14th.

Yesterday we dined at La Carlotta, another plantation of Germans of great extent, made eight years ago, in a hilly forest. The houses are scattered about. The parish church, inn, director's house, some shops and dwelling houses for handicraft men, form a very neat village on an eminence: as they have left standing all the

the evergreen oaks of any tolerable size, the face of the country is very handsome, the green corn being checquered with groves, clump, and single trees. About twenty or thirty acres is an allotment for a family, under the obligation of remaining on the spot ten years; during which period, they are subject to no taxes of any kind. At the expiration of the term, if they choose to settle here, the land is made over to them in fee, and they commence payment of a small quit-rent. The king furnishes them with seed corn, but they are obliged to replace it in his granaries after harvest; except the walls of a house, and some trifling instruments of husbandry, this is all the encouragement they meet with; and as this is by no means a sufficient help, and much of the soil is poor and hungry, and falls off at every crop, there is great reason to apprehend, that this colony will prove one of those ephemeral productions that so often spring up in monarchical governments, and almost immediately after birth, sink into their original nothing. Some hundreds of the Germans have died since the establishment, through poverty, intemperance, bad food, and change of climate.

The country, as you approach Cordova, is all bare, hilly, and arable. The view of the river, city, and woods, on the opposite hills, is extremely agreeable and picturesque.

LETTER

LETTER XXXIV.

Cordova, April 15th, 1776.

WE have ferreted out the few things in this city, that can be accounted worthy of any attention from a traveller; have ridden up and down the environs as often as the weather would permit, and have ftudied the mofque by day-light, and by torch-light; but ftill this temple is fo intricate a labyrinth, and contains fo many extraordinary things, that I fhall take one or two farther furveys of it before I attempt to defcribe it. The abundance of fubject-matter, and its celebrity, will entitle it to figure in a letter apart. This fhall be dedicated to objects of lefs importance, and when I fhall have informed you of the prefent ftate of the town, it will be proper to felect for you, from the beft author I have by me, fome curious particulars relative to its ancient hiftory.

The environs are delightful, and enjoy a rich variety of woods, hillocks, and culture, vivified by abundance of limpid water. The flat land produces olives and corn, and much of it is laid out in gardens, where the fruit-trees grow to a remarkable fize, and feem perfectly

fectly clean and healthy. The upper-grounds are over-run with evergreen oaks and pines, which the farmers grub up in the good spots to plant olive and carob bean trees in their stead. The farm houses are built in the midst of inclosures and orchards of orange-trees. Corn-land is let for so many measures of corn, either a fixed number for each harvest, or an indefinite quantity according to the crops; the highlands are all let out at a certain rent in cash.

The Guadalquivir runs before the town, which it has worn into a perfect half moon. A bridge of sixteen arches, defended by a large Moorish tower, leads from the south into Cordova, and near the end of the bridge stands the mosque, now the cathedral. The walls of the town are in many places just as the Romans left them; the method they have followed here in laying the stones is rather different from what I have observed in other Roman edifices. Here each long square stone is terminated and flanked by two thin ones set up an end.

The streets are crooked and dirty; few of the public or private buildings conspicuous for their architecture; the new hospital for the education of orphans, has something bold and simply noble in its cupola and portico. The palaces of the inquisition and of the bishop are extensive, and well situated.

We

We are juft returned from a bullfeaft, where no horfemen were allowed, as the animals were not of a breed fufficiently noble to try the lance upon. One poor bull that would not fight, was very dexteroufly run through the heart; two oxen were tormented a little, and then fent to the adjoining fhambles; and a fmall cow, after behaving mighty well as to jumping and fkipping, got a reprieve in confideration of her exceffive leannefs. It was too tirefome even to make us laugh, but we are in hopes of feeing this exhibition in greater perfection at Aranjuez. The motive of this paltry fpectacle is extremely laudable. The Corregidor (i. e. the triennial governor of the town, always a native of a different part of Spain from that wherein he is appointed to fuperintend the police) gives thefe little fhews to the people on Sundays and feftivals; and out of the profits and hire of the feats, raifes a fum fufficient to carry on the new walk he is laying out under the walls.

After the entertainment, the nobility paraded about in their coaches; and I was furprized to fee fuch elegance as I little expected in an inland town in Spain; very handfome Englifh and French carriages, fmart liveries, and excellent horfes. The nobility of this place live in a manner not to be met with any where elfe in the kingdom; if their union and mutual emulation in
rendering

rendering fociety agreeable be fuch as they are reprefented to me, they deferve the higheft encomiums from every lover of humanity : thirty families or more, meet every night at a houfe chofen by rotation, where the ladies do the honours of genteel refrefhments, merry good-natured converfation, and fome low cardplaying. The general run of the women feems to be handfome; fome we faw on the walks were extremely beautiful. We have been much preffed to frequent the affemblies; but as the weather is fo uncertain, we keep ourfelves ready in our boots and great coats, in order to feize every fair moment to get out and fee the town and country.

Having thus marked out the little that modern Cordova has to fhew, give me leave to carry you back to more remote times; to a period, when it figured to much greater advantage on the theatre of politics and commerce. This is not to be fixed at the time of its being a Roman colony [21], though it boafts of having given birth to Seneca and Lucan; nor in the ages during which it acknowledged the dominion of the Goths. To the Saracen Caliphs of the Ommiad family, Cordova is indebted for its glory; as we hear but little of it be-

---

[21] Strabo fays, that Corduba was founded by Marcellus, and was the firft Roman colony eftablifhed in Spain. Its Latin appellation was *Patricia*.

fore the year 755, when Abdoulrahman, only heir-male of the Ommiad line, paffed over from Africa, at the head of a few defperate followers, and found means to raife a rebellion in Spain. After a battle fought on the banks of the Guadalquivir, in which he overthrew the lieutenant of the Abaffid Caliph of Damafcus, Abdoulrahman became king of all the Moorifh poffeffions in the fouth of Spain, and in 759 fixed his royal refidence at Cordova.

Then began thofe flourifhing ages of Arabian gallantry and magnificence, which rendered the Moors of Spain fuperior to all their contemporaries in arts and arms, and made Cordova one of the moft fplendid cities of the world. Agriculture and commerce profpered under the happy fway of this hero; and the face of the country was changed from a fcene of defolation, which the long wars and harfh government of the viceroys had brought on, into a moft populous flourifhing ftate, exceeding in riches, number of inhabitants, activity, and induftry, any prior or fubfequent era of the Spanifh hiftory. He added new fortifications to the town, built himfelf a magnificent palace with delicious gardens, laid caufeways through the marfhes, made excellent roads to open a ready communication between the great towns, and in 786 began the great mofque, which he did not live to finifh.

During

During the course of two centuries, this court continued to be the resort of all professors of the polite arts, and of such as valued themselves upon their military and knightly accomplishments; while the rest of Europe was buried in ignorance, debased by brutality of manners, or distracted by superstitious disputes. England, weakened by its Heptarchy, was too inconsiderable even to be mentioned in the political history of the times; France, though it had a gleam of reputation under Charlemagne, was still a barbarous unpolished nation; and Italy was in utter confusion, the frequent revolutions and change of masters rendering it impossible for learning, or any thing good, to acquire a permanent footing in so unstable a soil; Greece, though still in possession of the arts and luxury of ancient Rome, had lost all vigour, and seemed absorbed in the most futile of all pursuits; viz. that of scholastic argument, and religious subtilties.

The residence of the Ommiad Caliphs, was long conspicuous for its supreme magnificence, and the crowds of learned men, who were allured to it by the protection offered by its sovereigns, the beauty of the country, the wholesomeness of the climate, and the variety of pleasures that returned incessantly in one enchanting round.

Cordova became the center of politeness, industry,

and genius. Tilts and tournaments, with other coftly fhews, were long the darling paftimes of a wealthy happy people; and this was the only kingdom in the weft, where geometry, aftronomy, and phyfic, were regularly ftudied and practifed; mufic was no lefs honoured, for I find that in 844, a famous mufician, called Ali Zeriab, came to fettle at Cordova, and formed feveral pupils, who were fuppofed to equal the moft celebrated performers that were ever known, even in the eaft. That architecture was greatly encouraged, we need no other proof than the great and expenfive fabrics undertaken and completed by many of these Spanifh monarchs: whatever faults may be juftly condemned in their manner by the connoiffeur, accuftomed to the chafte noble graces of the Grecian proportions; certainly nobody can behold what remains of thefe Moorifh edifices, without being ftrongly impreffed with a high idea of the genius of the artifts, as well as the grandeur of the prince who carried their plans into execution.

Thefe Sultans not only gave the moft diftinguifhed protection to arts and fciences, and to the perfons learned in any of them, but were themfelves eminently verfed in various branches of knowledge. Alkehem the fecond, collected fo immenfe a quantity of manufcripts, that before the end of his reign, the royal library contained

tained no less than six hundred thousand volumes, of which the very catalogue filled forty huge folios. The university of Cordova was founded by him, and under such favourable auspices, rose to the highest pitch of celebrity.

Abdoulrahman was succeeded by his son Hissem; whose passion for glory and architecture was not in the least inferior to that of his father. He put the finishing hand to the mosque, which the plunder of the southern provinces of France enabled him to complete in the course of a few years. Several historians have represented the terror of his name so great, that the inhabitants of the Narbonne, in order to purchase peace and liberty, agreed to transport from their city to Cordova, all materials necessary for the construction of the mosque. This story is hardly credible; Mariana supposes it to have been a sort of fine sand proper for mixing with lime, that the Narbonnese engaged to carry; but if there be any truth in the affair, I should imagine it to be more probable, that they furnished him with columns and other monuments of antiquity, which Narbonne abounded with, and which were undoubtedly employed in great quantities in the building of the mosque. The bridge over the Guadalquivir was a work of Hissem's, after his own plans.

Alkahem succeeded Hissem.

Abdoulrahman the second was also passionately fond

of building. He was the firft that brought fupplies of water to Cordova, by means of leaden pipes laid upon aqueducts of ftone. The quantity was fo confiderable, that every part of the palace, the mofques, baths, fquares, and public edifices, had all of them their fountains conftantly playing. A great many of thefe works ftill fubfift. He paved the whole city, and erected feveral mofques.

After him reigned Mahomet Almundar, Abdallah, and Abdoulrahman the third, who furpaffed all his predeceffors in fplendour, riches, and expence. His fubjects vied with each other in profufion and magnificence. I cannot give you a greater proof of the prodigious opulence and grandeur of the Arabians in the tenth century, than by enumerating the prefents made to this prince by Aboumelik, named in 938 to the poft of grand vizir. He caufed to be brought before the throne, and laid at the feet of his mafter,

Four hundred pounds of virgin gold.
Lingots of filver to the value of 4,20,000 zequins.
Four hundred pound of lignum aloes, one piece weighing one hundred and forty pounds.
Five hundred ounces of ambergreafe.
Three hundred ounces of camphire.
Thirty pieces of gold tiffue, fo rich that none but the Caliph could wear it.
Ten fuits of Khoraffan fables.

One

One hundred suits of fur of a less valuable sort.
Forty-eight sets of gold and silk long trappings for horses.
Four thousand pounds of silk.
Thirty Persian carpets.
Eight hundred iron coats of mail for war horses.
One thousand shields.
One hundred thousand arrows.
Fifteen led horses of Arabia, as richly caparisoned as those the Caliph was wont to ride.
One hundred horses of an inferior price.
Twenty mules with all their accoutrements.
Forty young men, and twenty girls of exquisite beauty, and most sumptuously decked out.

This display of riches was accompanied with a most flattering poem, composed by the minister in praise of his sovereign, who in return for this homage, assigned him a pension of an hundred thousand pieces of gold.

Abdoulrahman built a new town [11] three miles from Cordova, called Zehra or Arizapha, from the name of his favourite mistress. The palace was erected upon the plans of the most celebrated architect of Constantinople, at that time the best school and nursery of

---

[11] Supposed to have been at a place called Cordova la Vieja. There is nothing but a few ruins to support the conjecture.

artists

artifts in the world. In this edifice, were one thoufand one hundred and fourteen columns of African and Spanifh marble, nineteen of Italian, and one hundred and fourteen of moft exquifite workmanfhip, a prefent of the Greek emperor. The richnefs of the ftate-room exceeded the bounds of credibility. The walls were incrufted with marble, inlaid with golden foliages : in the middle was a marble bafon furrounded with various figures of animals fpouting water ; all thefe ftatues were gilt and enriched with precious ftones : the bafon was cut at Conftantinople, and the figures were efteemed the mafter-pieces of the moft expert fculptors of that city. Above the fountain, hung a famous pearl which the emperor Leo had fent to Abdoulrahman. The other apartments of the palace fell little fhort of this hall in magnificence. The moft retired part was allotted to his wives, concubines, flaves, and black eunuchs, in all fix thoufand. Over the principal enterance, in open defiance of the exprefs mandate of the prophet, ftood the ftatue of the fair Sultana, who gave her name to this new city, now become the conftant refidence of the court. Here the emperor was wont to take the diverfion of hunting, attended by twelve thoufand horfemen, accoutred with belts and fcimitars, imboffed with gold. At his return from the chace, he ufually retired to reft himfelf in a fplendid pavillion
erected

erected in the middle of the gardens, overlooking all the adjacent country. This banquetting house was supported by columns of the whitest marble ; the gilding and painting of the ceiling vied with the precious stones scattered over it ; and in the center was a vase, in which quickfilver supplied the place of water ; it shook with every motion of the room, and reflected the rays of the sun, which were admitted through some holes contrived in the roof.

You will no doubt be backward in crediting these relations ; and the inconceivable expence this prince must have been at in these undertakings, will be apt to stagger your belief. The town of Zehra, with the palace and gardens, cost him for twenty-five years, the annual sum of three hundred thousand dinars [23] ; add to this, the vast sums requisite for the maintenance of a seraglio of six thousand persons, a most numerous houshold, a guard of twelve thousand lancemen, and an incredible number of horses, and it can scarce be conceived where he could find revenues sufficient to answer such prodigious demands. All his life he kept on foot, and frequently sent into the field, very powerful armies. The salaries of the governors of provinces,

[23] Reckoning the dinar at 9s. 2d. the annual expence amounts to £.137,500 and in twenty-five years, this makes the sum of £.3,437,500 sterling.

towns, and forts; of the adminiſtrators of juſtice; the repairs of the fortified places, and the current outgoings of a formidable regular marine eſtabliſhment, are objects of ſuch expence, that it is eaſier to wonder than to believe, how they could be ſatisfied. But upon taking a review of the opulence of Spain at that epocha, of its trade, population, tributes, and taxes; that aſtoniſhment which we muſt be ſeized with, on the hearing of theſe accounts, will in a great meaſure ſubſide.

The Moors were then maſters of all the richeſt provinces of Spain, populous to an exceſs. In Cordova alone, they reckoned two hundred thouſand houſes, ſix hundred moſques, and nine hundred public baths [23].

The Arabian hiſtorian, from whom the preſent detail is taken, informs us, that in his time there were in Spain [24] eighty large cities, three hundred of the ſecond order, and that the number of villages and hamlets was not to be counted; upon the banks of the Guadalquivir, were no leſs than twelve thouſand villages; a traveller, in the courſe of a day's journey, met with

---

[23] In all probability, moſt of theſe houſes were very inconſiderable huts of one room, as the Moors never dwelt more than one family under the ſame roof.

[24] It does not appear from his account, whether he means the whole peninſula or only the portion of it ſubjeƈt to the Saracens.

three

TRAVELS THROUGH SPAIN.

three or four confiderable towns, and could not travel an hour without coming to a hamlet.

The revenues of the Ommiad caliphs in the time of Abdoulrahman the third, amounted annually to twelve million nine hundred and forty-five thoufand dinars, or about five millions five hundred and twenty thoufand fix hundred twenty-five pounds fterling. Befides this income in fpecie, a great number of impofts were paid in kind, which it is not poffible to afcertain or fix any average value upon; but it is certain they muft have been in proportion to the produce of the land, and confequently very great in a country inhabited by a numerous and indefatigable nation, devoted to agriculture, which they had carried to a pitch of perfection unknown to the reft of Europe [25].

The mines of gold, filver, and other metals, which Spain abounds with, were another inexhauftible fund of wealth to the Arabs, who kept a great number of miners conftantly employed. The difcovery of America and of its treafures, which feem to have brought contempt upon the riches of the old world, has deterred the

---

[25] This calculation of the Arabian hiftorian favours much of exaggeration; as the fums mentioned, far exceed all ideas we have of the quantity of gold and filver coin in circulation at that era: but I have given it in his words, without any farther comment.

kings of Spain from continuing to work the mines they have at home.

The extenfive commerce carried on by the Moors with other nations, brought an incredible flow of wealth into their country. I fhall not fpeak of their inland traffic, as I find nothing in their authors that can throw light upon it, or enable us to form any precife judgment of its extent and importance. I intend to confine myfelf to the operations of their foreign commerce, which was diftributed into various channels, many of them rendering an exceffive profit. It confifted either of the natural unwrought productions of Spain, or part of the fame productions manufactured at home, and exported to foreign markets.

Gold, filver, copper, raw-filk, oil, fugar, falfe cochineal, quickfilver, pig and caft iron, and above all, their filk and woollen manufactures, were the moft lucrative articles of exportation.

Ambergreafe, yellow amber, loadftone, antimony, falt, talc, marcaffites, rock chryftal, tuttie, fulphur, faffron, ginger, myrrh, and various other drugs, formed other objects of trade, which though inferior in value and quantity, produced neverthelefs great and clear returns.

Much coral was fifhed on the coaft of Andalufia, and that of Catalonia had a pearl fifhery.

Spain contained many mines of rubies and other precious

precious ftones; thofe of rubies near Malaga and Bejar, and that of amethyfts near Carthagena, were in the higheft repute.

Thefe different commodities were conveyed to Barbary, Egypt, and all the Eaft.

The temper of the Spanifh arms was held in the greateft repute by all the Africans; Spain was in a manner their arfenal from which they drew their cuiraffes, bucklers, cafques, fcimitars, and daggers.

The demand for raw-filk, and for the filk and woollen ftuffs of various colours made at Granada and Baça, and for the woollen cloths manufactured at Murica, was very great throughout Africa: there can be no doubt, but their trade with Egypt muft have been upon a more extenfive plan than that with Barbary; the Spanifh Arabs carried thither the goods of their country to barter againft thofe productions of Egypt, which Spain ftood in need of. The immenfity of their traffic with the Eaft, is not to be conceived; for reafons of ftate, the Ommiads conftantly endeavoured to keep upon the beft footing poffible with the court of Conftantinople, which they hoped would prove a check upon the enterprizes of the caliphs of Damafcus, who never ceafed repining at the difmembering of their empire by the firft Abdoulrahman. All the ports of the Grecian dominions were open to the Spanifh traders, who imported rich cargoes of merchandize adapted to the calls of that refined luxury, by which Conftantinople was then diftinguifhed; the profits upon fuch operations of commerce may eafily be fuppofed to have been prodigious.

Alkahem the fecond fucceeded his father. The Arabian writer relates the following fingular proof of courage given by a cadi, in reproving this prince for a piece of injuftice committed againft one of his fubjects.

A poor woman at Zehra, poffeffed a fmall fpot of ground contiguous to the royal palace. The caliph being defirous of extending his gardens that way, made propofals to the old woman to difpofe of her land for a fum of money; but fhe continuing deaf to every argument employed to induce her to part with the inheritance of her forefathers, the head gardener took by force what fhe refufed to yield to entreaty. The woman in an agony of defpair, flew to Cordova, to implore the fuccour of Ibn Bechir, the chief cadi of the city. This magiftrate immediately mounted his afs, taking with him a fack of extraordinary fize, and prefented himfelf before Alkahem, who was then fitting in a magnificent pavillion on the very ground in queftion. The arrival of the cadi, and the appearance of the wallet, furprized the fultan. Bechir having
proftrated

proftrated himfelf, entreated the prince to allow him to fill his fack with fome of the earth they were then upon. This requeft granted, and the bag full, the cadi defired him to help him to lift it on his afs. This ftrange demand was ftill more amazing than the reft: however the caliph confented; but upon putting his fhoulder to it, could not help complaining of the exceffive weight of the load. "Sir," replied the cadi, "this bag, which you find fo heavy, contains but a "very fmall portion of the earth which you have un- "juftly taken from a poor woman; how then do you "expect to be able at the day of judgment to fupport "the weight of the whole field you have had fo little "fcruple of ufurping." Far from being incenfed at this audacious rebuke, the caliph generoufly acknowledged his fault, and ordered the land to be reftored to the proprietor with every thing he had caufed to be erected upon it.

This monarch left a minor to fucceed him, and the kingdom to be governed by the famous vifier Mahomet Abenamir, firnamed *Almanzor* or *the defender*, from his great victories and wife conduct. His defcendants inherited from him the vifierfhip, and a power as abfolute as if they had been caliphs, until the weaknefs of the fovereigns encouraged, and the infolence of the minifters provoked the grandees to difturb the ftate
with

with their jealousies and dissentions; these broils occasioned such a series of civil wars and anarchy, as overthrew the throne of Cordova, and destroyed the whole race of Abdoulrahman. Thus the glorious edifice founded by the valour and prudence of that conqueror, and cemented by similar virtues in many of his successors, sunk into nothing, as soon as the sceptre devolved upon weak enervated princes, whose indolence and incapacity transferred the management of every thing to a visier. Many petty kingdoms sprang up out of the ruins of this mighty empire; and the Christians soon found opportunities of destroying, by separate attacks, that tremendous power, which when united had proved an overmatch for their utmost force.

But it is high time I should put an end to this long letter, which, I am afraid, you will look upon in no better a light than that of an Arabian night's entertainment: The writers of the Moorish history, though often contemporaries of the princes, whose lives they relate, may with good reason be suspected of exaggeration in their display of the wealth and atchievements of their heroes; but nevertheless, there must be some truth at the bottom, and their details cannot fail of being entertaining to every curious reader. My heart bleeds, while I tell you, that of all these glories, except the mosque, not even a ruin remains. Zehra, with

with all its delices, is erafed from the face of the earth; no one even knows where it ftood, and its very exiftence may pafs for a fable. The piety of the Chriftians in converting the mofque into a church, has preferved it from a fimilar fate.

That the wonders which have been the fubject of this letter, may obtain fome degree of probability in your eyes, I fhall haften to fketch out an exact defcription of that ancient place of worfhip.

LETTER XXXV.

Cordova, April 16, 1776.

I Did not intend fending you another letter from this city, as our plan was to have left it this morning by day-break; but there is no depending on the things of this tranfitory world, much lefs on the fkill of a Spanifh wheelwright. After waiting with impatience till he had completed the repairs of our fhattered chaife, which had been overturned the day we came from Eccija, we at laft received from him our travelling orders, and fet off in great fpirits; when, behold! directly

directly oppofite to the *Potro*, a place well known to Don Quixote's firft landlord, one of our wheels flew into fifty pieces, and brought us to the ground in the middle of the kennel: upon this, we had no choice left but of returning to our inn to pafs this day and to-morrow in the beft manner we can. I fhall employ it in writing to you what I intended fhould ferve to make a letter, to fill up part of my tedious hours in fome venta between Cordova and Madrid.

The *Potro*, our *ne plus ultra*, is nothing more than a large fountain with a paltry ftone ftatue of a *colt* on the top; when Cervantes wrote his Romance, Seville was the mart of Europe, and all the neighbouring places under the benign influence of commerce, were much more frequented and better known than at prefent; we walked on the playa of San Lucar, without feeing a fingle idle fellow, and the *compras* of Seville are now as empty as the fquare before the Potro of Cordova.

The mofque, in Spanifh called La Mefquita, from the Arabic word *mafgiad*, *a place of worfhip*, was begun by Abdoulrahman the firft, and deftined by him to remain to after-ages as a monument of his power and riches, and a principal fanctuary of his religion. His ideas were fublime, and he was fortunate enough to find an architect whofe genius was equal to the tafk of putting them in execution. He laid the foundation of
the

On the   U
of the   Za
or Sanctum   Sa

Section of the great Ile

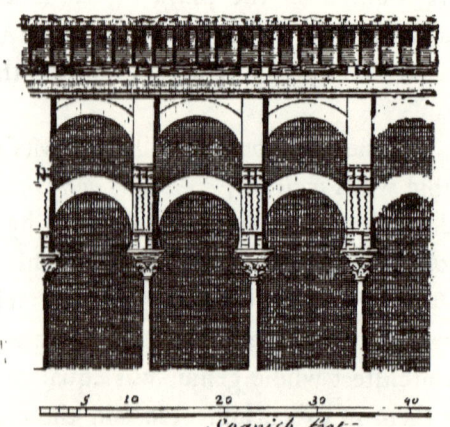

Spanish feet

A.S. del. 1776

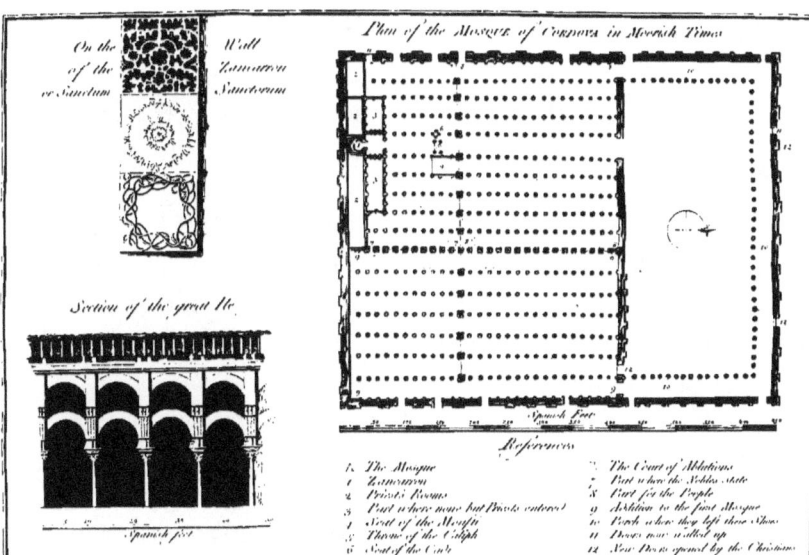

the work two years before he died: his son Hissem or Iscan finished the whole mosque about the year 800. It was more than once altered and enlarged by the Mahometans themselves, and has since undergone several changes since it became a Christian church. The greatest alteration was made in the fifteenth century, by building a cupola in the center upon Gothic arches, and scooping away part of the ancient edifice to form a large choir.

In the days of the Mussulmen, the mosque was a square building, with a flat roof upon arches, which did not rise more than thirty-five feet above the pavement. It was four hundred and twenty in breadth, and five hundred and ten in length, including the thickness of the walls. The roof was borne up by near a thousand columns according to some accounts, and by seven hundred and seventy-eight according to others, which formed nineteen iles from east to west, and twenty-nine from north to south, if we may trust to the description given by Morales, and many other historians; but I own I cannot see how there could ever have been more than seventeen, and the plans of the academy mark no more [25]. The columns were of the richest

---

[25] From my own observations, and an examination of the plans taken by the academicians, sent by the king to measure and draw this and other

richeſt marbles; the twenty-four gates were plated with bronze, emboſſed in a moſt curious manner. The principal entrance had its folding doors covered with plates of gold. Upon the higheſt cupola were three golden balls, bearing up a pomegranate and a flower de luce of the ſame precious metal. Four thouſand ſeven hundred lamps burned in the moſque every night, and conſumed in a year near twenty thouſand pounds of oil; it alſo required annually ſixty pounds of wood of aloes, and ſixty of ambergreaſe, for the perfumes.

Such is the deſcription of this famous temple left us in the writings of the Arabian and old Spaniſh authors.

I now proceed to give you a minute account of its preſent ſtate, after the notes I took down upon the ſpot with the utmoſt attention.

The ſtreets round the moſque are narrow, and ill calculated for affording a general view. But indeed there is nothing very ſhewy on the outſide. The walls are plain enough, and not very high: the roof is hid behind battlements cut into ſteps. On the eaſt

---

ancient buildings in the ſouth of Spain, I find the meaſurements given by moſt hiſtorians, who deſcribe the dimenſions of this church, to be extremely difficult to reconcile, and I believe erroneous, at leaſt not much to be depended upon; for which reaſon I have adhered to the plans above mentioned.

ſide,

side, the whole length is divided by buttresses into thirteen divisions, and about the same number on each of the other three sides. The doors opened in many of these compartments are ornamented with stucco of different colours. On the north side is a lofty belfry, a modern building, that has made a total alteration in the appearance of that front. Seventeen gates admit you into the church and cloyster. The cloyster, or court, which served the Mahometans for their ablutions, and as a place to leave their slippers in, before they entered the holy house, is an oblong square of five hundred and ten feet, (the length of the church) by two hundred and forty. A portico of sixty-two pillars environs it on three sides, about twenty-five feet wide. The middle is taken up with three handsome and copious fountains, groves of orange-trees, and some towering cypresses and palms, which form a most delightful retreat in the sultry hours. We have had occasion to experience the comforts of this shade at noon-day, when the natives being all retired to their *siesta*, we were left in full possession of this ancient fabric. Contrary to the custom of the rest of Spain, the doors are left open all day, and nobody finds fault with those that saunter about in the church out of idleness or curiosity.

Near the great gate, that leads from the cloyster into

the mofque, are three pieces of columns, each with an infcription, which vary from each other only in the name of the emperor, the reft of the words being alike in all three.

T.I. C.A.E.S.A.R. D.I.V.I. A.V.G.V.S.T.I. F.

D.I.V.I. I.V.L.I. N.E.P.O.S. A.V.G.V.S.T.V.S.

P.O.N.T.V.F.E.X. M.A.X. X.X.I. C.O.S.

V. I.M.P. T.R.I.B. P.O.T.E.S.T. X.X.X.V.I.I.

A.B. I.A.N.O. A.V.G.V.S.T.O. Q.V.I. E.S.T.

A.D. B.O.E.T.I.M. V.S.Q.V.E. A.D.

O.C.E.A.N.V.M.

L.X.I.I.I.I.

The others bear the names of Auguftus and Caius. What thefe kind of mileftones, and the Janus Auguftus were, I confefs I am not able to inform you, nor can I procure any information from Maffei's collection of infcriptions, as, inftead of explaining thefe lines, he doubts of there being any fuch exifting.

The grand entrance of the church is at the thirteenth ile from the eaft wall, which is rather wider and loftier than the reft, and the parts more decorated.

Nothing can be more ftriking than the firft ftep into this fingular, rather than beautiful edifice. To acquire fome idea of it, you muft reprefent to yourfelf a vaft gloomy labyrinth, like what the French are fo fond of

in

Part of the East Front

in their gardens, a fine *quincunx*. It is divided into seventeen iles, or *navès*, (each about twenty feet wide) by rows of columns of various marbles, viz. blue with white veins, yellow, red, red veined with white, grey, and Granadine and African green. These pillars are not all of the same height; for the Arabs having taken them from Roman buildings, served them in the same manner as the tyrant Procrustes did his guests: to the short ones they clapped on monstrous capitals, and thick bases; those that were too long for their purpose had their base chopped off, and a diminutive shallow bonnet placed on their head. However, the thickness of the shaft is pretty equal throughout, about eighteen inches diameter, and the capitals are generally barbarous imitations of those of the Corinthian order. A couple of arches, one above the other, rising from the columns, run along the rows; and from the same basis springs an arch that forms the roof of each ile.

By several alterations and additions, the Moors had divided the whole mosque into four parts, marked out by two lines of clustered pillars, crossing each other at right angles: three of these portions were allotted to the populace and the women; the fourth, in the south-east angle, was reserved for the nobility and clergy. In this last quarter was the zancarron, or holy chapel, where they deposited the books of the law. The door of of it faced the great gate, down the principal ile. The ornaments and architecture of this sanctuary, and of the throne of Almanfor, which is in front, at the diftance of fix intercolumniations from it, are very different from thofe employed in the other parts. Two ranges of columns that fupport the fcreen before this *penetrale*, are about fix feet high; the upper ones of red and white marble, the lower of green, with capitals moft minutely carved and gilt. The roof of the dark inner fanctuary is faid to be of one block of marble, eighteen feet wide: if fo, it is not only curious for its fize and quality, but alfo for the ingenuity of the architect, in placing it in fo perfect an equilibrium as to remain unfhaken fo many ages. The manner of cafting the arches, grouping the columns, and defigning the foliages of this fcreen and throne, (which is an exact repetition of it) is very heavy, intricate, and barbarous, unlike all the Moorifh architecture I faw at Granada. Indeed it is many centuries more ancient than any ornamental work at that place.

The zancarron is now the property of the duke of Alba, who has his family vault under it.

Behind this chapel, and on each fide of it, were the lodgings of the dervifhes, which now ferve for chapterhoufe, facrifty, and treafury. This church is extremely rich in plate, and has lately added to its ftore four ponderous

CHAPEL OF THE ALKORAN IN THE MOSQUE OF CORDOVA.

ponderous silver candlesticks, very nicely wrought: they were made in Cordova, and cost about eight hundred and fifty pounds sterling apiece.

It is scarce possible to ascertain the exact number of columns in the mosque, as they originally stood, because great changes have been made, many taken away, displaced, or built up in the walls of chapels, and several added when the choir was erected in the center of the whole. Were it in any other church, it would deserve great praise, for the Gothic grandeur of the plan, the loftiness of the dome, the carving of the stalls [27], and the elegance and high finishing of the arches and ornaments: but in the middle of the Moorish mosque, it destroys all unity of design, darkens the rest, and renders confused every idea of the original general effect of the building. Many chapels, stuck up in various parts between the pillars, interrupt the enfilade, and block up the passage. The worst of all, is a large chapel of the Virgin, that closes the main ile exactly in the middle; and the throne of Almansor is now occupied by a poor piece of legendary painting.

I can imagine no *coup-d'œil* more extraordinary than that taken in by the eye, when placed in such spots of the church as afford a clear reach down the iles, at right

---

[27] The stalls were carved after the designs of Cornejo of Seville. It took twelve years to finish the work, and one to put it up.

angles, uninterrupted by chapels and modern erections. Equally wonderful is the appearance, when you look from the points that give you all the rows of pillars and arches in an oblique line. It is a moſt puzzling ſcene of confuſion.

Light is admitted by the doors, and ſeveral ſmall cupolas; but neverthelefs the church is dark and awful: people walking through this chaos of pillars ſeem to anſwer the romantic ideas of magic, inchanted knights, or diſcontented wandering ſpirits.

In one of the cupolas hangs the tooth of an elephant; which, our guide told us, had formerly belonged to one of thoſe animals, that was particularly uſeful in carrying ſtones, and other materials, for building the moſque.

A very extraordinary circumſtance attending this church, which we have been thrice eye-witneſſes of, is, that when the foundlings given out to pariſh-nurſes die, they are brought into the cathedral, and laid upon a particular altar, that the chaplain may take them away to bury them. I went up to the firſt I ſaw, miſtaking it for a votive waxen ſaint, prepared for ſome ceremony; nor was I undeceived till I touched the poor little creature. The ſecond was laid down while we were there, and had all the ſymptoms of having been ſtarved to death. There are not leſs than five hundred children

loſt

loft to the population of Cordova every year in this manner, by neglect or ill treatment.

An officer took us out this afternoon to the bishop's country house down the river. The late prelate was very fond of it, and had made it a pleasant, comfortable retreat; but since his death it is become very ruinous. The revenues of the see amount to three thousand five hundred pounds sterling a year. As the bishops cannot devise by will, all they die possessed of escheates to the king.

I wish I could contrive a method of carrying you some of the fine earthen jars, called *buxaros*, which are made in Andalusiá. They are remarkably convenient for water-drinkers, as they are light, smooth, and handy: being not more than half baked, they are very porous, and the outside is kept moist by the water's filtering through: though placed in the sun, the water in the pots remains as cold as ice. The most disagreeable circumstance attending them is, that they emit a smell of earth refreshed by a sudden shower, after a long drought.

I am just informed that our wheel will require another day to be refitted; which is a terrible piece of news indeed this rainy weather; for every day the roads will grow worse and worse, and we are not able to ride about to see the environs. Were there such a thing as a book-a bookseller in this once learned city, I would buy Seneca, and try what consolation his philosophy affords in his native country.

LETTER XXXVI.

Santa Cruz, April 21, 1776.

I Write this from the Campo de Montiel, not very far from a *Lugar de cuyo nombre no quiero acordarme*[23] : Have passed over the Sierra Morena, and being now fairly entered into Don Quixote's own country, cannot resist the temptation of beginning a letter, let the end of it be written where it may so happen.

On the 18th we made our departure good from Cordova; but proceeded with fear and trembling, every moment peeping out to examine the state of our wheels, and, at each unmerciful jolt, biting our lips, and drawing up into our respective corners, to prepare for an overturn. Time gave us courage, and the anxiety passing off by degrees, we ventured to look out, and enjoy

[23] The first words in Don Quixote.

the fine vale of the Guadalquivir, which runs between two ridges of hills, covered with hanging woods and olive yards; several clear streams traverse the plain, and fall into the river. The ancient raised road, be it Roman or Moorish, was always most acceptable to us, whenever we got upon it; for it is a fine hard gravel above the level of dirt and water. Every brook had its bridge, but scarce one in twenty now remains.

At the bridge of Alcolea, where we passed to the south of the river, are kept the king's stallions. One or two of them are noble horses; but an Andalusian breeder values a horse for such points in the make, as would deter an English jockey from buying him. The former requires his horse to be forward and bulky in the shoulders, with his forelegs far back under his belly, and the tail set so low, as always to be squeezed close to his hams; he never suffers him to lie down, but keeps him constantly on a clean pavement sloping from the manger, with his forelegs close chained to the ground. You know Cordova has long been famous for its breed of horses, but it seems to be strangely fallen off; very few good looking ones are now to be met with. A gentleman of that city assured us, as indeed we had heard before, that the breed was much neglected, and little care taken to preserve it pure and genuine; the king having given the superintendence of his ftud to a ftranger, a foot officer, who perhaps never rode any thing but an afs or a mule in his life. Before this change, the employment was always held by a Cordovefe nobleman, who, as well as his friends, piqued himfelf upon breeding and exhibiting the choiceft horfes poffible; but now in difguft, they have entirely laid afide all thought or tafte for that purfuit, and feem quite indifferent about the animals they ride or drive.

For two days we travelled up the river. The country it waters is very rich and beautiful; the plains extending far and near, charmingly ftreaked with rows of olive-trees; towns and caftles near each other along the banks; the northern hills darkened with woods, and all the diftant eminences to the fouth, green with corn: this luxuriance of vegetation and fatnefs of foil, rendered the roads abominably deep; our baggage was obliged to be carried upon mules half a day to eafe the draught of the carriages. The cliffs along the river-fide fwarmed with flocks of a moft elegant water bird, called an *Abejaruxa* or Bee-eater: we fhot feveral of them, and longed much to be able to preferve them in their feathers, or to have time and opportunity to paint them for your infpection, as I am certain the fight of them would give you great pleafure. They are about the fize of a blackbird; their back is of a
light

light brown colour, shaded with burnished gold, growing more deep and ardent towards the head, ending in a pale yellow, mixed with a greenish blue about the beak, which is very long, black, sharp, and strait; a black stroke runs from the beak round the eye, which is of a bright scarlet colour; the throat is yellow; the breast, down which runs a narrow black line, is of a fine blue, that becomes lighter along the belly; the upper part of the tail is azure, the under brown; the wings of a brownish yellow, surrounded with a blue stripe, tipped with black.

At Carpio is a Moorish mill or engine, with three huge wheels, which raises water to a great height, and conveys it to enrich a large tract of level. The landscape near it is remarkably pleasing.

At Anduxar we took our leave of the Roman road, and of the river, which however we had now and then a distant peep of from the heights.

Yesterday we entered the Sierra Morena, a chain of mountains that divides Castille from Andalusiá; rendered famous by the wars of the Christians and Mahometans, but perhaps better known by being the scene where the immortal Miguel de Cervantes has placed the most entertaining adventures of his hero. As we were near the eastern extremity, the land, though very high, and commanding a vast prospect to the south,

south, did not in the least resemble a ridge of mountains, such as the Alps, the Pyreneans, or many others. It did not appear much more broken and elevated than many parts of England, which are well inhabited and cultivated.

The journey was very agreeable up the course of the Rio de las Piedras, a clear roaring torrent, tumbling over a bed of rocks, through glens of beautiful woods: the wastes are covered with a profuse variety of flowering shrubs; particularly cistus of many sorts, among which the gum-cistus or rock-rose is the handsomest: they gather manna from it in spring, by beating the bushes with small twigs, to which the viscous substance of the plant adheres. Sumach also grows in great abundance on these hills; it is cut down in August, the leaves, flower, and stalk, are all pounded together, and used in lieu of oak-bark in dressing hides.

We now entered the new Colony of La Carolina, and its dependencies, planted eight years ago by the king, in a very extensive tract of woody mountainous country. The first settlers were Germans; but from eating unwholsome herbs, and drinking too much wine and brandy, above half of them died, and now the inhabitants are the mixture of Germans, French, Savoyards, Catalans, and other Spaniards. The reach of land in cultivation, and full of houses and villages, where

where there was nothing before but forefts, the retreats of banditti, extends at leaft three leagues in length, and, I believe, very little lefs in breadth. They talk of ten thoufand families being already fettled here; but I do not fee how it is poffible there can be any thing like that number.

La Carolina, the capital of all the colonies, ftands on a fine hill that towers over the whole fettlement, and indeed over moft part of the provinces of Granada and Cordova. For the fake of thus overlooking the reft of the plantations, they have placed it in a fpot deficient in wood and water; and reduced themfelves to the neceffity of digging an incredible number of wells for the purpofes of drinking, and watering their gardens. The whole town is new from the foundations, for there was not a cottage there eight years ago, the ftreets are wide, and drawn in ftrait lines, but the ground is not fufficiently levelled; the houfes are upon an uniform plan, without the leaft decoration: the church fronts the principal fouth road; and a tower placed at each angle marks the extent of the town, which is to be an exact fquare: the market place and another fquare, are very fpacious and fhewy. All the flat on the crown of the hill before the town is laid out in kitchen gardens, and planted with avenues of elms, which are to ferve hereafter for public walks.

I never

I never saw a scene more pleasing to the eye, or more satisfactory to the mind of every person that feels himself interested in the welfare of his fellow-creatures: his humanity must exult at the probability of their lot being so much ameliorated: for my part, I enjoyed the most agreeable sensations at the sight of this absolute creation, this new world risen out of the very heart of desolation and solitude; every thing seems so alive, so green, neat and thriving; in a word, so unlike the rest of this unactive kingdom. About a year ago, the department or district of the town of La Carolina, contained near eight thousand souls, but I was not able to obtain any exact information of the extent comprized under that denomination; three hundred Catalan manufacturers came to settle here in the course of last year: cloth and other manufactures seem to go on briskly; but I fear there is an inconstancy, a languor in the pursuit of projects, inherent in the very essence of the Spanish government, that will greatly retard the further progress of this colony; in the beginning, they spare neither pains nor expence to carry on a scheme, as may be seen here, where it is astonishing to behold how much has been done in a very short space of time. Our master muleteer, who had never been here since the Miquelets were sent to scour the country, and destroy the gang of robbers, that harboured hereabouts, could

could scarce believe his eyes, and did nothing but raise his hands to heaven and cross himself, as if he had got into a land of witches. It was no small enhancement of the merit of the place, to find an excellent inn and good dinner, and to regale ourselves upon excellent cow's milk and butter, to which we had been long strangers; for though they have cows in many parts of Spain, they seldom milk them, but keep them for breeding, and fattening in their old days for slaughter.

Now I have shewn you the fair side of La Carolina, I cannot, as a just and impartial correspondent, avoid informing you of the vices of its constitution, the defects in its establishment and direction, with the reasons I have for suspecting it will fall off every year, 'till it dwindles away to a petty Spanish town, just kept alive by the monies spent at the inns by muleteers and passengers.

The foreigners complain, with what justice I know not, of not having been treated with the indulgence and tenderness an infant colony requires; if any of them expressed discontent, or seemed desirous of returning to his native country, he was instantly secured, and chastised by a long and severe imprisonment. Many families were two or three years before their allotments were made out, during which time they were obliged to work gratis for the other settlers; unmarried people were allowed no share of land, but employed as servants to the rest; when the poor Alsacians or Savoyards had the good fortune to be placed upon a rich patch of soil, and had brought it into tolerable condition, they were frequently ousted by the governor, their habitation transferred to a Spanish family, and themselves sent to improve a more bleak and barren part of the hills. The king gives all new-comers one year's seed corn, two cows, ten goats, some implements of husbandry, and some houshold stuff, which is generally infinitely worse than his majesty intends it should be: he pays them a stipend for their maintenance for the first three years. Some few foreigners, having numerous families grown up, thrive and improve in their circumstances, but the rest will in all probability leave the country as soon as the time of their contract expires, provided they be allowed to remove. The Spaniards have gradually got possession of the best plantations, and the town of Carolina has scarce any other inhabitants. The worst of all is, that there seems to be no outlet from this settlement, in case their manufactures should arrive at any degree of perfection, for it is on every side extremely remote from the sea, and many days journey by land from the great cities of Spain, where the consumption of their commodities

might

might be expected to turn to any confiderable account.

A little north of Carolina, we paffed through a new village called Las Navas de Tolofa, from the old name of the defile in the neighbouring mountains; where, in 1212, Alfonfo the ninth, king of Caftille, Peter the fecond, of Aragon, and Sancho the feventh, of Navarre, with their joint forces, attacked and cut to pieces the army of Mahomet, king of Morocco. Hiftorians gravely tell us, that there fell no lefs than two hundred thoufand Moors, more than half their army, with the lofs of only twenty-five Chriftians. In a letter faid to have been written by Alfonfo to the Pope, this lift of the flain is given. I always thought it a moft extraordinary ftory, but now that I have feen the field of battle, I look upon it to be full as wonderful how three hundred and fifty thoufand Moors, without reckoning the Spanifh forces, could contrive to fqueeze themfelves into fuch a heap of mountains jumbled together, where you could not find twenty yards of level ground for fome miles round the fpot.

The evening was very fine, and the hills fteep, which induced us to walk moft part of the way. Having got a good diftance before the carriages, among fome woody dells, we began to be in great hopes and conftant expectation of fome *Cardenio* or *Dorothea* bolting out upon us. While we were amufing ourfelves with fuch Quixotic reveries, the found of a guitar fuddenly ftruck our ears. At a turn of the road, clofe by the fide of a fweet murmuring brook, we met with about a dozen well dreffed men, and as many fmart, handfome damfels, dancing upon a platform of large level ftones. The females that were not bufy dancing, were feated under fine hanging woods, on a natural amphitheatre of rocks. The principal men came very politely up to us, and invited us to partake of their fport, while a very pretty girl prefented us with fweetmeats and fugar-plumbs. A jolly friar feemed to do the honours of this *fête champêtre*, and to have the privilege of throwing his handkerchief at which of the fultanas he pleafed; for they all courted his fmiles and careffes. We ftayed fome time with this merry crew, who danced feveral fequidillas, and fang feveral fongs at our requeft. They preffed us much to go back up the hill, and pafs the night with them at the houfe they belonged to, where they intended to be very frolicfome: but as it began to rain, we declined the kind offer, and parted with our new friends, whofe mufic and jovial fhouts we had the pleafure to hear re-echoed by the rocks, almoft during our whole walk up to our inn at Miranda.

This morning, the heavieft of our trunks being put
upon

upon mules, to lighten the chaifes, we croffed the Sierra Morena, at the pafs called *El Puerto del Rey*. The road is far from bad, though fteep; but the mountain is as dreary and difagreeable as any thing can well be. The heavy rain did not render us more indulgent to its ill-favoured afpect. In Cervantes's days, there were perhaps noble woods to cover all this nakednefs, as here and there fome venerable pines and chefnut-trees remain, fad monuments of ancient forefts.

All the Mancha before us feems to be a bare corn-country, ugly and tedious beyond expreffion. For my part, unlefs it be to look out at a venta, or peep about for an adventure at the meeting of the crofs-roads, I intend fleeping all the way to Madrid.

LETTER XXXVII.

Madrid, April 27, 1776.

WE perceived a very fevere alteration in the climate as foon as we defcended the Sierra Morena, and entered the Mancha: from the beginning of fummer we were in a manner thrown back to the laft months

months of winter. In Andaluſiá, the vines were all in leaf, and their fruit ſet; the flowers of the ſhrubs falling off to make way for the ſeed. On the northern ſide of the mountains ſcarce a freſh leaf was to be ſeen, or a bud in the vineyards; the poor ſtarved buſhes, with juſt a flower or two blown; the weather cold and raw: in a word, it is difficult to conceive ſo ſudden and ſo thorough a change of ſeaſons as that which we experienced in this journey.

The Mancha is an immenſe plain, interſected by different ridges of low hills and rocks: not an incloſure of any kind, except mud-walls about the villages: and really I can almoſt ſay, there is not a tree to be ſeen from the Sierra Morena to Toledo, nor from the banks of the Tagus to Madrid: a few dwarfiſh evergreen oaks, huddled together in nooks of hills, and ſome ſtumpy olive-plants, ſcarce deſerve the name of trees. All this vaſt tract of open country is cultivated in corn or vines: there cannot be an uglier. The villages are large; few or no ſingle houſes; and not a *venta* that I could fix upon for the ſcene of any action in Don Quixote. We lay at Puertolapiche, a ſmall village mentioned by Cervantes; but I think he omits telling us what adventure was atchieved there. In ſhort, with all the helps of imagination, and reading the book all the way, the country did not raiſe one agreeable idea, nor tempt me to take
a ſingle

a single sketch of any part of it. The houses are built with mud and gravel. The women cover their heads with coloured handkerchiefs, and their necks with laced palatines.

Val de Peñas produces a very pleasant red wine, the most drinkable, for common use, of any in Spain. The provision of wine for the king is kept in hogsheads; the remainder of the vintage in skins. The best wine sells at the rate of twenty reals the arroba.

The badness of the weather hindered us from riding a few miles out of the road to visit *Los Ojos dela Guadiana*, where that river, after running eight leagues under ground, rises up to day, and thence takes its course towards Estremadura. We passed over the subterraneous river at the Venta de Quesada, where the well in the yard communicates with it. Straw, or any kind of light stuff, dropped into the well, is hurried away with such rapidity by the stream, that you will not bring up a single straw, though you let down the bucket almost instantaneously. The incurious Spaniards have made so few experiments upon this phenomenon, that we could procure no further intelligence on this head. The Manchegos have a pretty song about these eyes of the Guadiana, which, however, they declare to be much less wonderful than those of their mistress. At Consuegra, a most beautiful gipsy girl, with the sweetest eyes in the

the world, sung it to us, and danced sequidillas to the tune with admirable agility and expression. She was quite *Preciosa the little gipsy*, with her soft voice and affected lisp. It is a pity her beauty was much impaired by her mode of dressing, which gave her a most prominent belly, a defect few Spanish women are free from, and a flat low breast, which they esteem a great perfection in a lady's shape.

Toledo is the strangest city you can imagine in point of situation; something like Durham, or Richmond in Yorkshire, but not equal to either in beauty, as it is totally bare of wood.

The Tagus, after winding at large through a fine plain, which a little more wood would render very agreeable to the eye, comes at last to be wedged in between two ramparts of high steep rocks: the passage is very narrow, and before the river gets out again into a broad bed and open ground, it almost returns to the place where it entered the defile. On this rocky peninsula stands the city, exceedingly ill built, poor, and ugly. The streets are so steep, that no stranger in his sober senses would venture up or down them in a carriage.

The Alcazar, or ancient palace, which was burnt down by the allied army in the beginning of the century, is placed on the highest point of all. It is a noble

noble extensive building, and has just undergone a thorough repair, at the expence of the archbishop, who has fortunately taken a turn towards employing some portion of his great revenues in works of public utility, such as this palace, a new road to Aranjuez, and a street in the town [19]. It is supposed that the Alcazar will be converted into an hospital or orphan-house. The architecture is chaste and unaffected; the inner court is very grand; its colonnade of granite columns, of the Corinthian order, makes a noble appearance; the chapel is lofty and narrow, which renders it convenient to attend divine service, as there is a balcony in each story of the house that leads into it. The stables are under the kitchens and offices, and are large enough to contain a very considerable number of horses. The garret story is one open gallery for playing in, above

[19] The see of Toledo is said to be worth four hundred thousand ducats a year; but there are large deductions to be made. Besides the proportion the infant Don Lewis receives, and pensions to different people, it pays annually fifteen thousand ducats to the monks of the Escurial, notwithstanding Philip the second granted to them no less than thirty villages in their neighbourhood. The Spanish court finds many ways of lessening the revenues of the church, by pensions, donations to hospitals, charitable foundations, and premiums to the societies of agriculture. There is not a bishopric in the kingdom but has somebody or other quartered upon it; and I believe the second-rate benefices are in the same predicament. Out of the rich canonries and prebends are taken the pensions of the new order of knights of Carlos tercero.

eighty yards in length. In the middle ſtories are ſeveral large halls, the moſt ſpacious of which meaſures about one hundred and ſixty feet by thirty-ſix.

The cathedral has nothing particularly beautiful on the outſide above the common run of Gothic churches: it is not to be compared with many we have in England. The ſteeple is in the ugly ſtyle of the Flemiſh and German ſpires, a heap of blue turrets piled one upon another. The inſide is well lighted and chearful, neither heavy, nor confuſed with too many ornaments: the decorations added of late years are not in the beſt of taſtes, but in richneſs of gilding without a competitor. The wealth of the archbiſhop and chapter diſplays itſelf in the profuſion of gold laviſhed on the walls; they have gilded the iron rails, the Gothic arches, and even drawn lines of gold to mark the joints of the ſtones with which the pillars of the choir are built.

The group of angels, called *El tranſparente*, which is fixed behind the choir, and eſteemed by the Toledans the glory of their church, is at beſt but a clumſy, ill-deſigned monument, remarkable for nothing but the fineneſs of the marble and other materials.

One of the greateſt vexations a curious perſon experiences in travelling through Spain, is the ſcarcity, the non-exiſtence of tolerable *Ciceroni*; thoſe you meet with are generally coblers, who throw a brown cloak

over

over their ragged apparel, and conduct you to a church or two, where they cannot give you the least satisfactory information concerning its antiquities or curiosities. This is literally the case at Toledo: but to make amends, they lead you to a hole in a pillar, where the host was hidden all the time that the Saracens were in possession of the city, though the whole fabric has been built from the ground since the expulsion of the Moors; for Saint Ferdinand laid the first stone of the present church in 1226. They also shew you the stone on which the Virgin Mary stood, when she came to pay a visit to Saint Ildephonsus, and which is worn through by the fingers of the pilgrims. Ask them any thing about the Mosarabic chapel, and what is done there, they will tell you, as they did us, that mass is said there in Greek. That you may not accuse me of being as barren of instruction as our conductors, I shall put together the chief points wherein the [30] Mosarabic rite differs from that of the Roman missal. The former liturgy was constantly used by the church of Spain, down to the pontificate of Gregory the seventh, in the eleventh century: it had been confirmed by several Spanish councils, commented upon and illustrated by Saint Isidore of Seville: but the policy of the court of

---

[30] The Mosarabic rite is so called from its having been observed by the Christians that remained in the provinces conquered by the Arabians.

Rome, and its influence over the mind of Alphonfus the fixth, who had lately conquered Toledo, overcame the obftinate attachment of the Spanifh clergy. Notwithftanding the prowefs of the Mofarabic champion, who came off victorious in the fight (for it was agreed to try the merits of the two liturgies by fingle conibat) notwithftanding the flames were not more indulgent to the Roman than to the Gothic ritual, when, in hopes of a decifive miracle, the two books were thrown into the fire before the king, notwithftanding the clamours raifed by the natives, the ancient rite was abrogated in the greater part of the kingdom. It fubfifted in fix parifhes of Toledo as late as the fifteenth century, but is now reftrained to the fingle chapel of St. Euftatiá, in the cathedral, where Cardinal Ximenes, unwilling that his church fhould lofe all remembrance of its ancient forms, made a foundation for thirteen priefts and three clerks, who officiate every morning according to the Mofarabic manner.

In effentials this ritual agrees perfectly with Rome, but in many outward forms differs widely. I fufpect it varied much more in its original ftate; for it is hardly credible the difpute could have been fo obftinately maintained for fuch trifling deviations as what now fubfift. But indeed that would not amount to an undeniable proof; we know that the church has always

looked

looked upon the refiftance to its authority to be of more confequence than the difference in outward ceremonies.

The prayers before mafs are not the fame; not always the fame portions of fcripture read on the fame feftivals. In the Roman miffal are two leffons, one from the Old Teftament or the Epiftles, and one from the Gofpels : the Mofarabic gives three, one from the Old Teftament, another from the Epiftles, and a third from the Gofpels. The Romans fay the creed before the offertory, the others after the confecration.

Toledo has lain in the route of moft of thofe travellers that have written on Spain ; and in them you will find ample accounts of every thing remarkable. As I hate repetitions, and would willingly avoid them whenever it is poffible, give me leave to refer you to the works of thofe gentlemen. One circumftance only I cannot refufe myfelf the fatisfaction of acquainting you with, though I make no doubt but it is an anecdote to be met with in twenty books of travels. In the convent of St. Francis, founded by Ferdinand and Ifabella, the firft novice received was Ximenes, who, in the courfe of the fame reign, rofe to be cardinal, archbifhop of Toledo, and prime minifter of Spain. His hiftory, as well as that of Don Juan de Padilla, have lately acquired redoubled luftre from the pen of Dr. Robertfon ; in whofe

admirable

admirable life of Charles the fifth is to be found every neceffary information relative to the revolt of Toledo.

From the ancient capital of New Caftille to within half a league of Madrid, the prefent feat of government, the roads are as bad as in any part of the kingdom, and the country extremely ugly. I do not imagine the moft pitiful city in the peninfula can cut a more defpicable figure than this metropolis of all the Spains does from the oppofite hills, as you approach it on the fouth fide; neither tree, villa, nor garden, until you arrive at the avenues of the town; the corn-fields run up clofe to the houfes; in fhort, the whole landfcape round you is the bareft and moft melancholy I ever beheld: but as foon as the trees of the walks fhut out the profpect of the neighbouring country, the appearance of Madrid is grand and lively; noble ftreets, good houfes, and excellent pavement, as clean as it once was dirty.

The court is abfent from Madrid, fo that our ftay here will be no longer than will be fufficient to reft ourfelves, and get our things put in order for our appearance at Aranjuez.

LETTER XXXVIII.

Aranjuez, May 3d, 1776.

THIS place is twenty miles from Madrid; the road to it extremely fine; but the trees planted on each fide are as yet too young to fhut out the abominable country it paffes through. The prefent king made it at the vaft expence of one hundred and thirty thoufand pounds fterling. The new bridge over the Xarama, at the defcent into the plain, is very long and grand.

Aranjuez has great beauties, and would pleafe you much; for here are numberlefs avenues of aged elms on a perfect level; green banks to reft upon, near a fine meandring river; fountains and fhady groves; plenty of milk and butter, and vegetables in great perfection.

The fituation of this place renders it one of the moft agreeable refidences I know belonging to a fovereign prince. It ftands in a very large plain, furrounded with bare hills, which to be fure, are exceffively ugly; but they feldom appear, being very well hidden by the noble rows of trees that extend acrofs the flat in every direction. The compartments between the avenues are
railed

railed off, and laid down in pasture and meadow, for the supply of the large dairy of cows established here by the present king. That part of the vale which stretches out towards the cast is left in a ruder state, and, except some few fields of corn, is mostly forest-land, through which the Tagus winds in a deep shady bed. The walks and rides along the banks, through the venerable groves, and under the majestic elms that overhang the roads, are luxuries unknown to the rest of Spain. The beauties of the scenery are enhanced by the flocks of many-coloured birds that flutter and sing on the boughs, by the herds of deer, which amount to no less than seven thousand head, and by the droves of buffaloes, sheep, cows, and brood mares, that wander uncontrouled through all these woods. The wild boars are frequently seen in the evenings in the streets of the town.

The finest avenue, called the *Calle dela Reyna*, is three miles long, quite strait from the palace gate, crossing the Tagus twice before it loses itself in the thickets, where some noble spreading elms and weeping poplars hang beautifully over the deep still pool. Near this road is a flower-garden for the spring, laid out with great taste by Mr. Wall during his ministry. The gay variety of flowers at this time of year is particularly pleasing to the eye; but its beauty soon fades on the approach of summer. As the weather grows hot, the company that chooses to walk retires to a garden in an island of the Tagus, on the north side of the palace. This is an heavenly place, cut into various walks and circular lawns, which in their primitive state may have been very stiff and formal; but in the course of a century, Nature has obliterated the regular forms of art; the trees have swelled out beyond the line traced for them, and destroyed the enfilade, by advancing into the walks, or retiring from them. The sweet flowering shrubs, instead of being clipped and kept down, have been allowed to shoot up into trees, and hang over the statues and fountains they were originally meant to serve as humble fences to. The jet-d'eaus dash up among the trees, and add fresh verdure to the leaves. The terraces and balustrades built along the river, are now overgrown with roses, and other luxuriant bushes, hanging down into the stream, which is darkened by the large trees growing on the opposite banks. Many of the statues, groupes, and fountains, are handsome, some masterly, the works of Algardi: all are placed in charming points of view, either in open circular spots, at a distance from the trees, or else in gloomy arbours, and retired angles of the wood.

The west front of the palace is handsome: two new wings, which are to be brought out from the main body,

body, will increase its bulk, but, I am afraid, will not add much to its beauty. The first part of the building was erected by Philip the second, who purchased the estate, planted many of the avenues, and, in order to extend his chace, or to indulge his splenetic disposition, had all the vines that grew on the hills rooted up. By that means he drove away the inhabitants, and rendered the environs of his villa a perfect desart. These hills are full of springs, that throw up large quantities of a strong purgative salt.

The apartments are good, but contain no great number of paintings or statues. There is an Annunciation in the chapel, by Titian, and Mengs has painted some holy subjects in the bed-chamber, and an allegorical piece of Time and Pleasure, in the ceiling of the theatre. In a Franciscan church lately finished, the picture of San Pasqual, by the same hand, is much admired.

The town or village formerly consisted of the palace, its offices, and a few miserable huts, where the embassadors, and the attendants of the court, endeavoured to lodge themselves, as well as they could, but always very uncomfortably; many of the habitations were vaults half under ground. What determined the king to build a new town, and to embellish the environs, was an accident that happened at the nuncio's; a coach broke

Palace of ARANJUEZ

broke through the ceiling of his dining-room, and fell in upon the table. The court then began to apply very confiderable fums to the purpofe of erecting proper dwellings, for the great number of perfons that flock to the place where the fovereign refides; near ten thoufand are fuppofed to live here two or three months in fpring; the king keeps one hundred and fifteen fets of mules, which require a legion of men to take care of them. Half a million fterling has been laid out at Aranjuez, fince the year 1763; and it muft be acknowledged, that wonders have been performed; feveral fine ftreets drawn in ftrait lines with broad pavements, a double row of trees before the houfes, and a very noble road in the middle; commodious hotels for the minifters and embaffadors; great fquares, markets, churches, a theatre, and an amphitheatre for bull feafts, have been raifed from the ground. Neatnefs and convenience have been more ftudied and fought for than fhew in the architecture, but altogether the place has fomething truly magnificient in the coup-d'œil.

This afternoon we had a very pretty entertainment on the river. The prince of Afturias, and his attendants, embarked in a galley richly decorated, preceded and followed by other fmaller barges, adorned in a lefs fplendid, though ftill a very gay manner. They rowed from his banqueting-houfe up into the woods, where the meandrings of the river are exceedingly beautiful, forming fine sweeps and reaches with green banks, shaded by aged trees that hang in various clumps over the stream. Crowds of holiday-folks in their best apparel, lined both sides of the Tagus, and were no small addition to the rural shew.

The pleasures of Aranjuez are walking or riding in the morning, going to court, dining at some of the open tables kept by the great officers of state, a game at cards, a drive along the avenue, and the Italian opera. The ministers are quite easy in their behaviour, and their houses free from ceremony and restraint; that of the prime minister, the marquis Grimaldi, is superlatively so: he keeps an open house, where we are always sure of meeting with a numerous company, cards, and conversation; the master of it is always glad to see us, and shew us every civility the place admits of: I am afraid we do not attend as much perhaps as we are in gratitude bound; for there are so many temptations at our own embassador's, that it is with difficulty we can bring ourselves to sacrifice the pleasures we find at his house to the duties imposed upon us by society. The easy frankness, affability, and friendship, with which Lord G. treats us, make us loath to waste elsewhere the hours we can pass so agreeably under his roof.

LETTER

LETTER XXXIX.

Aranjuez, May 6, 1776.

WE have juſt finiſhed our round of preſentations, which in ſo numerous a royal family, is a work of more days than one; as I know you expect a minute account of each of thoſe that compoſe it, I am ſorry I am incapable of ſatisfying your curioſity, in as ample a manner as I could wiſh; you ſhall have a deſcription of their perſons, and as much of their characters, as I have learned from well-informed people, in whoſe judgment I can confide. I beg you will conſider how hard it is to diſcern the true character of the great, as your intelligence can only flow to you through the ſuſpicious channel of many jarring paſſions and intereſts. It is impoſſible for a ſtranger to ſeize a good likeneſs in ſo ſhort a time, and to tranſmit to others a faithful repreſentation, of a prince, that does not admit him to a familiar intercourſe. I don't know but ſovereigns are the moſt difficult characters to define in a whole nation; for all princes appear pretty nearly alike; their mode of life is uniform; by ſeeing none but inferiors about them, they acquire a great indifference in their

manner

manner, and seldom betray in their countenance any of those strong emotions that mark the various feelings of men obliged to bustle through the world; their passions lack the relish which arises from delays and difficulties; what the French call *Ennui*, wearisomeness, is, methinks, the grand malady of princes, and therefore amusement is their main pursuit in life. In the princes of the House of Bourbon, the passion of fowling predominates; yet in the Spanish royal family, there are some who toil at the gun with more reluctance than the farmer's boy does at the plough; have a taste for arts and sciences, and wish for nothing more than to be freed from the obligation of following the diversion.

The ceremony of presentation is performed as the king rises from table. Charles the third is a much better looking man than most of his pictures make him; he has a good-natured laughing eye; the lower part of his face, by being exposed to all weather, is become of a deep copper colour; what his hat covers, is fair, as he naturally has a good skin; in stature he is rather short, thickly built about the legs and thighs, and narrow in the shoulders. His dress seldom varies from a large hat, a plain grey Segovia frock, a buff waistcoat, a small dagger, black breeches, and worsted stockings; his pockets are always stuffed with knives, gloves, and shooting tackle. On Gala days, a fine suit is hung upon his shoulders,

shoulders, but as he has an eye to his afternoon sport, and is a great œconomist of his time, the black breeches are worn to all coats. I believe there are but three days in the whole year that he spends without going out a shooting, and those are noted with the blackest mark in the calendar; were they to occur often, his health would be in danger, and an accident that was to confine him to the house, would infallibly bring on a fit of illness. No storm, heat, cold, or wet, can keep him at home; and when he hears of a wolf being seen, distance is counted for nothing; he would drive over half the kingdom rather than miss an opportunity of firing upon that favorite game. Besides a most numerous retinue of persons belonging to the hunting establishment, several times a year all the idle fellows in and about Madrid, are hired to beat the country, and drive the wild boars, deer, and hares, into a ring, where they pass before the royal family. A very large annual sum is distributed among the proprietors of land about the capital, and near the country palaces, by way of indemnification for the damage done to the corn. I was assured that it costs seventy thousand pounds sterling for the environs of Madrid, and thirty thousand for those of Saint Ildefonso. In order to be entitled to this reimbursement, the farmers scatter just as much seed-corn over their grounds, as will grow up into something like a crop;

but

but they do not always give themselves the trouble of getting in the scanty harvest, being sufficiently paid for their labour by the royal bounty.

Being naturally of an even phlegmatic temper, the king is sure to see events on their favorable side only; and whenever he has determined in his own mind that a measure is proper to be pursued, he is an utter enemy to alteration. As far as I can judge, by comparing the different accounts I have had, he is a man of the strictest probity, incapable of adopting any scheme, unless he is perfectly satisfied in his conscience that it is just and honourable; of such immoveable features, that the most fortunate or the most disastrous occurrences are alike unable to create the smallest variation in them: rigid in his morals, and strenuously attached to his religion; but he does not suffer his devotion to lay him open to the enterprizes of the court of Rome, or the encroachments of his own clergy; on the contrary, they have frequently met with rougher usage at his hands than they might have expected from a free-thinker. The regularity of his own life renders him very strict about the conduct of his children, whom he obliges to be out fishing or shooting as long as he is absent on the same business; this he does to prevent their having time or opportunity to harbour bad thoughts; and truly I believe he goes out so constantly himself, in order to

keep

keep down the vigour of his own conſtitution. He seldom addreſſes himſelf to any young men of his court; but delights in converſing and joking with elderly perſons, and ſuch as are of his own age, eſpecially monks and friars. He is very partial to Naples, and always ſpeaks of that country with great feeling.

Since his acceſſion, many great works have been completed; noble roads made to all the palaces round the metropolis; ſeveral others undertaken in more remote provinces: he has finiſhed the palace at Madrid, and added conſiderably to thoſe of the Pardo and Aranjuez; built new towns at Aranjuez, the Eſcurial, and Saint Ildefonſo; and planted a great deal at Aranjuez. The marquis of Grimaldi has the merit of having ſuggeſted and conducted moſt of theſe improvements, and of having urged on the king, who, although he has naturally no great reliſh for the arts, thinks it the duty of a ſovereign to encourage them.

The prince of Aſturias is of an athletic make, his countenance rather ſevere, and his voice harſh. He ſeemed in a great hurry to get away from us; but the princeſs ſtayed chatting a great while. She is not handſome, being very ſickly, but ſeems lively, and genteely ſhaped, with a very fine hand and arm. If ſhe lives to be queen, I dare ſay ſhe will render this court a very gay one; for ſhe appears to like to go abroad, and converſe

verse with strangers. When she walks out, all persons that have been presented, and chance to be in the way, are expected to join her company, and escort her as long as she thinks proper. Her mildness and good-nature have softened much of her husband's roughness of manner; and of late he seems to have more pleasure in sitting with her in a domestic way, than in trudging over the heath in quest of game.

Don Gabriel is a tall well-looking man, but timid to excess. He possesses many talents, but his constant avocations out of doors prevent his applying to study as much as he could wish. I have seen some good pictures done by him with the flock of cloth, and have heard much of his classical learning, and turn for mathematics.

Don Antonio appears to be very well pleased with the active life of a sportsman.

The Infanta Maria Josepha has reason to envy every country wench she sees roaming at liberty; for confinement, etiquette, and celibacy, are likely to be her lot during life.

Don Lewis, the king's brother, after having been a cardinal and an archbishop, is now on the eve of matrimony with a pretty Arragonese girl, whom he took a fancy to last year, as she was running across the fields after a butterfly. As he has made a collection of natural

ral hiftory, this fimilarity of tafte made a great impreffion upon him. This wedding, which the king has confented to with reluctance, has produced a total revolution in the marriage-laws of Spain. A new pragmatica or edict is publifhed, to prevent all matches betwixt perfons of unequal rank and quality; by this decree, the old cuftom is abrogated. Heretofore it was out of the power of parents to hinder their children from marrying whom they liked, and the church interpofed to oblige them to make a fuitable fettlement upon the young couple.

Don Lewis's bride is not to be allowed the title or rank of a princefs of the blood, nor are her children to be deemed qualified to fucceed to the crown; he is to refide near Talavera, where I make no doubt but he will lead a happy life, as he has a great tafte for mufic and natural hiftory; his cabinet already contains a very valuable collection of rarities, efpecially fuch as are found in the Spanifh dominions. This prince is chearful, humane, affable, and full of pleafantry; good qualities that render him the darling of the nation.

The king and all the males of his family wear the enfigns of a great variety of military orders. On their left breaft is a row of ftars like the belt of the conftellation of Orion: they are alfo decorated with the blue ribband of the French order of the Holy Ghoft, and the infignia of the Burgundian golden fleece. They have befides the Neapolitan red fafh of Saint Januarius, the red croffes of Calatrava, founded in 1158, of Saint Iago, dating from 1175, and of Montefa, inftituted in 1317, and the green crofs of Alcantara, invented in 1176. After all thefe badges, comes the blue and white ribband of the Conception or Carlos tercero, eftablifhed by the prefent king, on the birth of the late fon of the prince of Afturias.

LETTER XL.

Aranjuez, May 28, 1776.

IN the courfe of laft week, we faw the king's ftallions, fome of which are beautiful creatures. Before I came into Spain, I thought handfome horfes were to be met with in every part of the kingdom, but to my great furprize, found them very rare in all the provinces; fo little attention has there been paid to the breed of that generous animal, formerly the boaft of Spain.

At Villamejor, a few miles from hence down the Tagus,

Tagus, his majesty has a stable of a less noble, but not less useful race of stallions, that of Jack-asses. These beasts are of a shape and size you can have no idea of: they are fourteen hands high, and have such monstrous large heads, thick legs, and rough coats of long hair over their whole body, that scarce a trace remains of the figure of an animal. They say these *Garañones*, as the Spaniards term them, are extremely furious in the covering season; I am sure at present, they are the most stupid of their dull species. Each ass covers twenty mares, and costs near thirty thousand reals, about two hundred and eighty pounds sterling. They are bred in the mancha.

The way to Villamejor lies along the vale through a considerable new farm, called the *Campo flamenco*, lately taken in by the marquis Grimaldi, and laid out in a grand scale. On an eminence stands the farm house, with large rooms for the royal family to take a hunter's repast in. The road up to it is a shewy, royal work, but might have been spared had the building been erected a little lower, or had it been intended for the reception of none but common husbandmen.

In our return in the evening we overtook the bulls intended for the next day's feast or fight. They appeared very peaceable and tractable. Whatever may be said of their ferocity, when irritated in the *arena* by darts, fire, and lances, I am apt to think they can never

ver be so terrible or dangerous as our vicious bulls in England. Those I have seen wanted size and weight, and did not appear to me to have any real fury in their nature, 'till it is raised by repeated provocations, and the desultory attacks of so many adversaries. To bring them quietly along the roads from their pasture, the drovers employ certain white oxen, trained up to be decoys; these go along with the bulls, 'till they lead them into the stables under the amphitheatre.

I have now been a spectator of several *Fiestas de Toros*, but cannot bring myself to have any relish for the diversion. Whatever they may have been in former times, they are certainly but a poor exhibition at present, though the crowds of people assembled in a circle, and agitated in a most tumultuous manner, must be allowed to be an interesting and curious spectacle. None of the royal family ever appear at these favorite amusements of the Spanish nation: the nobility no longer pique themselves upon their strength, courage, or dexterity, in these rough exercises; and the fair condescend to yield up their hearts and persons to lovers that have given no proofs of their prowess, but in combats of a softer nature: the consequence is, a total want of emulation: no gentleman cares to hazard his life in a trial of skill that promises no advantage to him of any kind. The shew is conducted with great œconomy and niggardliness; none but the worst of horses are bought for the

the day; and the mercenary gladiators no longer ſtudy the moſt dexterous, but the moſt ſecure way of deſtroying the bulls, being allowed ſo much a head for each beaſt they ſlaughter. The money paid for boxes and ſeats, is appropriated to the building or endowing of ſome hoſpital.

The coup-d'œil of the amphitheatre, filled with ſo many ſpectators of all ranks, is very ſtriking. They are ſo very noiſy and impatient till the ſhew begins, and in ſuch violent commotion while it laſts, that one is kept in perpetual alarm and flurry of ſpirits for the firſt or ſecond time of aſſiſting at this diverſion. Contrary to the cuſtom of the ancient Romans, who placed the ſenators next to the *podium*, the nobility ſit here in wooden galleries and boxes, the mob on benches below, next the arena. A row of ſoldiers, behind the circular parapet wall, or paliſado, hold out halberts and bayonets, to keep the beaſts within the liſts: but it ſometimes happens that a bull, while yet in full vigour, will take a run, and leap over into the crowd on the benches. The confuſion it creates is very great; but as the bull is itſelf hampered and diſabled by the ſeats and woodwork, it can do but little miſchief before it is diſpatched [31].

The

[31] In ſome of the liſts delivered out with an account of an approaching bull-feaſt, notice is given, that people are permitted to flap their hats in the ſun. Since the revolt of Madrid (when all hats were ordered to be worn

The common method of conducting a bull-feast is as follows: One or two *Toriadors*, dressed in rich jackets, broad-brimmed hats, and breeches and boots made of a tough, impenetrable leather, and holding under their right arm a long ashen lance (tipped with a broad shallow-pointed head, that can only enter skin-deep) parade on horseback round the lists, and pay their devoirs to the governor of the place. They then retire to their post, almost in front of a large door, which is opened to let out the bull. The fellow that opens it takes care to climb up immediately into the gallery; for it is not unusual for the bulls to stop short as soon as they get out, and make a home-thrust at the porter: some rush forth with the utmost impetuosity, and run directly at the horsemen; others gaze around, and take their measures with more circumspection.

The cavalier presents the head of his horse to the bull, and with the lance, which cuts along its shoulders, pushes it away to the right, at the same time bearing off his horse to the left: his antagonist is driven out of the line by the violence of the thrust, and its horns pass behind, without hurting either horse or rider. When the man is mounted on a nimble, spirited,

worn cocked up, wherever the court resides) the common hangman is commanded to wear his slouched, that others may not be tempted to let theirs down, for fear of being mistaken for him.

and

and docile fteed, there is no difficulty in this evolution, as the motions of both animals coincide in giving additional force to the well-directed ftroke: but if the horfe is numb or refractory, the bull is likely to ftrike him in the flank, and throw both horfe and cavalier to the ground.

There is another way of attacking, with a kind of forked dagger. The horfeman ftands clofe by the door, and as the bull fprings forward into the lifts, he plants the weapon in the back of its neck, and kills it on the fpot. Should he mifs his aim, there is fcarce a poffibility of his efcaping from the enraged animal; for which reafon this mode of combat is feldom practifed.

To take off the bull's attention, and to make fport, feveral nimble fellows on foot run about and tofs darts with curled paper tied to them, which, fticking in the head and fhoulders, drive the poor creature to madnefs, and caufe a great effufion of blood. This light infantry is often in imminent danger, obliged to run for its life, and fave itfelf by flying into the receffes in the palifadoes, or by jumping over the parapet: it fometimes happens that neither the fhouts of the multitude, nor the affaults of the other runners, can call off the bull from the purfuit of one particular fellow; who has then nothing to truft to but his own agility, being totally unprovided with offenfive as well as defenfive weapons.

When the governor thinks a victim has afforded sufficient diversion, leave is given to put an end to its life. A well-made champion steps forth, with a short brown cloak hung upon a stick held out in his left hand, and a strait two-edged sword in his right; the blade is always of the finest Toledo temper, and the hilt covered with leather. This *Matador* advances up to the bull, and provokes it to action; as the bull darts at him, and makes a push obliquely, with its eyes shut, he turns it off with the cloak, retiring a little on one side to be ready for the return. On the second attack, he holds the sword in an horizontal position, with such steady aim, that the furious beast rushes upon the point, and by its own impetuosity forces it up to the hilt. The sword enters at the collar-bone, and either pierces the heart, or cuts the great artery. Sometimes the bull drops down dead instantaneously; sometimes stands a few minutes, heaving and spouting a torrent of blood out of the mouth and nostrils.

When the bull proves so cowardly, or so exhausted with fatigue and loss of blood, as to refuse to run at the matador, it is difpatched by stabs in any part of the body, or worried by bull-dogs. The last bull of each fiesta is *embobado*, that is, his horns are muffled, and all the mob is let in, with sticks in their hands, to learn the trade, to beat the animal, or to be bruised and tossed about

about themselves. Three mules, adorned with streamers and bells, draw off the slaughtered bulls and horses between each battle.

I have been thus particular in my account of a bullfight (though you may find descriptions of it in almost every book that treats of Spain) because most of those I have read talk of royal feasts and exhibitions, which are very different things from the common shews now a days. Our last was a very bloody one: two bulls killed seven horses, but luckily no men lost their lives, though many had hair-breadth escapes. I never saw any thing so weak and inactive as the poor horses were; they had not agility enough to avoid one stroke: and of all horrible sights, that of the bull's tearing out their entrails, and tossing them about with its horns, was the most nauseous and shocking I ever beheld. Both the bulls were hacked to death in a very awkward manner; but the spectators were mightily delighted with the barbarity and bloodshed. We were the other night at a puppet-shew, that ended in the representation of a bullfight; the mob in the pit was to the full as violently affected, as riotous, and noisy, as they could possibly have been at the real spectacle.

Last year a negro from Buenos Ayres, where he had been trained up from his infancy to hunt the wild cattle of the desart, exhibited some very extraordinary feats of strength and dexterity: he took a long rope, with a running noose, and throwing it over the horns of a bull, brought it close to a strong stake, fixed in the middle of the area, where he tied it tight, till he had fastened a saddle on its back, on which he seated himself; he then cut the cord, and let the beast run about and exert ineffectual efforts to shake off so unusual a load by the most furious movements. When fatigue had sufficiently tamed it, he drove this uncommon steed against another bull, which he soon dispatched, and then at one blow struck the beast that he was mounted upon, dead. The violence of this exercise generally brought on him a dangerous spitting of blood.

The princes and their attendants are now very busy preparing, by daily rehearsals, for the *Parejas*; which we cannot stay to see, as they are seldom exhibited till the middle of June.

These Parejas are a kind of dance on horseback, in imitation, perhaps, of the Trojan games described by Virgil in the fifth book of the Æneid; or more probably of some tournament in the times of Moorish chivalry.

The prince of Asturias, Don Gabriel, Don Antonio, and Don Lewis, have revived them, and each heads a squadron of twelve young gentlemen, arrayed in the ancient Spanish dress; the divisions distinguished by the particular

particular colour of their cloaths, feathers, and horse furniture. They parade with music before them in a large tilting yard near the palace; separate themselves into detachments, and perform various intricate figures, resembling those of a stage dance. The docility and elegance of the horses, the splendour and gaiety of apparel of the riders, more than any thing there is in the game itself, render it entertaining for the first time of seeing; but it languishes from a want of that action, that spirit, which interests us so strongly in all public sports, when the actors exert uncommon strength and skill, and are, or seem to be, in some kind of danger. However, it is a pompous spectacle, and may produce very salutary effects, by rousing the nobility from their lethargy, and encouraging them to be a little more attentive to the breed and education of their horses.

LETTER XLI.

Madrid, June 4, 1776.

SINCE our return from Aranjuez, the mornings have been employed in turning over a multitude of books and prints, and in taking extracts of such parts as tend to elucidate the history, literature, or antiquities of Spain. In the afternoons, we have spent our time in visiting the most remarkable edifices of the city; if you except the royal palaces, there are few buildings worthy of attention, nor do I believe there is in Europe a capital that has so little to shew as Madrid; having never been the see of a bishop, it has of course no cathedral, nor indeed any church, that distinguishes itself much from the common herd of parishes and convents. Allowing some few exceptions, I think I may safely pronounce the outward architecture of them all to be barbarous, and their manner of ornamenting the inside as bad as that of the worst ages; most of them were erected or retouched during the term of years that elapsed between the middle of the seventeenth century and the year 1759, a period in the history of

Spain,

Spain, when all arts and sciences were fallen to the lowest ebb of depravement; the effect of the degeneracy of manners, the want of public spirit, and the disorder and weakness of a decaying monarchy. These vices in the political system under the three last princes of the Austrian line, could not be removed immediately on the accession of another family; the wars that shook the very foundations of their throne for the first ten years of this century, kept all polite arts groveling in the dust; and when they ventured to raise their heads again, and court the favour of the sovereign, there seems to have been a total want of able professors to second their efforts, and assist them in returning to the paths of good sense and true taste. No mad architect ever dreamed of a distortion of members so capricious, of a twist of pillars, cornices, or pediments, so wild and fantastic, but what a real sample of it may be produced in some or other of the churches of Madrid. They are all small, and poor in marbles as well as pictures. Their altars are piles of wooden ornaments heaped up to the ceiling, and stuck full of wax lights, which more than once have set fire to the whole church. The convents which may be said to possess a good collection of pictures, are those of Saint Pasqual and of the bare-footed Carmelite nuns. The former has a fine Titian, a capital Guerchino, and many other pieces by

esteemed

esteemed Italian masters. In the sacristy of the latter, is a numerous collection of paintings by various hands, many of which are of superior merit. The tombs of Ferdinand the sixth and of his queen Barbara, in the church of the visitation, are almost the only sepulchral monuments of any consequence.

The first king that made any long abode in Madrid, was Henry the fourth. Before his reign, this was but an insignificant place, with a small castle for the convenience of the princes that came to hunt the bear in the environs, which were then as woody as they now are naked. Its situation on a hill overlooking many leagues of country, open on every side to a wholesome circulation of air, and abundance of good water, induced the emperor Charles the fifth to build an ample palace here, which he intended to make his chief residence, as he thought the climate best adapted to his constitution. The sovereign being once fixed at Madrid, the nobility soon abandoned their hereditary castles and houses in other cities, to follow the court. They were under the necessity of settling in the houses they found ready built; and for that reason, added to the supine indifference that seized the Spaniards during the last two-thirds of the seventeenth century, and near half of this, most of the great families still continue to inhabit vast ranges of ugly fabrics not distinguishable from the

the common houses in the streets, except by their larger dimensions.

The palaces of the grandees that contain either statues or pictures of value, are few in number.

In that of Medina Celi are many precious monuments of antiquity in marble, the remains of a great collection brought from Italy, by one of the Dukes of Alcalá.

The duke of Saint Estévan possesses many of the best works of Luca Giordano.

In the gallery of the marquis of Santiago, Murillo has painted the life of Jacob and a Madonna, which may be reckoned among the most capital of the Spanish school.

At the Duke of Alba's is to be seen a very famous picture of Corregio, called the school of Cupid; it represents Venus giving the God of Love to be tutored by Mercury. There is also an holy family, said to be by Raphael; a charming Venus, by Velasquez, lying half reclined with her back to the spectator, and her face reflected in a mirror she holds in her hand. Among the portraits, the most curious are those of Anna Bullen, and the great Duke of Alba. Here are also very fine hangings, executed after the Cartoons of Raphael, which, with the Venus of Correggio, once formed part of the collection of that nice connoisseur and unskilful monarch, Charles the first of England.

These pictures naturally lead me to speak of the royal palace; which I should have mentioned first, had I not wished to dispatch the lesser objects, that I might have nothing to think of that could interfere with the description of the noble collection in the new palace.

The old palace was burnt down to the ground in 1734, and Philip Juvara commissioned by Philip the fifth to give a plan for rebuilding it in the most splendid manner. The model he made is still existing, but was rejected on account of the immensity of the size, and the greatness of the expence, as well as of the want of sufficient room to place it, the king being determined on account of the air, to have it rebuilt on the exact spot where the old one stood. Juvara dying before he could prepare a second design, his disciple Sachetti produced that which has been carried into execution; both his and his master's plans have the defect of being clumsy and confused in the windows, pilasters, and ornaments; where they have aimed at simplicity, they have sunk their architecture under a load of stone, and where they have studied to be rich and light, they have generally given into the capricious rather than the beautiful.

It is all of white stone. Each of the fronts being four hundred and seventy feet in length, by an hundred high, this pile towers over all the country, where nothing intercepts the view for many miles. The entrances.

trances and ground-floor appear more like those of some mighty fortress, than of the peaceable habitation of a powerful monarch, an hundred leagues removed from his frontiers. The range of large glazed arches round the inner court, resembles the inside of a manufactory: this is the more unpardonable, as they had at no great distance in the Alcazar of Toledo, as elegant a colonnade as the nicest critic could desire. The beautiful circular court of Granada might have suggested noble ideas to the architect, but probably at that time, the very existence of such a thing was a secret at Madrid.

The stair-case was meant to be double, but it was afterwards judged more convenient to shut up one flight, as the remaining half answered every purpose. At the foot of the stairs I shall leave all my spleen, and prepare myself with unfeigned satisfaction to describe to you the beauty and grandeur of the upper apartments. I know no palace in Europe, fitted up with so much true royal magnificence. The ceilings are chef-d'œuvres of Mengs, Corrado, and Tiepolo. The richest marbles are employed with great taste in forming the cornices and socles of the rooms, and the frames of the doors and windows. What enhances the value of these marbles, is the circumstance of their being all produced in the quarries of Spain, from whence it is the opinion of a learned writer, that ancient Rome was supplied with many of the precious materials that enriched her porticoes and temples. At least, there is no presumption in asserting, that the bowels of the earth in Spain contain most of those species of marbles, alabasters, &c. that are to be seen in the ruins of the mistress of the world, whatever might be the countries from which they were drawn. Porphyry is found near Cordova; the finest jasper near Aracena; the mountains of Granada furnish a beautiful green, those of Tortosa a variety of brown marbles; Leon and Malaga send alabaster; Toledo, Talavera, Badajoz, and Murviedro, abound in marbles of different colours; and most parts of the kingdom afford some specimen or other of jasper, besides the amethyst and its radix, for which Spain is celebrated above most other countries.

The great audience chamber is one of the richest I know. The ceiling, painted by Tiepolo, represents the triumph of Spain; round the cornice the artist has placed allegorical figures of its different provinces, distinguished by their productions, and attended by several of their inhabitants in the provincial habit; these form a most uncommon picture, and a curious set of *Costumi*. The walls are incrustated with beautiful marble, and all round hung with large plates of looking-glass

TRAVELS THROUGH SPAIN.

in rich frames. The manufactory of glafs is at Saint Ildefonfo, where they caft them of a very great fize; but I am told they are apt to turn out much rougher and more full of flaws than thofe made in France.

A collection of pictures, by the greateft mafters of the art, adorns the walls of the inner apartments; but even this vaft fabric does not afford room for all the riches his Catholic Majefty poffeffes in this branch. The detail and catalogue of a number of paintings is fure to fatigue a reader who has never feen, nor can ever rationally expect to fee them; therefore it is incumbent upon me to felect only a few of my favorites from my memorandums.

The gallery of the Efcurial is faid to be ftill more valuable, efpecially as the famous picture of Raphael of the carrying the crofs, called the Spafimo di Sicilia[31], remains in this palace unplaced, and confequently unfeen.

Of the works of Titian, the moft remarkable are, a Bachanalian woman lying on her back, afleep; the liquor has diffufed a glow over her beautiful face, and her body is divinely handfome; one of the greateft painters of the age has often declared, he never paffed before this picture without being ftruck with admira-

---

[31] Raphael painted it for the Church of the Madonna dello Spafimo, or the mother of Dolours, in Sicily.

tion.

tion. Some boys playing, full of grace and a charming variety of attitudes.

Rubens: Chrift and St. John Baptift, lovely children. A prieft on horfeback, carrying the viaticum to a fick perfon, accompanied by Rodolph earl of Hapfburgh, one of the mafter-pieces of his pencil.

Murillo: A vintager, winefeller, holy family, two boys; all in their different characters, excellently painted with a rich mellow colour.

Vandyke: The feizing of Chrift in the garden, a ftrong compofition; feveral portraits abfolutely alive.

Spagnolet: Ifaac feeling Jacob's hands; very capital.

Velafquez: Many portraits. His genius fhines moft confpicuous in the equeftrian figure of the Conde Duque Olivarés, prime minifter of Philip the fourth, which I really think the beft portrait I ever beheld: I know not which moft to admire; the chiaro fcuro, the life and fpirit of the rider, or the natural pofition and fire of the horfe. Another of a young prince alfo on horfeback, is a beautiful piece: the little cavalier fits upright, and feems proud of his exalted ftation; but the fixed ferious caft of his features, betrays the apprehenfion he feels of his prancing fteed. The water-feller of Saville, an admirable old figure; fome women fpinning; and Velafquez himfelf drawing the portrait of an Infanta.

Mengs:

Mengs: Many fine things, which, even in this rare collection, do not seem intruders; most of them represent devout lugubrious events, the most gloomy of which, such as the flagellation and crucifixion, have been chosen by the king to adorn his bed-chamber. Among the profane and allegorical subjects he has treated, I was much delighted with four light airy genii over the doors, representing the different parts of the day.

The last pictures I shall mention, in order to close my catalogue with eclat, are an holy family, and a Christ praying in the garden, by Correggio, not inferior to any of the small-sized works of that child of the graces. Of the last-mentioned piece I have seen more than one repetition. In the Capodimonte collection near Naples, is one exactly similar.

I have passed over many excellent pictures by a crowd of Italian and Flemish painters, that would hold the first rank in most other galleries.

In the magazines and store-rooms lie unsorted, a number of pictures, sufficient to furnish such another suite of apartments.

At the bottom of the palace-yard is an old building, called the Armeria, containing a curious assortment of antique arms and weapons, kept in a manner that would have made poor Cornelius Scriblerus swoon at every step;

no notable houfe-maid in England has her fire-grates half fo bright as thefe coats of mail; they fhew thofe of all the heroes that dignify the annals of Spain; thofe of St. Ferdinand, Ferdinand the Catholic, his wife Ifabella, Charles the fifth, the great captain Gonfalo, the king of Granada, and many others. Some fuits are embóffed with great nicety. The temper of the fword-blades is quite wonderful; for you may lap them round your waift like a girdle. The art of tempering fteel in Toledo, was loft about feventy years ago, and the project of reviving and encouraging it, is one of the favourite fchemes of Charles the third, who has erected proper works for it on the banks of the Tagus.

As the new palace ftands on the brow of a fteep hill, and is hemmed in very clofe behind by the buildings of the town, it became neceffary to open a communication with the vale of Mançanarés below, that his Majefty might go into the country without paffing through the whole city of Madrid. In order to effect this, they have cut a broad road, with an eafy afcent from the river to the palace, and adorned it at the foot of the hill with a kind of triumphal arch, dedicated to St. Vincent. This expence might have been faved, as well as the many thoufands of dollars buried in the vaults and fubftructions that ferve as foundations to the ponderous mafs of buildings which compofe the palace,

had

had the kings thought proper to re-build or embellish their house at the Buenretiro, on the hill east of Madrid [33]. Instead of being crampt for room, even for a walk or a terrace, they would there have had a large garden ready planted, and space behind to stretch out

[33] The finishing and fitting up of the new palace has, in all probability, saved Madrid from ruin, by fixing the court of Spain to this spot. The king intended to have removed it for ever to Seville and the southern provinces, after the sedition of Madrid, when the populace rose in consequence of the order for cleaning the streets, and the prohibition of slouched hats and large cloaks. His surprize, resentment, and indignation, would certainly have induced him to retire for ever from so barbarous a metropolis, to the milder climate of Andalusiá, had not his minister, unwilling that so much treasure should have been lavished in the improvements of the palaces in Castile to no manner of purpose, and loath to abandon to destruction so many darling creations of his own, prevailed on his royal master to conquer his anger, and alter his determination. But the king still retains so much spleen against Madrid, as to dislike to sojourn in it; and indeed, he escapes from it as often as decency will allow him. It was said at the time, that many persons of rank were mingled in disguise among the mob, to encourage them to proceed to extremities; but this seems a groundless report. It is very remarkable, that during the greatest ferment of the sedition, all parties retired, as if by mutual consent, about dinner-time, to take their usual nap or meridiana; after which they returned to the charge with fresh vigour, and redoubled fury, resumed their clamours, and repeated their outrages. The military force finally quelled the tumult, and the king carried his point. Every blackguard now loiters about with his hat pinned up triangularly; but the moment he gets out of town, and beyond the bounds of the proclamation, he indulges himself in flapping it down on all sides.

their improvements as many miles as they could wish. The air in both situations must be equally good, and for any thing there is to see in the adjacent country, which is the only difference the new palace can boast of, I should think it rather a disadvantage than a recommendation: surely the view from the retiro towards the best part of the city, with a full command of the public walks, is much grander and more agreeable than a stretch over twenty leagues of ill-cultivated depopulated hills.

The palace of the Buenretiro is now stript of all its best pictures and furniture. The buildings are poor; and unworthy of a sovereign, so that few parts of it could have been preserved in any judicious plan. The only remarkable things about it are the theatre, where Farinelli sang before a court, which he may be said to have governed as prime minister; a bronze statue of Charles the fifth; and an equestrian one of Philip the fourth, cast by Tacca at Florence; the posture of the horse curvetting, supported by his hind feet and tail, is very ingenious; and it appears difficult to conceive how the artist could contrive to preserve the equilibrium of such a mass, entirely thrown out of its perpendicular. The gardens are agreeable, and open to the public; one of the great ornaments of Madrid, is the fine iron railing that divides them from the walks of of the Prado, and the road up the hill to the gate of Alcala, a new arch defigned by Sabatini; this gate is rather heavy, but perhaps its fituation requires the parts to be very folid, in order to produce a grand effect from the proper point of view; at leaft it enfures to them, an almoft eternal duration.

In the fhallow vale between the retiro and the town, which has not the leaft fuburb of any kind belonging to it, the prefent king has finifhed the Prado, which in a few years, provided they manage the trees properly, will be one of the fineft walks in the world. Its length and breadth are great, the avenues drawn in an intelligent noble ftyle, the foot paths wide and neat, the iron railing and ftone feats done in a grand expenfive manner. All the coaches in Madrid drive in the ring here; and though the abfence of the court leffens the appearance more than two-thirds, yet laft night I counted two hundred carriages following each other. On the declivity of the retiro, they mean to plant a botanical garden.

The view from this walk is, as it fhould be, confined; for the winds are fo fharp and boifterous, and the landfcape fo horrid all round the city, that no place of public refort could be comfortable, unlefs it were, like this, fhut in from all diftant views, and fheltered by the hills from the blafts that fweep over the highlands of Caftille. To the weft, it has the town, the three principal ftreets of which terminate in the Prado; there are three noble openings, excellently paved, and clean even to a nicety, indeed fo are moft of the ftreets of Madrid fince the edict for paving and cleaning them; the foreigners that refided here before that time, fhudder at the very recollection of its former filth. Some of the natives regret the old ftinks and naftinefs, as they pretend that the air of Madrid is fo fubtile, as to require a proper mixture of a groffer effluvia to prevent its pernicious effects upon the conftitution. The extremes of cold and heat are aftonifhing in this place, and the winds fo fearching, that all the Spaniards wear leathern under-waiftcoats to preferve their chefts, for they pervade every other kind of cloathing. In fummer the duft is intolerable.

To the eaft and north the heights of the retiro defend the Prado from cold. The walk extends from the gate of Saint Barbara to that of Atocha, and there joins an older avenue of trees, which reaches down to the new canal and the banks of the Mançanarés. This canal is a late undertaking, that has hitherto anfwered very well: near two leagues of it down the valley is navigable; and the tranfporting of lime, ftones, and other materials for building, the plantations of mulberries and other trees, and the fale of a right of
angling

angling, have already produced substantial advantages. The king has almost completed his communication highway between the Aranjuez road and the gate of Saint Vincent. It crosses the ends of the bridges called, on account of the places they lead to, the bridges of Toledo and Segovia; they are long and lofty, but decorated in the most wretched of all tastes; many writers have ridiculed them as immense piles of arches thrown over an insignificant rivulet, but the truth is, the Mançanarés sometimes swells to a great height, and pours down a terrible volume of water; the sands it has already washed down have almost choaked up some of the arches, and these high bridges may in time prove too low for the little brook.

In the broken banks south of the river are found large quantities of pebbles, called Diamonds of Saint Isidro. They cut them like precious stones, and ladies of the first fashion wear them in their hair as pins, or on their fingers as rings. They have little or no lustre, and a very dead glassy water. The value of the best rough stone does not exceed a few pence.

Opposite the new gate below the palace, is the royal park of the Casa del campo. The villa is a building of no consequence; the woods are wild and pleasant, though not so extensive as they might be made with a little attention: in the court is a grand equestrian statue of Philip the third, by John of Bologna; and in the rooms are many pictures, among others the original of Callot's temptation of Saint Anthony. In the menagery are some Vicuñas or Peruvian sheep, from whose wool a very fine silky cloth is woven, and made up into winter cloaths without being dyed; it is of a rich brown colour, and sells very dear.

LETTER XLII.

Madrid, June 5, 1776.

IT has been my constant study, during our tour round Spain, to note down and transmit to you every peculiarity that might throw light upon the distinctive turn and genius of the nation. Experience has taught me to look upon this method as the best, and indeed the only sure guide to the knowledge of a people; but at the same time, has made me sensible how imperfect an idea is to be acquired by a transitory view, in a progress of a few months. Customs that struck me at first as unaccountable, from my ignorance of motives and situations, have frequently since appeared to

me

me not only proper and rational, but absolutely so much in the common course of things, that I have wondered how I came to put them down as extraordinary. The mistakes I have found myself guilty of in several little remarks made in the first part of my journey, have rendered me very cautious of deciding upon matters, where I could not come at a knowledge of their causes. I therefore very early learned to mistrust my senses, and applied where I expected to have my doubts resolved, and the reasons of modes and usages explained to me. Accordingly I omitted no opportunity of drawing information from the natives of all ranks; from strangers long established in Spain, and from those who having resided but a few years here, were more likely to be sensible of the singularities of the national disposition. I cannot say my endeavours have been crowned with much success. Were I to draw the picture of the Spaniards from the manyfold sketches traced by their countrymen, every province in the kingdom would in its turn appear a Paradise, and a Pandæmonium, a seat of holy spirits, and a receptacle of malicious devils; the most contradictory accounts, enforced by the most positive asseverations, have been repeatedly given me of the same places. I have often found the virtue one province prides itself in, as being the specific mark of its inhabitants, not only refused

them

them by a neighbouring country, but the very oppofite vice impofed upon them as their characteriftic. The Englifh, French, and other foreigners, living in Spain, are in general but indifferently qualified to decide upon thefe matters: as long as they retain the prejudics they brought from home againft every thing that clafhes with their native cuftoms, they are but partial judges; and when once they fall into the ways of the place where commerce has fixed their lot, they become fuch thorough-paced Spaniards, that they can neither perceive the particularities you fpeak to them of, nor affign reafons for ufes that are grown habitual to them.

As I am not afhamed to acknowledge my infufficiency, I frankly confefs it is not in my power to give what you may think a fatisfactory character of the Spaniards. Were I inclined to flatter my felf-love, I might add, that I do not efteem any of thofe who have already written on the fubject, much better qualified than myfelf. What I can venture to fay, amounts to very little.'

The Catalans appear to be the moft active ftirring fet of men, the beft calculated for bufinefs, travelling, and manufactories. The Valencians a more fullen, fedate race, better adapted to the occupations of hufbandmen, lefs eager to change place, and of a much more timid, fufpicious caft of mind than the former.

The Andalusians [34] seem to me the great talkers and rodomontadoes of Spain. The Castillians have a manly frankness, and less appearance of cunning and deceit. The new Castillians are perhaps the least industrious of the whole nation; the old Castillians are laborious, and retain more of ancient simplicity of manners; both are of a firm determined spirit. I take the Aragonese to be a mixture of the Castillian and Catalan, rather inclining to the former. The Biscayners are acute and diligent, fiery, and impatient of controul; more resembling a colony of republicans, than a province of an absolute monarchy. The Galicians are a plodding pains-taking race of mortals, that roam over Spain in search of an hardly-earned subsistence.

The listless indolence equally dear to the uncivilized savage, and to the degenerate slave of despotism, is no where more indulged than in Spain; thousands of men in all parts of the realm are seen to pass their whole day, wrapped up in a cloak, standing in rows against a wall, or dosing under a tree. In total want of every excitement to action, the springs of their intellectual faculties forget to play; their views grow

---

[34] Andalusiá is derived from the Arabic, and means a *dark evening western country*. It was a name generally given by the Saracens to all Spain, and agrees with that of Hesperia, which it was known by among the Greeks.

confined within the wretched sphere of mere existence, and they scarce seem to hope or foresee any thing better than their present state of vegetation; they feel little or no concern for the welfare or glory of a country, where the surface of the earth is engrossed by a few over-grown families, who seldom bestow a thought on the condition of their vassals. The *poor* Spaniard does not work, unless urged by irresistible want, because he perceives no advantage accrue from industry. As his food and raiment are purchased at a small expence, he spends no more time in labour, than is absolutely necessary for procuring the scanty provision his abstemiousness requires. I have heard a peasant refuse to run an errand, because he had that morning earned as much already as would last him the day, without putting himself to any further trouble.

Yet I am convinced that this laziness is not essentially inherent in the Spanish composition; for it is impossible without seeing them, to conceive with what eagerness they pursue any favourite scheme, with what violence their passions work upon them, and what vigour and exertion of powers they display when awakened by a bull-feast, or the more constant agitation of gaming, a vice to which they are superlatively addicted. Were it again possible, by an intelligent, spirited administration, to set before their eyes, in a clear and forcible
manner,

manner, proper incitements to activity and industry, the Spaniards might yet be roused from their lethargy, and led to riches and reputation; but I confess the task is so difficult, that I look upon it rather as an Utopian idea, than as a revolution likely ever to take place.

Their soldiers are brave, and patient of hardships; wherever their officers lead them, they will follow without flinching, though it be up to the mouth of a battery of cannon; but unless the example be given them by their commander, not a step will they advance.

Most of the Spaniards are hardy; and when once engaged, go through difficulties without murmuring, bear the inclemencies of the seasons with firmness, and support fatigue with amazing perseverance. They sleep every night in their cloaks on the ground; are sparing in diet, perhaps more from a sense of habitual indigence, than from any aversion to gluttony; whenever they can riot in the plenty of another man's table, they will gormandize to excess, and not content with eating their fill, will carry off whatever they can stuff into their pockets. I have more than once been a witness to the pillage of a supper, by the numerous beaux and admirers which the ladies lead after them in triumph, wherever they are are invited. They are fond of spices, and scarce eat any thing without saffron, pimento, or garlic; they delight in wine that tastes strong of the pitched skin, and of oil that has a rank smell and taste; indeed, the same oil feeds their lamp, swims in their pottage, and dresses their sallad: in inns the lighted lamp is frequently handed down to the table, that each man may take the quantity he chooses. Much tobacco is used by them in smoking and chewing. All these hot drying kinds of food, co-operating with the parching qualities of the atmosphere, are assigned as causes of the spare make of the common people in Spain, where the inn-keepers are almost the only well-fed, portly figures to be met with.

The Spanish is by no means naturally a serious, melancholy nation: misery and discontent have cast a gloom over them, increased, no doubt, by the long habit of distrust and terror inspired by the inquisition; yet every village still resounds with the music of voices and guitars; and their fairs and Sunday wakes are remarkably noisy and riotous. They talk louder, and argue with more vehemence than even the French or Italians, and gesticulate with equal, if not superior eagerness. In Catalonia, the young men are expert at ball; and every village has its *Pelota* or ground for playing at fives; but in the south of Spain, I never perceived that the inhabitants used any particular exercise. I am told,

told, that in the ifland of Majorca they ftill wield the fling, for which their anceftors, the Baleares, were fo much renowned.

Like moft people of fouthern climates, they are dirty in their perfons, and over-run with vermin.

The very mention of horns is an infult, and the fight of them makes their blood boil. As their conftitution may be faid to be made up of the moft combuftible ingredients, and prone to love in a degree that natives of more northern latitudes can have no idea of, the cuftom of embracing perfons of the other fex, which is ufed on many occafions by foreigners, fets the Spaniards all on fire. They would as foon allow a man to pafs the night in bed with their wives or daughters, as fuffer him to give them a kifs; and indeed, I believe the ladies themfelves would look upon that favour as a certain prelude to others of greater confequence. Next to accufing a Spaniard of wearing horns, nothing can give him fuch offence, as to fufpect him of having an iffue.

I was furprized to find them fo much more lukewarm in their devotion than I expected; but I will not take upon me to affert, though I have great reafon to believe it, that there is in Spain as little true moral religion as in any country I ever travelled through, although none abounds more with provincial protec-

tors,

tors, local Madonnas, and altars celebrated for particular cures and indulgences: Religion is a topic not to be touched, much lefs handled with any degree of curiofity, in the dominions of fo tremendous a tribunal as the Inquifition. From what little I faw, I am apt to fufpect, that the people here trouble themfelves with very few ferious thoughts on the fubject; and that, provided they can bring themfelves to believe that their favourite Saint looks upon them with an eye of affection, they take it for granted, that, under his benign influence, they are freed from all apprehenfions of damnation in a future ftate; and indeed, from any great concern about the moral duties of this life. The burning zeal, which diftinguifhed their anceftors above the reft of the Catholic world, appears to have loft much of its activity, and really feems nearly extinguifhed. It is hard to afcribe bounds to the changes a crafty, fteady, and popular monarch might make in ecclefiaftical matters. The unconcern betrayed by the whole nation at the fall of the Jefuits, is a ftrong proof of their prefent indifference. Thofe fathers, the moft powerful body politic in the kingdom, the rulers of the palace, and the defpots of the cottage, the directors of the confcience, and difpofers of the fortune of every rank of men, were all feized in one night, by detachments of foldiers, hurried like malefactors to the

fea-ports,

sea-ports, and banished for ever from the realm, without the least resistance to the royal mandate being made, or even threatened. Their very memory seems to be annihilated with their power.

We found the common people inoffensive, if not civil; and having never had an opportunity of being witnesses to any of their excesses, can say nothing of their violent love, jealousy, or revenge, which are points most writers on Spain have expatiated upon with great pleasure. I believe in this line, as well as in many others, their bad as well as good qualities have been magnified many degrees above the truth.

The most furious example of passion and cruelty that I heard of, happened a few years ago at San Lucas. A Carmelite friar fell desperately in love with a young woman, to whom he was confessor. He tried every art of seduction his desires could suggest to him; but to his unspeakable vexation, found her virtue or indifference proof against all his machinations. His despair was heightened to a pitch of madness, upon hearing that she was soon to be married to a person of her own rank in life. The furies of jealousy seized his soul, and worked him up to the most barbarous of all determinations, that of depriving his rival of the prize, by putting an end to her existence. He chose Easter week for the perpetration of his crime. The unsuspecting

pecting girl came to the confessional, and poured out her soul at his feet; her innocence served only to inflame his rage the more, and to confirm him in his bloody purpose. He gave her absolution and the sacrament with his own hands, as his love deterred him from murdering her, before he thought she was purified from all stain of sin, and her soul fit to take its flight to the tribunal of its Creator; but his jealousy and revenge urged him to pursue her down the church, and plunge his dagger in her heart, as she turned round to make a genuflection to the altar. He was immediately seized, and soon condemned to die; but lest his ignominious execution should reflect dishonour on a religious order, which boasts of having an aunt of the king of France among its members, his sentence was changed into perpetual labour among the galley-slaves of Portorico.

The national qualities, good and bad, conspicuous in the lower classes of men, are easily traced, and very discernible in those of higher rank; for their education is too much neglected, their minds too little enlightened by study or communication with other nations, to rub off the general rust, with which the Spanish genius has, for above an age, been, as it were, incrustated. The public schools and universities are in a despicable state of ignorance and irregularity.

Some

Some feeble hope of future reformation is indulged by patriots; but time muſt ſhew what probabilities they are grounded upon [35].

The reigns of Charles the fifth and Philip the ſecond, were the times of great men and good authors, the Spaniſh Auguſtan age; and perhaps continued a few years under Philip the third. Since thoſe days, it is difficult to point out any original work of learning or merit, except thoſe of Cervantes and la Vega, who ſurvived the reſt of the geniuſes of that period.

Hitherto the academies, and ſocieties of *friends to*

[35] Since I left Spain, a reform has taken place in the great colleges, notwithſtanding a ſtrenuous oppoſition. In 1771 Cedulas had already been iſſued out for viſiting and examining the great foundations; as his majeſty had been informed of the decline of the Univerſities for above a century, of the great diſorders that had crept into their conſtitutions, and of the contagion which had ſpread among other literary bodies, to the great prejudice of public education, and of the ſtate. The Cedula for the reformation is ſigned in April 1777. The colleges to be reformed are, Santa Cruz in Valladolid, Saint Ildefonſo in Alcala, Saint Bartholomé, San Salvador de Oviedo, Santiago de Cuenca, and Santiago del Arzobiſpo, in Salamanca. Theſe ſix colleges were linked together in a ſtrict union, and formed a more powerful and compact body than the Jeſuits. They had ſufficient intereſt to procure for their own members moſt of the good things in church and ſtate, and had a majority in every council and tribunal of Spain. Inſtead of maintaining poor ſcholars and profeſſors, their immenſe rents, tythes, and dues, were portioned out among themſelves. They are reduced to their original inſtitutions: their old ſtatutes are confirmed, or new modelled to the times; and poverty, which for many years had been a ſure plea for excluſion, is reſtored to its primitive claim.

their country, the *Amigos del pais*, have gone on but flowly in their improvements in literature and agriculture. I doubt they have not yet got into a proper method; for they undertake many things, and finifh none. Their great dictionary is a glaring proof of my aflertion. They have now in hand an edition of Don Quixote, with prints taken from original drawings of the dreffes and landfcapes of the country, which has employed all their engravers for fome time paft; but they will, in all probability, be called off to fome new fcheme before this be ready for publication. The works of Calderon have been lately reprinted; and they have begun a new edition of Lopez de la Véga, on excellent paper, and with very fine types; Printing feems of late, to be the branch they moft excel in.

The catalogue of living authors is confined to a very fmall number.

Don Francifco Perez Bayér, preceptor to the infants and archdeacon of Valencia, may be placed in the firft line of Spanifh literati. He is author of a diflertation on the Phenician language, added to the tranflation of Salluft by the infant Don Gabriel. He is a man of learning, a very good Greek and Latin fcholar, well acquainted with the Hebrew and Arabic tongues, and moreover a modeft man, of a friendly and communicative difpofition; he has travelled through Italy, and

and acquired more enlarged notions with respect to foreigners, than usually fall to the share of the Spaniards.

Don Gregorio Mayans y Sifcar, of Valencia, formerly librarian at Madrid, and now an honorary *Alcalde de corte*, is likewise a scholar of great knowledge and liberal sentiments. He has published several editions of classic authors, grammars, dissertations, tracts and commentaries on the civil law, a life of Cervantes, of Dean Marti, and others.

Don Miguel Casiri's Bibliotheca Hisp. Escurial, certainly entitles him to some merit in the knowledge of Oriental literature. He is of a Syromaronite family, from mount Libanon, but born at Tripoly, and educated in the Maronite college at Rome.

Don Pedro Rodriguez Campomanés, fiscal of the council of Castille, is likewise a man of letters. He has published something on most subjects in and out of his profession, from *Guias de postas y caminos*, to translations of Arabic and Greek. He assisted the Conde de Aranda in expelling the Jesuits, and seems well inclined to reform the other religious societies. This has made him many ecclesiastical enemies; [36] and it is said,

---

[36] Freedom of speech on religious matters had risen to such an height in the coffee-houses of Madrid, that at last it reached the ears of the king, who sent for the inquisitor general, whom he reproached with his supine-

he has been admonished by the inquisition, which to the great astonishment of all the world, has lately acquired fresh strength, when most people were tempted to think it had lost its sting. Perhaps it is but a last effort before its final dissolution. The fiscal is of an active enterprising genius; he has lately published five or six volumes of ill-digested materials for the improvement of his country. Many of his schemes are good, but he lashes away at every thing in a bold loose manner. The origin of these books was a small tract, called Industria popular. which has brought forth four others, each three times as big as its parent, under the denomination of *appendixes*, *education*, and *second appendixes*. He is perhaps the ablest and most disinterested lawyer

ness in a concern of so important a nature. The bishop answered, that he looked upon his office as next to a sinecure; not having any expectation of support from government, should he attempt to exert his authority. The king gave him such assurances of being seconded by the secular arm, that the holy office seized upon an advocate, tried him for speaking against purgatory, and condemned him to eight years imprisonment in a convent. They might as well have hanged him; for the infamy that follows every accusation before that tribunal, even when the accused is declared innocent, is so great in the eyes of all persons whatever, that a man of any spirit had better be dead than thus lost in the esteem of the public. In order to make a display of their revived power, the inquisition summoned many great officers and others, suspected of free-thinking, to attend the trial, and be witnesses of the impartiality and candid behaviour of the court, and at the same time, of its resolution to enforce its authority by chastisement.

in Spain, a country where every civil and criminal process is determined by weight of metal and interest, which they term *Empeños*. When a servant of Lord G's was wantonly murdered by an invalid soldier, the secretary of state told his lordship, that if he chose to have the offender hanged, there would be no difficulty, as a poor soldier could have no friends to apply or make empeños for him. In cases like these, justice may sometimes take its course, if they are not too lazy to execute it.

Don Antonio Ponz is publishing a tour through Spain, in which he enters into very prolix details; but as he writes for the instruction of his countrymen, whom the objects he treats of ought principally to interest, his minuteness cannot be imputed to him as a fault. His observations have already produced some good effects in correcting abuses, suggesting useful works, and reforming the vicious taste of the Spaniards in many points of architecture.

Don Antonio Ulloa, who in company with the late Don George Juan, travelled into Peru to assist the French academicians in ascertaining the figure of the globe, published an account of their tour; he has also given a treatise upon the native Indians of South America; in which he has degraded their capacities and sentiments almost to a level with the instinct of the brute species.

Mr.

Mr. Bowles, though not a Spaniard, is certainly to be ranked among the Spanish writers; his natural history of Spain, though rather an introduction, and an assemblage of dissertations, than a complete work, has opened the career, and I hope will excite other persons learned in the secrets of Nature, to impart to the public their discoveries in the same study. Spain is so rich in all articles of natural history, that it alone affords as much matter for such a work as many other kingdoms put together.

I do not know whether I ought to mention Medina Conti, though a very learned man. He began his excavations in 1734, and all the inscriptions he published, except a few Roman ones, are arrant forgeries. Bayer, and the French Benedictine monks of Saint Maur, helped to detect him. I do not find he had any other object in view, than hopes of preferment; to secure the king and his confessor, he forged the sentiments of the ancient council, which establishes the doctrine of an immaculate conception of the Virgin Mary. He was also concerned for the clergy in the famous law-suit of the Voto de Santiago, of which the following is a succinct account. In the year 938 Abdoulrahman, the third king of Cordova, made an irruption into Castille, and by the rapidity of his progress, and the multitude of his troops, threatened the Christians with
utter

utter deftruction. In this emergency Ramiro the fecond, king of Leon, implored the fuccour of Saint James the apoftle, and vifited his tomb at Compoftilla, in folemn penitential proceffion. The clergy have, by *all manner* of ways, endeavoured to prove, that in thankful remembrance of Santiago's kind affiftance, by means of which he obtained a complete victory over the Moors, Ramiro the fecond obliged all his fubjects to pay a portion of the produce of all their lands to the church of Compoftilla, or, as it is worded in Spanifh, *A la paya de cufta medida de pan, vino y de mas femillas por cada junta que tubieren de labranza.* All this is flatly denied by the adverfe or lay party, on the ftrength of the negative argument, that there is no proof; nay more, they call in queftion the very exiftence of the battle. The demand of the church is pretty large, for they pretend that not only what Ramiro then poffeffed, but alfo all that his fucceffors have acquired fince, becomes fubject to the tax. On the other hand it is contended, that allowing all the ecclefiaftical affertions to be true, the poffeffors of land of thofe times only would be liable to fuch a tribute, as it would be abfurd to fuppofe Ramiro could have a right to give away what did not belong to him. The proceedings are already fwelled to the fize of a folio volume, and probably will increafe, for it is not likely there fhould be an end put to the litigation,

gation, as long as the firſt place in the council of Caſtille is filled by a canon of Santiago.

It is not in my power to extend the liſt of writers.
The common education of an Engliſh gentleman would
conſtitute a man of learning here; and ſhould he underſtand Greek, he would be quite a phænomenon[37].

As

[37] Though I make no doubt but the nation is much improved ſince
1722, yet I don't think it will be improper to tranſcribe ſome of the Dean
of Alicant's ſtrictures upon his countrymen at that period, as a Spaniard
is very good authority, when he finds fault with Spaniards. Theſe are his
words in a letter to Count Scipio Maffei of Verona: "No country, except
Italy, abounds more with ancient monuments than Spain: in every province you meet with remnants of bridges, aqueducts, temples, theatres,
circuſſes, amphitheatres, and other public edifices; moſt of which have
been reduced to their preſent deplorable condition by the outrages of the
inhabitants, rather than by the injuries of time. Such is the nature and
ſpirit of the Spaniards, that to overthrow the monuments of the Pagans
or Romans, is accounted among them one of the moſt meritorious acts of
piety, and moſt efficacious in drawing down upon them the bleſſing of the
Almighty. Alas! ſuch prepoſterous devotion! But how can it be other-
wiſe in a kingdom which is ruled by the ſtupid idle monkiſh tribe; where
it is thought a crime to deviate an inch from the rules laid down by the
hooded blockheads. Whatever they ſputter out, is revered as oracles of
old, iſſuing from the Delphic tripod. The ſluggards, puffed up with this
nauſeous adoration, thunder out the pains of hell againſt all ſuch as ſo
much as look with attention on an ancient ſtatue. When any thing of the
kind is dug up, their barbarous hands ſeize, break, deface it; and, left the
pure light of the ſun ſhould be defiled by the ſight of ſuch an abomina-
tion, it is burnt to lime, or buried again in the ground. If the buſt of an emperor, a philoſopher, or an orator, ſhould happen to be diſcovered, they cry
out, "'tis an idol! away with it! deſtroy it!" and inſtantly it undergoes the

fate

As to the nobility I wonder how they ever learned to read or write; or having once attained so much, how they contrive not to forget it. It is difficult to say what they pass their time in; or what means, besides inattention to business, they employ in running through their immense incomes. In the great houses one custom may contribute to extravagance; a servant once' established is never discharged, unless for some very enormous offence; he and his family remain pensioners as long as they live: the Duke of J. pays near ten thousand pounds sterling a year in wages and annuities to servants. The Grandees, one or two excepted, are diminished by a series of distempered progenitors to a race of pigmies, which dwindles away for lack of heirs, and tends gradually to an union of all the titles and estates upon the heads of one or two families. I think

fate of Dagon. The vulgar demolish all inscriptions, as they believe their characters are designed to confine some unclean spirits as guardians over hidden treasures. Immense are the quantities of inscriptions that have been defaced, or thrown back into the holes where they had lain hidden for so many ages. Superstition and ignorance combine to demolish every thing of the kind. Many were sent to France; and during the late war of the Succession, two English travellers freighted two ships with ancient monumental and historical inscriptions, which they had collected near Terragona."

Since the time of Dean Marti, Don John Celaya, rector of the university of Valencia, directed a number of Roman inscriptions to be buried in the foundations of the bridge of Serranos; and a much later instance of barbarism of the same kind, was exhibited by the Franciscan friars of S. Maria de pina, at Oliva.

the Conde de Altamira has no lefs than nineteen Grandeefhips centered in his perfon. Though they all ftyle themfelves *de primera claſſe*, as it were, by way of diſtinctive pre-eminence over others of a lower degree; yet I believe no fecond or third clafs exifts, and it would be a very grofs infult to fuppofe any of them were of an inferior rank to the reft of the *corps:* fome difference may perhaps be made in the degrees of popular refpect paid to the defcendants of the heroes that make a figure in the Spanifh annals, and fuch Grandees as have been honoured with the dignity in later times. A Grandee can marry none but his equal. They all *thou* each other; and affect to appear backward in mixing in other company.

The Spanifh women are in general little and thin; few are ftrikingly beautiful, but almoft all have fparkling black eyes, full of expreffion. It is not the fafhion here, as in France, to heighten their *eclat* with paint. They are endowed by nature with a great deal of wit and lively repartee, but for want of the polifh and fuccours of education, their wit remains obfcured by the rudeft ignorance, and the moft ridiculous prejudices. Their tempers having never been fafhioned by polite intercourfe, nor foftened by neceſſary contradiction, are extremely pettifh and violent. They are continually pouting for fomething or other, and put out of humour by the mereft trifles. Moft of the ladies about court

court are the reverfe of handfome, and do not feem to have any ambition of paffing for clever or accomplifhed; not one talent do they poffefs; nor do they ever work, read, write, or touch any mufical inftrument; their *Cortejo*, or gallant, feems their only play-thing. I believe no country exhibits more bare-faced amours, and fuch an appearance of indelicate debauchery as this. The account given me of their manner of living in their family way, as foon as they come out of the convent, and before they have fixed upon a lover to fill up their time more agreeably, is as follows: they rife late, and loiter away the remains of the morning among their attendants, or wear it out at church in a long bead-roll of habitual unmeaning prayers; they dine fparingly, fleep, and then drefs to faunter for a couple of hours on the Prado. They are never without fome fort of fugar-plumb or high-fpiced comfit in their mouths. As foon as it is dark, they run to the houfe of fome elderly female relation, where they all huddle together over a pan of coals, and would not for the world approach the company that may occafionally drop in; it would throw them into the greateft confufion, were they to be requefted to join in the converfation. The hour of the affembly paffed, they hurry home to their maids, and with their help fet about dreffing their own fuppers by way of amufement.

LETTER XLIII.

Segovia, June 10, 1776.

PREVIOUS to our departure from Madrid, we received from the minifters, by the particular order of his majefty, every permit and paffport that could conduce to the comfort of our journey to the frontiers of France. We have leave to take out with us what fpecie we pleafe, and the mules and horfes we have purchafed in the kingdom; our baggage is to pafs unfearched. I think it my duty to acknowledge, with a grateful fenfe of the diftinction, that during our ftay near the court, the king fhewed a very flattering anxiety that we fhould meet with no difficulties of any kind; and more than once enquired whether we had been fhewn fuch and fuch things, and whether we were pleafed with our reception, or in want of any thing to render the place agreeable. We are not a little proud of the honour; and I hope you will think our vanity too excufable to be any impeachment of the foundnefs of our underftanding.

On the fixth we left Madrid. As we paffed through the ftreets, we found great preparations made for the
proceffion

procession of Corpus Christi; among the rest, sets of girls dressed out in ribbons, dancing round may-poles.

We travelled through the park of the Casa del Campo, and over a bare corn country, leaving the forests of *El Pardo* and *La Sarsuela*, two royal hunting seats, on the right hand. The last miles of the road to the Escurial, which is exceedingly good, is also uncommonly pleasant, being carried through a very noble wood, where the deer are continually crossing and recrossing before you.

The aspect of this celebrated convent, situated in a corner of a lofty ridge of mountains, struck us with awe and pleasure. As we could not see the inside that evening, we enjoyed ourselves in walking round the gardens and fields. The landscape is very grand, for at a single view you command one of the largest edifices in the world, a boundless extent of woodlands, and a clear prospect of Madrid; and beyond all a vast tract of country that loses itself gradually in the horizon.

There are many minute descriptions of the [38] Escurial,

---

[38] Etymology of the word Escurial as explained by Casiri in his Bib. Hisp. Esc. "This is an Arabick word, meaning a place full of rocks, and the nature of the country agrees perfectly with it. It is to be written with an U and not an O, as the common way is. Those that derive it from the Scoria of iron forges, have no authority for supposing that there ever were any such iron works in that neighbourhood. Sarmiento very strangely interprets it, a Beech-grove, *Esculetum*."

extant

extant in all languages; let it therefore suffice to give you a general idea of this stupendous fabric and its treasures.

You have read that it was built by Philip the second, in consequence of a vow he made to Saint Laurence before the battle of Saint Quintin, which was fought on the tenth of August 1557. Though this story of the vow seems a little apocryphal, it may be supposed that Philip, in memory of so signal a victory gained by his troops over the French, might choose to dedicate to Saint Laurence, the patron of that day, the mausoleum he intended to erect in consequence of his father's dying request, therein to deposit the bones of that emperor, and of the empress Isabella. It was begun in 1562, and consists of several courts and quadrangles, which altogether are disposed in the shape of a gridiron, the instrument of the martyrdom of Saint Laurence: the apartment where the king resides forms the handle. The building is a long square of six hundred and forty feet by five hundred and eighty; so that allowing besides four hundred and sixty for the projection of the chapel and king's quarter, the whole circumference comes to two thousand nine hundred Spanish feet. The height up to the roof is all round sixty feet, except on the garden side, where the ground is more taken away. At each angle is a square tower two hundred

hundred feet high. The number of windows in the weft front is two hundred; in the eaft front, three hundred and fixty-fix. The orders employed are Doric and Ionic ; but the outward appearance of this vaft mafs is extremely plain, and I am forry to fay, in my eyes, very ugly. With its narrow high towers, fmall windows, and fteep floping roof, it certainly exhibits an uncouth ftyle of architecture; but the domes, and the immenfe extent of its fronts, render it a wonderful grand object from every point of view. The beft fide to fee it from, for I tried them all, is about half a mile down the hill on the Madrid road, as you are then fo much below it that the building hides the bleak mountain, which preffes very clofe upon it behind; the green fields and woods behind it, and the place you ftand in, make a good contraft, and fet it off to the beft advantage.

The church, which is in the center of all, is large, aweful, and richly, but not affectedly ornamented. The cupola is bold and light. The high altar is compofed of rich marbles, agates, and jafpers of great rarity, the produce of this kingdom. Two magnificent *Catafalques* fill up the fide arcades of this fanctuary: on one the emperor Charles the fifth, his wife, daughter, and two fifters, are reprefented in bronze, larger than life, kneeling; oppofite are the effigies of Philip the fecond, and of his three wives, of the fame materials, and in the fame devout attitude.

Underneath.

Underneath is the burial-place of the royal family, called the Pantheon. Twenty-five steps lead down to this vault, over the door of which is a very classical inscription, denoting that

> *Hic locus sacer mortalitatis exuviis Catholicorum Regum, &c.*

was intended by Charles the emperor, resolved upon by Philip the second, begun by Philip the third, and compleated by Philip the fourth. The mausoleum is circular, thirty-six feet diameter, incrusted with fine marbles in an elegant taste. The bodies of the kings and queens lie in tombs of marble, in niches, one above the other. There are twenty-six of these urns, but as yet only thirteen are filled; the two last kings, and all the queens that died without issue, being buried elsewhere. The plan of these sepulchres is grand, and executed with a princely magnificence; but I own I could not help finding them too gay, too light, and too delicately fitted up for the idea we are apt to form of a chapel destined for the reception of the dead. Accustomed to feel a kind of horror on our approach to any place that reminds us of the painful dissolution of our being, we naturally expect something serious and aweful in the appearance of such a repository.

The princes and princesses of the royal family lie in two side-vaults near the entrance of the Pantheon.

The collection of pictures dispersed about various parts

parts of the church, facrifty, and convent, furpaffed my expectations; and I think I may venture to pronounce it equal, if not fuperior to any gallery in Europe, except that of Drefden. Formed out of the fpoils of Italy, and the wafted cabinet of that unfortunate dilettante Charles the firft of England, it contains fome of the moft capital works of the greateft painters that have flourifhed fince the revival of the art. It would be a very ufelefs trouble for me, and no entertainment to you, were I to copy out a catalogue of them, as you may find it at full length in many books. I fhall juft note down fome of the principal pictures in the order we faw them, under the guidance of one of the Hieronymite monks.

In the Aulill. A glory by Titian, in which he has introduced Charles the fifth and Philip the fecond, as fuppliants, not as faints: there is a great and noble effect in this large compofition. By the fame hand, a burial of Chrift, and a Saint Margaret, which they have fpoilt by painting a cloth to cover her naked thigh, which the fcrupulous thought an indecent and dangerous fight in a convent of the votaries of penance and chaftity: thefe are high coloured and ftrongly painted. A very fine piece, by *El Mudo*, of fome Chriftians coming by ftealth in the night to carry off the body of Saint Laurence; the fears, caution, and filence, of thofe employed, are admirably expreffed; and the light given by a fingle torch is diftributed with great judgment over the whole; the faint's body feems to be roafted to a turn.

In the Chapter-houfe. By Spagnolet, a Saint John playing with a lamb, and fmiling with exquifite grace. An annunciation, a chef-d'œuvre of Baroccio. Chrift giving his bleffing, a fine half length, by Titian.

In the Vicar's Hall. Jacob's fons fhewing him Jofeph's bloody garment, efteemed the beft picture of Velafquez: indeed the compofition, expreffion, and intelligence, of Chiaro-fcuro are wonderful; the agony and furprize of the father is life itfelf.

· In the Prior's Hall. A dead Chrift, by Rubens; the figure of Mary Magdalen, and the dead body are painted in his beft manner. The Centurion kneeling to Chrift, by Paul Veronefe; the beft picture of the Venetian fchool in the Efcurial: the characters are noble, the architecture magnificent. The crowning of thorns by Vandyke, in which the tents, femitents, and tranfparency of colour, are more admired than the choice of his figures; the boy peeping through a grate, is incomparable, almoft a deception. An holy family, by Rubens; which would ftrike one more were it not fo near another on the fame fubject, by Raphael, which by its grace and beauty eclipfes all the merit of the

Ultramontane

Ultramontane master. Another Madonna in glory, by Guido; one of the most precious pictures in the collection: the Virgin is full of soft majesty, the Christ supernaturally pensive. The ceilings of these rooms are executed with great airiness, taste, and beauty, after designs made in imitation of those of the Vatican.

In the Outward Sacristy. The piece that pleased me most, is a Riposo, by Titian; in which the back-ground is one of the finest landscapes imaginable.

In the Sacristy are so many capital pictures, I scarce know which to give the second place to, for the first is undoubtedly due to the *Madonna della Perla*, by the divine Raphael. This was part of the spoil of the English royal collection; the king of Spain was so much enchanted with it, when it was brought to him, that he gave it the name of *Perla mia*, by which it has been distinguished ever since. The Virgin Mary is presented, sitting with her right hand, holding the infant Jesus under the arms, who has one leg upon her knee, and the other resting upon some white linen thrown carelessly over a cradle. The Virgin's left hand reposes on the shoulder of Saint Anne, who kneels by her daughter's left side, and forms a most perfect groupe, with the figures and the cradle; the old saint leans upon her hand, which is supported on the knee of the Madonna. Saint John Baptist advances on the other side

side to offer some fruit in a skin; Jesus reaches out his hand to take it, but at the same time turns round to look at his mother, with all the joy and graceful simplicity natural to a beautiful child of that age. Behind is a small figure of Saint Joseph among ruins; the fore-ground is rich in flowers, the back-ground in variegated landscape; the characters of face divine; the folds of the drapery large and flowing; the colours harmonious; the lights thrown in admirably; and the figures and attitudes beyond all powers of description[39]. After this, I can with difficulty bring myself to remember or reflect on the other valuable pictures in the hall, such as a Madonna giving suck, by Guido; an apparition of Christ to Mary Magdalen, by Corriggio; Christ and the Pharisee, by Titian; another holy family, by Raphael; another, by Andrea del Sarto (which for design, composition, and beauty of tints, may be ranked with his master-pieces); a visitation, by Raphael; a washing of the feet, by Tintoret. I should never have done if I were to describe minutely the beauties of the above-mentioned pieces; I must content myself with saying, that they are chef-d'œuvres of those divine masters; and that any one of them would give a

[39] Raphael is thought by many to have painted the Madonna, and his Scholars the rest upon his designs.

name

name and relief to the best private collection. At the end of the Sacrifty is an altar, called *La santa Forma*; this is a kind of Tabernacle or *Custioda*, of gems, marbles, woods, and other precious materials, inlaid in gilt bronze; in which, rather than in the excellence of the workmanship, or taste of the design, consists the merit of this rock of riches. Before it hangs a curtain, on which Coello has represented Charles the second, and all his court in procession, coming to place this *Forma*. This is undoubtedly one of the most curious collections of portraits in the world; for all the persons are drawn with the greatest strength of colour and truth of expression, and are said to be perfect resemblances not only of the monarch and grandees, but even of the monks, servants, and guards.

In the Old Church, so called, because divine service was performed in it while the other was painting; a martyrdom of Saint Laurence, and a Mater Dolorosa, by Titian, are capital. Here also hangs the celebrated *Madonna del Pesce* of Raphael, one of the most valuable pictures in the world. I do not know how Amiconi came to doubt of its originality; but his arguments are sufficiently refuted, and justice done to the picture, in a letter from Mr. Henry, published three years ago, in the Viago de España, by Ponz. The personages that compose the subject are the Virgin Mary seated, with her

son

son in her arms; on her right, the angel Raphael introduces Tobit, who kneeling presents the fish, which gives name to the whole; on the other side, stands Saint Jerome, in the habit of a cardinal, kneeling near a lion. This picture was brought from Naples, by order of Philip the fourth. Mr. Henry rates it above all the rest of the collection. Some connoisseurs have preferred the *Perla*, but I believe without sufficient cause.

The statues, busts, and medallions of the Escurial, are not in any great number, nor very remarkable for their excellence. The statue of Saint Laurence in the church is good and simple. Many have taken it for an antique, but the only part likely to be so is the head, and that I suspect to have belonged to a Bacchus; were it the statue of Saint Denis, this would not surprize me, as in the many stops he made to rest himself, when he carried his head about, he might be supposed to have mislaid his own, and taken up another in its stead.

They shewed us some original writings of saints; among the rest a wretched scrawl of Saint Teresa, the mystical reformatrix of the Carmelite nuns.

The Library contains a most precious collection of manuscripts, many fine drawings, and other curiosities, which we had not leisure to peruse as much as we could have wished.

Notwithstanding

Notwithstanding the coldness of the exposition of this convent, the king, for the sake of hunting, passes here several months of the year. To make the place less inconvenient to his attendants and the nobility, he has built an entire new town adjoining to it; but in spite of all he can do, the Escurial will always remain a most uncomfortable habitation for winter residence.

From the Escurial we came along the south foot of the mountains that separate the two Castilles, crossed the great Burgos road, and took up our night's quarters at a venta in the heart of the rocks and mountains, among forests of aged nodding pines. Next morning, we travelled many hours over the woody heights of the *Puerto* or passage of *Fuenfrio,* where the snow was still very deep on the summits of the mountains. Some of the turns and views through the groves are charming; now and then such prospects over the plains of Old Castille, the town of Segovia, and the palace of Riofrio[40], opened upon us, as astonished us by their beauty and novelty. We arrived for dinner at Saint Ildefonso, and found orders had been sent before for our immediate admission to the palace, water-works, and other curiosities of the place.

[40] Begun, but never finished, by Elizabeth Parnese, Queen Dowager of Spain.

This palace was much embellished and favoured by Philip the fifth, who spent much treasure in forcing Nature, and rendering it in some sort an imitation of what he remembered to have seen in the garden of Versailles. His son Ferdinand abandoned it to his mother in law. The court now comes here in the hot months of summer, as it is a remarkable cool spot, being fenced from the hot south winds by a ridge of very high snowy mountains, and situated in the bottom of a vale open to the north. But this situation exposes it to such sudden and frequent changes of temperature and seasons in the course of a few hours, that it is often necessary to shift from cloth to silk, and from silk to cloth, twice or thrice a day; and these transitions are sometimes productive of colics, and other serious disorders.

A romantic brook rolls over the rocks at no great distance from the town, through a large tract of thickets, and serves his majesty as a fishing-place. A walk is cut along the sides for a mile or two, and very much resembles modern English improvement. The quantity of fine water is one great recommendation to Saint Ildefonso. The palace is patch-work, and no part of the architecture agreeable. In the apartments is a very numerous collection of pictures; but that we had just left at the Escurial made us perhaps undervalue these.

these. I took notes of some that pleased me, but I will not pretend to say they are the only ones worthy of admiration. A small head of Portia, by Guido, a most pathetic countenance. Saint Anne teaching the Virgin Mary to read; a charming picture, by Murillo, mellow, true, and expressive. A Magdalen's head, by M. Angelo; S. Francis Xaverius, by Spagnolet; a Boy, by Murillo; a Roman Charity, by Spagnolet; Landscapes, by Claude Lorrain and Wouvermans; Animals, by Rosa di Tivoli.

In the Gallery below are many fine statues, busts, and bass-reliefs. The best are, a groupe of Castor and Pollux sacrificing; one of them has his left arm over the shoulder of his brother, and with his right pours something out of a patera on an altar, where the other twin is lighting a torch with his right, while he brandishes another with his left hand; this is a noble piece of antiquity. A Venus kneeling on a tortoise, and anointing her head with a phial of ointment. Seneca seated. Mercury with a boy. A bust of Alexander dying, and another of Antinous.

The gardens are in the formal French style; the trees are poor starved limes, for the soil is so shallow, and the rocks so compact and near the surface, that they can strike no root. To plant them, the old king had squares in the rock blown out with gunpowder, and worked with tools, then filled with earth. You may eafily imagine they have not thriven much, and indeed they are with difficulty kept alive by frequent renewals of foil and waterings.

The water-works furpafs all thofe I ever faw, not excepting the fineft at Verfailles. Not having any memorandums of their different heights, I do not know but thofe in the French king's gardens may throw the water up higher; but I very well recollect, that the Seine-water, which they fpout out, is of a muddy colour, falling down like a ftinking thick fog. Thefe jet-d'eaus of Saint Ildephonfo, fend forth a ftream as clear as cryftal, whereon the fun-beams play in the moft beautiful prifmatic tints; it falls around like the fweeteft fineft dew. The defigns of the fountains are elegant, efpecially that of the Frogs; a centrical one, where fixteen fpouts play in a regular combination; the great cafcade; the bafket, remarkable for its idea and fymmetry; it delighted us much: but the fountain of Diana furprized us with the richnefs of its decoration, and the fulnefs of its ftream; the lofty column of water iffuing out of the trump of Fame, exceeded all our conceptions of the power of hydroftaticks; the gardener mentioned a height to us that I durft not commit to paper on his authority, but I confefs the water went up to fuch an extraordinary elevation, that it was no longer in my power to guefs at the number of feet. Thefe fountains are fupplied by two

refervoirs

reservoirs at the foot of the mountain. One of them is allotted solely to the fountain of Diana. The larger which is emphatically called *El Mar*, is a very pretty lake, which with the hanging woods and a small building on the edge, forms a very pleasing subject for a landscape painter.

On our return to our lodgings, we were not a little entertained with the modest request of a friar, just alighted with some company from a carriage. He desired we would order the water-works to be played off again immediately for them, as it had not been possible for them to arrive in time to go into the gardens with us, and they intended travelling that night as far as Segovia. It was with great difficulty we could convince him, that it was a thing not to be done that evening, for want of time, and that the keepers would expect a very handsome present, if they set them agoing without orders from court.

Below the town is the manufactory of plate-glass belonging to the crown, carried on under the direction of Mr. Dowling; two hundred and eighty men are employed. The largest plate they have made is one hundred and twenty-six Spanish inches long; the small pieces are sold in looking-glasses all over the kingdom; but I am told the king makes no great profit by it; however it is a very material point to be able to supply his subjects

subjects with a good commodity, and to keep in the country a large sum of money that heretofore went out annually to purchase it from strangers. They also make bottles and drinking-glasses; and are now busy erecting very spacious new furnaces to enlarge the works. To provide fuel for the fires, they have put the pine-woods under proper regulations and stated falls: twenty-seven mule loads of fir-wood are consumed every day; and four loads cost the king, including all the expences of cutting and bringing down from the mountains, about forty reals.

LETTER XLIV.

Saint Jean de Luz, June 19, 1776.

THE first object in Segovia that attracts the eye, is the Aqueduct; as the road from Saint Ildefonso runs near it a considerable way through the suburbs. It is perfectly well preserved, and does not seem leaky in any part. From the first low arches to the reservoir in the town, its length is two thousand four hundred Spanish feet; its greatest height (in the Plaza del Azo-

bejo

Castle of Segovia.

Passage of the Bidasoa.

1. River Bidasoa. 2. Island of Conferences 1659. 3. Passage 4. Spain. 5. Spanish custom-house 6. France 7. French custom-house

bejo at the foot of the walls) is one hundred and four; it is there compofed of a double row of arches, built of large fquare ftones without mortar, and over them a hollow wall of coarfer materials for the channel of the water, covered with large oblong flags. Of the lower range of arcades, which are fifteen feet wide by fixty-five high, there are forty-two. The upper arches are one hundred and nineteen in number; their height twenty-feven Spanifh feet, their breadth feventeen; the tranfverfal thicknefs or depth of the piers eight feet. This Aqueduct is not only an admirable monument of antiquity for its folidity and good mafon's work, which have withftood the violence of fo many barbarians, and the inclemencies of the feafons during fo many ages, but alfo wonderfully beautiful and light in its defign. I do not think the Pont du Gard equal to it in elegance of proportions. Antiquaries have not agreed upon the epocha of its erection; fome attribute it to the time of Trajan, and others are willing for the honour of their country to give the credit to Hercules. The Romans certainly were the builders of it, but no infcription leads to the knowledge of the precife period of their empire, in which it was conftructed: perhaps a perfon accuftomed for years to ftudy among the ruins of Rome, the different modes of building adopted in different ages by that people, might be able from an infpection of the

ftone-stone-work, to determine the æra. It is likely to remain in its prefent ftate as long as Segovia exifts; for the fituation of that city on a dry rock renders this fupply a thing of indifpenfable neceffity.

The Cathedral, dedicated to Niceftra feñora de la Paz, is one of the handfomeft churches in Spain, in the lateft Gothic manner. The infide is majeftic, and remarkably clear of the embarraffments of altars and chapels fo common throughout the kingdom. The high altar is rich and fhewy.

The Alcazar, or Caftle, ftands in one of the fineft pofitions poffible, on a rock rifing above the open country; a very pretty river wafhes the foot of the precipice, and the city lies admirably well on each fide on the brow of the hill; the declivity is woody, and the banks charmingly rural; the fnowy mountains, and dark forefts of Saint Ildefonfo, compofe an aweful back-ground to the picture. Towards the town there is a large court before the great outward tower, which you are as well acquainted with as I am; the prifon of Gil Blas is fo well defcribed by Le Sage, that the fubject requires no farther explanation. The reft of the buildings form an antique palace, which has feldom been inhabited by any but prifoners fince the reign of Ferdinand and Ifabella, who were much attached to this fituation. There are fome magnificent halls in it, with
much

much gilding in the ceilings, in a femi-barbarous tafte. All the kings of Spain are feated in ftate along the cornice of the great faloon; I know not whether they are like the princes whofe names they bear, but if that refemblance be wanting, I am fure they have no other merit to claim. The royal apartments are now occupied by a college of young gentlemen cadets, educated at the king's expence in all the fciences requifite for forming an engineer. The grand mafter of the ordnance refides at Segovia, which is the head eftablifhment of the Spanifh artillery.

Another court of the palace is allotted as a prifon to eleven Algerine Reis, or captains of fhips. Their crews work in the arfenal of Carthagena. Thefe Turks are very handfome portly figures, with clean looks, and well-combed beards; they are well treated, and left to themfelves. Moft of their time is fpent in converfation, walking up and down a long gallery, fmoking, and playing at chefs, except when they go down at ftated hours to fetch water for their own ufe. Confinement apart, their lives pafs in eafe and tranquillity. As foon as they faw us walking about the court, they immediately knew us to be Englifhmen, moft of them having been feveral times at Gibraltar, and being well acquainted with the Britifh character of face; it being the hour of fetching water, and the door open, they flocked

flocked about us with great demonstrations of joy, and tears of pleasure starting into every eye. They kissed our hands, and called us *Ingles buens bueno Amigos*, over and over again, with difficulty prevailing upon themselves to leave us to go about their work at the well. My man S. G. by our orders, followed one of the principal men among them, and in lingua Franca, which indeed is the common jumble of tongues he makes use of at all times, gave him an account of the Spanish defeat before Algiers. They had heard of the preparations for the expedition, and had been much cast down with the thoughts of it, but had begun to entertain some hopes of a miscarriage, as many months had elapsed since they knew of the departure of the fleet, and not a syllable concerning its success had dropped from any of their guards. The venerable old Musulman raised his hands to heaven, and seemed to look upon the pains and irksomeness of slavery, to be more than repaid by the exquisite sensations he enjoyed in this happy moment. When his informant added, that the Algerines had lost a great number of camels, the Turk turned upon him with a, "What talk ye to me of Camels? had they killed thousands of them, there would still remain enough, and the beasts themselves must be proud of dying to save their country." After shaking them all by the hand, and leaving a present to

buy

buy tobacco, we took our leave of our *allies*, who followed us down the portico with longing eyes and a thousand benedictions; which, if their prophet has any jurisdiction over the roads, will preserve us from overturns and broken limbs.

The mint is below the Alcazar, a large building, the moſt ancient place of coinage in the kingdom. The machines for melting, ſtamping, and milling the coin, are worked by water. I believe that of Seville has at preſent more buſineſs, as being nearer the ſource of riches, the port of Cadiz, where the lingots of America are landed.

The unevenneſs of the crown of the hill, gives a wild look to this city. Moſt of the ſtreets are crooked and dirty; the houſes wooden and very wretched: nor do the inhabitants appear much the richer for their cloth manufactory. Indeed it is not in a very flouriſhing condition; but what cloth they make is very fine.

The country hereabouts has the reputation of being the beſt for feeding the kind of ſheep that gives the celebrated wool; but as thoſe flocks wander over many other parts of the kingdom, and are not bred here, I do not ſee any right Segovia has to this excluſive claim. A ſmall quantity of it is manufactured in the country, and through miſmanagement, lazineſs, or lack of hands, the greateſt part of the wool is carried to France;

France; and, at Orleans and other places, made up into caps and cloths, many of which return to Spain for fale.

The country grew fandy as we advanced into Old Caftille. In general it is extremely open, but now and then we came to woods of pine-trees, efpecially near the rivers. It appears much better land, and more populous, than New Caftille, for the villages ftand pretty thick in moft parts of it. At Villa de Santa Cruz, the only thing we remarked was a cow's tail, in which the hoftefs ftuck her combs; as this was the firft inftance we had met with of a cuftom which prevailed in Sancho Pança's time, and was of fuch fervice in furnifhing the barber with a falfe beard, we took particular notice of it. You know how fond I am of the fat fellow, and how happy I muft be to find any thing that explains and exemplifies the traits of his inimitable hiftory.

Olmedo, which I think is a place that occurs in Gil Blas, is a ruined town in a fine plain, rich in corn and pafturage, in droves of brood mares, and flocks of black fheep; fome pine woods, in one of which is a grand monaftery of Bernardines, bound the horizon very agreeably. We flept on the tenth at Hornillo, a fmall village on the river Aldaya, the banks of which are prettily wooded, and form many interefting points of view.

The

The next morning we came through a very sandy tract of forest land, to a hill from which we discovered the plains of Valladolid, and the course of the Duero; a fine river, that falls into the ocean at Porto, in the kingdom of Portugal. Beyond a chain of bare white hills, at one of their angles, stands the town of Simancas, where, in 938, was gained that signal victory over the Moors, which gave rise, as is pretended, to the voto de Santiago. The archives of the realm were deposited, by Philip the second, in the castle of Simancas, where they still remain. Valladolid is a very large rambling city, full of edifices; which, during the reign of Philip the third, who made it his constant residence, were the palace of his great officers and nobility. Being abandoned by their owners, who have followed the court in all its different emigrations, they are fallen to decay, and exhibit a picture of the utmost desolation: the palace of the king is so ruined, that I could with difficulty find any body to shew me the spot where Philip had resided. The private houses are ill-built and ugly. The great square, some streets built upon porticos, many colleges and convents, are still grand, and denote something of the magnificence of a place that had been long honoured with the presence of its monarch; but in general, Valladolid has the appearance of having been run up in a hurry to receive the court, and that it was meant to be rebuilt afterwards at leisure, of more durable materials than bad brick and mud, the composition of most of its present houses. The Dominican convent, a gothic edifice, is the most remarkable in the city. The university is in the last stage of a decline, and trade and manufactures at as low an ebb. It is melancholy to behold the poverty and misery painted in the meagre faces, and displayed in the tattered garments of the common people; the women go quite bare-headed.

We passed the river Puiserga at Cabeçon, which has the reputation of producing the best wine in the province. The soil is clay mixed with sand, and most of it planted with vines. The hills are composed of strata of clay and marle; great scarcity of wood; but a much more chearful look in the country than in any part of New Castille: the number of small towns or large villages rather considerable; on most of the hills, ruined towers and remains of ancient castles. We travelled up the Puiserga for many miles, through a broad vale, bare of trees, but tolerably well cultivated; we crossed and recrossed the river several times; the largest bridge is near Torquemada, of twenty-two arches. The houses hereabouts are built with pieces of clay squared and baked in the sun, but their concoction is very imperfect.

On the 13th we came to a much more agreeable country, better provided with wood, and more thronged with habitations; on every steeple one or two storks' nests; those birds seem to be held in the same veneration here as they are in the Low Countries. That morning we arrived at Burgos, the ancient capital of the kingdom of Castille, but long since abandoned by its princes to obscurity and decadency. The approach to it, up a long valley, is rather pleasing: the castle, the ancient broken walls sloping down from it, and lower down the cathedral, terminate the prospect in a picturesque manner. The dress of the women differs from all those we have seen elsewhere; and were there any smartness in their manner, any beauty in their faces, or even the usual bright Spanish eye to peep out from under their veil, it would be a very becoming garment for a country girl: but all those we saw were the ugliest awkward hoydens in nature; they wear large clumsy shoes, almost as bad as the French sabot, a brown gown thrown back and tied behind, a blue and white apron, and a large flowing white veil fastened with blue ribands. The montero caps of the men are all faced with red or blue.

Before we entered Burgos, we passed by the famous Abbey delas Huelgas, one of the best endowed in Spain. Its nuns are all noble, and the abbess almost a sovereign princefs, by the extent of her territories, the number of her prerogatives, and the variety of her jurifdictions. The convent is not a fhewy building; the fituation is low and unpleafant. The little river Alarcon feparates the fuburbs from the city; which is built in a very irregular manner, on the declivity of a fteep hill, commanded by an antique caftle, once the abode of the counts, and afterwards of the kings of Caftille.

As foon as the petty fovereigns of Afturias ventured to fteal out of their mountainous faftneffes and retreats, to extend the limits of their little kingdom at the expence of the Mahometan caliphs, their conquefts feem to have been entrufted to the care of generals or counts. As the kings of Leon and Afturias were always bufied in warfare, if men of ftrong bodies and valiant fpirits, and if princes of a weak conftitution and an unwarlike turn, were unable to form any ftrong oppofition, thefe counts gradually encroached upon the royal perogative, and converted a precarious delegated command into the folid eftablifhment of hereditary power. By thefe means, about the clofe of the tenth century, the counts of Caftille became entirely independent of the crown of Leon, in the time of Ferdinand Gonzales, and during the minority of Ramiro the third, king of Leon. Some authors have advanced, that the Caftillians at one time had formed themfelves

into

into a commonwealth, governed by two judges, one appointed to fuperintend all civil affairs, and the other to command the troops. But the proofs alleged to fupport this opinion, are extremely weak and fufpicious; it is however a favourite ftory in Caftille.

The male line of Gonzales failed in the perfon of Garcias Sanchez, who was murdered by fome exiled noblemen; and his fifter Munia transferred the fovereignty to her hufband Sancho the Great, king of Navarre. This prince was the common ftock of all the princes that afterwards governed the feveral monarchies of Spain. The title of king of Leon was foon abforbed, or at leaft fuperfeded in point of rank, by the new one of Caftille.

Over the city gate are fome ftatues of the judges or counts, ftill objects of great veneration in the eyes of the patriotic Caftillian.

The cathedral is one of the moft magnificent ftructures of the gothic kind, now exifting in Europe; but although it rifes very high, and is feen at a great diftance, its fituation in a hole cut out of the fide of the hill, is a great difadvantage to its general effect. Its form is exactly the fame as that of York-minfter, which I look upon to be the criterion according to which the beauties or defects of every Gothic church are to be eftimated. At the weftern or principal front are two
fteeples

steeples ending in spires, and on the center of the edifice rises a large square tower, adorned with eight pinnacles; on one side of the east end is a lower octagon building, with eight pyramids, which correspond exactly to the Chapter-house at York. We were struck with the resemblance between these buildings; both were embellished with a profusion of statues; most of those at York were destroyed in the first emotions of iconoclastic zeal; those of Burgos are still in full possession of the homages of the country, and consequently entire; several of them are much more delicate than one would expect, considering the age they were sculptured in. Santiago, the patron of this cathedral, stands very conspicuous on his war-horse among the needles of the main steeple; and the Virgin Mary is seated in solemn state over the great window of the west porch. The foliage-work, arches, pillars, and battlements, are executed in the most elaborate and finished manner of that style which has usually been called *Gothic*; of late this appellation is exploded, and that of *Arabic* substituted for it. I confess, I see some reason to doubt of the propriety of this second epithet. In the buildings I have had opportunities of examining in Spain and in Sicily, which are undoubtedly Saracenic, I have never been able to discover any thing like an original design, from which the

the Gothic ornaments might be supposed to be copied. The arches used in our old cathedrals are pointed; those of the Saracens are almost semi-circular, whenever they are not turned in the form of an horse-shoe. The churches of our ancestors shoot up into spires, towers, pinnacles and filigree work, and no such thing as a cupola seems ever to have been attempted; the mosques and other buildings of the Arabians, are rounded into domes and coved roofs, with now and then a slender square minaret terminating in a ball or pine-apple; the Arabic walls shine with painted tiles, mosaics, and stucco, none of which ever appear in our ancient edifices; the pillars in the latter are generally grouped many together, and from a very small member of an entablature springs one or two arches; in the former, the columns stand single, and if placed more than one together to support some heavy part, they never touch, or as it were grow into each other; there is always a thick architrave at least to support the arch, and commonly an upright piece of wall to resist the lateral pressure. Whenever it happens, as in the great divisions of the mosque at Cordova, that four pillars are joined together, it is by means of a square wall or pier, at the four angles of which are placed the columns, perfectly separated and distinct. In all the varieties of capitals I have taken drawings of, I never found one exactly

actly the same in design or proportions, as our Gothic ones in the churches of England, or in those of France, at least such as I have examined; viz. Saint Denis, Amiens, Rouen, Bordeaux, Tours, and others. The Christian structures are extremely lofty, and full of long windows with painted glass; the porches and doors are deep recesses, with several arches one within another, crowded with little saints and angels. Now every thing is different in the mosque of Cordova, the only one I have ever seen, but which I think may be fairly deemed a proper sample of Arabian sacred architecture, to establish a judgment upon; whether we consider its antiquity, being built before the ninth century; its present state, which, some parts excepted, is exactly as it was a thousand years ago; or lastly the princely hands that raised it. It was erected by Abdoulrahman the first, probably upon the designs, and under the inspection of the ablest architects of the age, and according to the method of distribution observed in holy edifices built in Arabia and Egypt. Here, and I have reason to think it is so in most, if not all, mosques, the elevation of the roof is trifling, not a seventeenth part of the length of the iles; there are no windows of any size, and what there are, are covered with filigree-work in stone, so as never to admit any great quantity of light, which was received from sky-lights and cupolas,

polas, and from the occafional opening of the doors: the finking back of the arches over the gates is fcarce perceptible, as they are almoft of an equal projection with the wall of the building. From all thefe differential marks, I am inclined to fufpect that our old ftructures have been new-named, and Mahometanifed without fufficient proof of their Arabic origin. At the fame time I acknowledge it is difficult to find them a more fatisfactory and genuine pedigree.

The beft age of that ftyle of conftruction began in England in the reign of Henry the third, for till then we built in the clumfy manner called Saxon, deftitute of every recommendation but folidity; the new tafte came in all probability from France, introduced by fome Provençals that followed the queen. If you fuppofe it imported into that kingdom by thofe that returned from the crufadoes, we muft of courfe fet it down as an eaftern invention. The queftion is what part of the eaft it came from, and whether it was the fame as that employed by the Arabians. If there were clear proofs of its being a branch of the Arabic architecture, it would ftill appear extraordinary, that its very firft inroduction into Chriftendom fhould be attended with fo great a variation from the models it was meant to imitate; and that any prince or learned prieft that thought it worthy of being employed in his country, fhould immediately fet about new fafhioning it in all its points. We may, if we pleafe to indulge our fancy, fay that fome fublime genius ftarted out from the dufty gloom of a monaftic library, altered and improved upon the hints he found in books of Arabian architecture, fubftituted bold and aftonifhing ideas of his own; found bifhops, princes, and abbots, willing to adopt them; and built churches in a ftyle entirely new, and apparently original. We may fuppofe him to have formed a fchool of other monks, the only architects of thofe ages among the Chriftians; and that thefe pupils gradually new modelled the precepts of their mafter, and reduced his method to certain rules; which afterwards ferved as guides through all the fantaftic mazes of our ecclefiaftical architecture. Some perfons have fufpected it to have been the manner practifed by the eaftern Chriftians, and not adopted by the Arabs; who might difdain to have any thing fimilar in their places of worfhip, with thofe of a conquered people. Others have been of opinion, that it comes originally from Perfia, or further eaft; and fome again maintain it to be an European invention, or at leaft a barbarous mode of building brought by fome great genius to the elegant perfection we behold in our cathedrals.

thedrals. The argument would require a great number of comparisons, confrontations, and combinations, to find out the connection between the two manners: such a disquisition belongs more properly to a treatise than to a letter, of which it has already engrossed too large a share.

In a narrow lane near Burgos we were detained for some time by the passing of many small carts, coming down from Aragon with spears for bull-fighting, iron, and chairs. These are the carts that suggested to Cervantes the idea of Merlin's chariot in the second part of Don Quixote. Their wheels make a creaking or grinding, which I can compare to nothing but the noise of iron mills and fire engines. It is the loudest and most piercing sound imaginable; and before you are acquainted with the cause, it is not possible to guess what produces it.

We proceeded along the river side, through a well wooded handsome vale. The Carthusian convent stands beautifully on a round hill; its old chapel answers the idea of a fine object in an English garden. Behind it rises a long ridge of green hills, over which appear the snowy summits of some very distant mountains. We slept at a poor place, where we were much diverted with the head attire of the married women; it consists of a black periwig, faced all round with the wool of a black lamb, ending behind in two long plaited tresses,

that

that reach down to their rumps. Previous to their nuptials, they are obliged to make up this elegant kind of helmet, which renders their natural uglinefs ftill more horrible.

All the fourteenth we travelled from vale to vale, over the bare hills that feparate them. The moft fertile is the vale of Saint Mary, where the corn was uncommonly ftrong and healthy, but the roads fo bad as to put us frequently in danger of an overturn. At length all thefe alternate plains and hills brought us to the foot of the Sierra del Oca; a lofty ridge of mountains that runs from weft to eaft, and feems to block up all further progrefs. As our muleteers had informed us that we were not to climb the mountain, we were long confidering where the pafs could poffibly be. Pancorvo proved to be the place; a long village in a defile that winds through the Sierra, with immenfe piles of rock impending on every fide. It wears a moft aweful tremendous afpect, which was heightened by the black clouds that hung upon the fummits of its cliffs, and foon after burft in a violent ftorm of thunder and rain.

On the fifteenth having paffed through with great eafe, as the road is extraordinarily good, we defcended into the fruitful plains of the Ebro. This noble river did not appear to us much lefs here at Miranda, than it did above two hundred and thirty miles lower, at

Tortofa,

Tortofa, where we croffed it eight months ago. The bridge was deftroyed laft year, and a ferry now fupplies its place; and is likely to do fo long, for this is not the country for fpeedy repairs. Miranda is well fituated, but its buildings are poor, and its gates and ftreets fo narrow that a carriage cannot pafs through them. The plain is of great extent, bounded to the weft by the blue mountains, where the Ebro takes its rife. In thefe flats, which are frequently overflowed, the foil is a rich loam, where they cultivate a large quantity of oats, a grain not much fown or ufed in the fouthern provinces. We afcended the hills to a gravelly country planted with vines, and at Puebla de Triviño, bade adieu to all bad roads, and villainous inns; for here we entered Alaba, a divifion of Bifcay, and immediately came to the fineft road imaginable, made at the expence of the province, and carried through the whole fignory of Bifcay, to the frontiers of France. Their only fault is being rather narrow in fome places, which indeed is excufable from the mountainous and difficult paffes they have been conveyed over, where more fpace is fcarce to be contrived. Every thing round us now affumed a different appearance; inftead of the bare depopulated hills, the melancholy defpondent countenances, the dirty inns, and abominable roads, that our eye had been accuftomed to for fo many months;

we

we here were revived by the fight of a rich ftudied culture, a clean-looking, fmiling people, good furniture, neat houfes, fine woods, good roads, and fafe bridges.

Bifcay is the country of the ancient Cantabri, fo imperfectly fubdued by Auguftus, and fo flightly annexed to the Roman empire. Their mountains have in all ages afforded them temptations and opportunities of withdrawing themfelves from every yoke that has been attempted to be impofed upon them. Their language is accounted aboriginal, and unmixed with either Latin, French, or Spanifh. It is fo totally different from the Caftillian, that we feldom met with any of the peafants that underftood one word of Spanifh. The Bifcayners are ftout, brave, and choleric to a proverb. The beft failors in Spain belong to the ports of Bifcay, and its mountains produce a very valuable race of foldiers. Their privileges are very extenfive, and they watch over them with a jealous eye. They have no bifhops in the province, and ftyle the king only *Lord of Bifcay*. The men are well-built and active, like all mountaineers. The moft fingular thing in their drefs is the covering of their legs; they wrap a piece of coarfe grey or black woollen cloth round them, and faften it on with many turns of tape; it anfwers precifely the idea I have of Malvolio's crofs-gartering in the Twelfth-night. The

women

women are beautiful as angels, tall, light, and merry; their garb is neat and paftoral; their hair falls in long plaits down their backs, and a veil or handkerchief, twifted round in a coquetifh manner, ferves them for a very becoming head-drefs: on Sundays they generally wear white, tied with rofe-coloured knots.

The firft Bifcayan inn we ftopped at, is delightfully fituated near the banks of the romantic Sahorra. We were very lavifh of our praifes upon the fmart habiliment of the landlord's daughters, his own civility, and the cleanlinefs of every thing in his houfe.

We came in the evening an eafy journey to Victoria, through the fineft plains perhaps in Europe. I cannot find words to exprefs its wonderful fertility, the crowds of villages in fight on all the little eminences, the noble woods that ftretch round the corn-lands, and the happy bufy looks of the crowd which we met returning from market; every cottage has its little garden, neat and flourifhing.

Victoria is placed on a hill, and makes a figure from all the environs; but the ftreets are narrow and gloomy, the houfes being built of a very dark-coloured ftone.

Having traverfed the rich plains beyond the capital of Alava, we afcended the hills into the woods, which confift of oak, beech, and chefnut. They purfue here the fame method as the inhabitants of the French fide of the Pyrenees, that of planting their timber-trees; wherever an old one is felled, they take care to replace it with a young fet about four feet high.

Near Salinas, a village inhabited by the workmen of the iron forges, we entered the very heart of the mountains; which would be impaffable from the fteep afcents and rapid flopes, had they not leffened the difficulties by proper windings of the road, and by great attention to the keeping of it in perfect repair. The tops of all thefe mountains are crowned with forefts, or covered with paftures; the acclivities cultivated as far as their nature will allow, and the deep vallies thronged with villages, hamlets, iron-works, orchards, and gardens. The timber of the mountains, and the iron fmelted in the forges, employ a great number of hands, and give life and fpirit to the whole province. The little towns are full of good houfes, built by thofe whofe induftry and enterprizes have been rewarded with fuccefs. Thefe manufactories and undertakings diffufe opulence among the middle clafs of men, and enable them to indulge the patriotic vanity of fettling comfortably in their native hamlet.

Having winded along a charming valley for many hours, and repeatedly croffed a beautiful river, we paffed over a high chain of mountains at the Puerto de Villareal. We there enjoyed fine but not extenfive
views

views of a mountainous well-wooded country. We then defcended into the charming valley of Tolofa, a large town, which like all thofe we paffed through, fwarms with inhabitants. The landfcape on every fide is divine, and approaches the neareft to thofe of La Cava in the kingdom of Naples, or thofe of Tivoli in the Roman ftate, of any I recollect having met with in the courfe of my travels.

Early on the eighteenth we gained the fummit of a woody hill, from whence we overlooked the Bay of Bifcay, Fontarabia, Andaye, the courfe of the Bidaffoa, the province of Labour in France, and a prodigious range of the Pyrenees. A more delightful profpect never exifted, even in the divine imagination of Claude Lorrain.

About eleven we arrived at the Bidaffoa; a broad clear ftream, that iffues with great majefty out of a valley among the mountains, and flows through the marfhes into the fea. The water was fo low that the carriages paffed through the river; but we took the ferry-boat, and landed in France.

THE END.

www.ingramcontent.com/pod-product-compliance
Lightning Source LLC
Chambersburg PA
CBHW021420300426
44114CB00010B/579